THE OBAMA HATE MACHINE

ALSO BY BILL PRESS

THE OBAMA HATE MACHINE

THE LIES, DISTORTIONS, AND
PERSONAL ATTACKS ON THE PRESIDENT—
AND WHO IS BEHIND THEM

BILL PRESS

THOMAS DUNNE BOOKS

ST. MARTIN'S GRIFFIN ≈ NEW YORK

THOMAS DUNNE BOOKS.
An imprint of St. Martin's Press.

THE OBAMA HATE MACHINE. Copyright © 2012 by Bill Press. All rights reserved. Printed in the United States of America. For information, address St. Martin's Press, 175 Fifth Avenue, New York, N.Y. 10010.

www.thomasdunnebooks.com
www.stmartins.com

The Library of Congress has cataloged the hardcover edition as follows:

Press, Bill, 1940–
   The Obama hate machine : the lies, distortions, and personal attacks on the president—and who is behind them / Bill Press.
      p. cm.
   ISBN 978-0-312-64164-1 (hardback)
   ISBN 978-1-4299-4125-9 (e-book)
   1. Obama, Barack. 2. Right-wing extremists—United States. 3. United States—Politics and government—2009– I. Title.
   E908.P77 2012
   973.932092—dc23

                                                             2011046508

ISBN 978-1-250-03102-0 (trade paperback)

First St. Martin's Griffin Edition: August 2012

10 9 8 7 6 5 4 3 2 1

To Milo, Prairie, Django, Willow, and Silas.
What joy!

CONTENTS

ACKNOWLEDGMENTS

It may seem like a lonely undertaking, but it's not. Every nonfiction book is a collaborative effort that builds and grows on the work of those who have plowed the same ground before.

To that end, I thank especially my good friends at Think-Progress, the communications arm of the Center for American Progress. Editor-in-Chief Faiz Shakir has built the Web site into one of the country's most dependable sources of information on public policy. And, simply by reporting the facts of their vast political contributions, indefatigable researcher Lee Fang has made life hell for the Koch Brothers—to which exercise I am only too happy to add my contribution.

As they did with my last book, David Brock and his amazing crew at Media Matters helped enormously, too. In addition to being a fierce media watchdog, they pump out a steady, dependable flow of research for those of us in talk radio.

I'm proud again to publish with the imprint of Thomas Dunne Books. A special word of thanks to Tom Dunne for his personal inspiration, insights, and additions. Nobody loves or knows politics better. It's a joy to work with Tom's associates Rob Kirkpatrick, Margaret Smith, Joe Rinaldi, Nadea Mina, and other professionals at St. Martin's Press.

My work is made easier every day by the outstanding assistance of producers Peter Ogburn and Dan Henning and the support of colleagues Eric Burns, Karl Frisch, and David Shuster.

For this, our sixth book together, thanks most of all to researcher Kevin Murphy and agent and friend Ron Goldfarb. You could not ask for more committed partners and collaborators.

And, as always, a special word of thanks to Carol.

THE OBAMA HATE MACHINE

INTRODUCTION

The single most important thing we want to achieve is for President Obama to be a one-term president.

—SENATE MINORITY LEADER MITCH McCONNELL, OCTOBER 24, 2010

A NEW BEGINNING

Inauguration Day, January 20, 2009. For those who traveled to the nation's capital, as well as for those who watched at home, it's a day we'll never forget. Washington had never seen a crowd so big or so happy.

An estimated 1.8 million people crowded in front of the United States Capitol to witness the swearing-in of Barack Obama as the forty-fourth president of the United States. The mass of humanity stretched from the western steps of the Capitol all the way to the Washington Monument, a mile and a half away.

It was a bitterly cold morning, but nobody seemed to mind. There were smiles everywhere. People greeted total strangers with hugs and high fives. Police officers and National Guard troops, out in record numbers, got in the spirit of the occasion. They smiled and posed for photographs with Obama supporters. To help pass the time before the ceremony began, crowds broke out chanting "Yes, we can" and "Fired up, ready to go!"—the signature slogans of the Obama presidential campaign.

Indeed, there was magic in the air. For the first time, people sensed the reality of the "hope" and "change" they had believed in and enthusiastically voted for. And they understood they were participating in a very special event: not only the inauguration of a new president but a young president, with a young family—and, most significantly, 143 years after the end of slavery, America's first African-American president. Everybody knew they were watching history being made.

But what few, if any, in that huge crowd on the Mall realized was that, at that very hour, a different kind of history was also being made—and not so far away: in the headquarters of the Republican National Committee, just south of the Mall; in the offices of K Street lobbyists, just a few blocks north; and in the corridors of the Capitol building itself.

Even while Barack Obama was taking the oath of office, conservative political operatives were busy plotting how to bring down this new young president. They embarked on a twofold agenda: not only to cause his entire political agenda to fail but also to destroy him personally. To that end, they unleashed a barrage of personal attacks and a litany of hate uglier than those directed against any other president in modern times.

CHANGING THE TONE

There is nothing wrong or unusual about pursuing a different political agenda. That is, after all, the job of the opposition party: to oppose.

Similarly, no president should be spared criticism. No president has. But even if Barack Obama is not the first, nor the last, president to face such criticism, the personal attacks directed against him, for whatever reason, have been more relentless and uglier than those against any other president in our lifetime, certainly any president since Abraham Lincoln.

It began during the presidential campaign of 2007 and 2008. It intensified once he was in the Oval Office. And it only continues to accelerate the closer we get to November 2012. In the past, the "loyal opposition," whether led by Democrats or Republicans, was usually conducted as a constructive, not a destructive, response. With regard to any serious problem facing the nation, both sides might have come up with different ideas on how to fix it, but they still agreed there was a problem that needed fixing. They both had the same goal, just different ways of getting there.

In order to balance the budget, for example, Democrats usually favored a combination of taxes and spending cuts; Republicans insisted on spending cuts alone. On immigration, most Democrats wanted to secure the border, while at the same time providing some path to citizenship for millions of immigrant families settled in this country for a long time; many Republicans simply wanted to seal the border and send anyone here illegally back home. Everybody understands that, in such a system, neither side gets everything it wants. Both parties have to give a little, or compromise. Slowly, albeit imperfectly, progress is made.

That's how government works. Or rather, that's how government used to work. This was true no matter who was in the White House, and no matter whether a Democrat or Republican was majority leader of the Senate at the time: Bob Dole, George Mitchell, Howard Baker, Tom Daschle, or Trent Lott. After each election, winners and losers sat down together, decided on the agenda for the next session of Congress, and got down to work, solving problems.

Yes, that's how it used to be. Not always, of course. Newt Gingrich, certainly no Howard Baker kind of Republican, adopted a take-no-prisoners approach to politics. And under his direction, Republicans started road testing a new, more virulent form of opposition: trying to break the president—at that time, William Jefferson Clinton—personally. They accused him of dubious crimes (Whitewater) and even outright murder (Vince Foster), shutting down the government if they could not have their way, plunging the United States into an impeachment crisis, and forcing us all to sort through Clinton's dirty laundry once they had latched onto a sex scandal—evidence of which, alas, was only too easy to find in Monica Lewinsky's closet.

But however badly behaved the opposition was under Clinton—and let's remember, they were bad—things got even worse for President Obama. Never before in U.S. history had so many on the Right insinuated that the president was not even an American, or that he was a socialist, a fascist, a tyrant, or some combination of all three. Never before had so many tried to claim the president was illegitimate. Perhaps this was because they disagreed with him. Perhaps it was because he was so popular and successful. Or, perhaps, it was just because he was black.

From the very beginning of the Obama administration, Senate majority leader Mitch McConnell and the then House minority leader, John Boehner, made it clear they had a different agenda. Instead of working together on any issue, they would automatically oppose anything President Obama or congressional Democrats put forward—even if it happened to be legislation identical to proposals previously submitted to Congress by President George W. Bush, which they had enthusiastically supported.

Boehner made that point very dramatically in the first weeks of the new administration. On January 9, 2009, he and other House leaders sent Obama a letter, inviting him to meet with the House Republican Conference to discuss his proposal to stimulate the economy and rescue the country from the brink of depression. It's important that we meet soon, they told Obama, "in keeping with your campaign pledge to work in a bipartisan manner and change the partisan tone in Washington, D.C."

Much to their surprise, perhaps, their invitation was welcomed with an "enthusiastic yes" by former House Democratic leader Rahm Emanuel, then serving as Obama's new White House chief of staff. The meeting date was set for Tuesday, January 27.

Hopes were high for changing "business as usual" in Washington. Even Boehner rhapsodized that "the president is sincere in wanting to work with us, wanting to hear our ideas, and trying to find some common ground."

Well, that's what he was saying publicly. But as the then press secretary, Robert Gibbs, recounted, Boehner was singing a different tune behind closed doors. The morning of their meeting, before Obama had been offered a chance to explain his economic package, even before he'd climbed into his limo for the drive to Capitol Hill, Boehner told his 178 Republican colleagues that he was going to oppose Obama's plan—and that they should, too. And they did, in lockstep.

So much for "changing the partisan tone in Washington, D.C." Boehner proved he had zero interest in bipartisanship—which, after all, if it's going to work, must be a two-way street. In the summer of 2011, Boehner and McConnell carried that same refusal to compromise into negotiations over raising the debt ceiling: willing to see the United States default on its obligations for the first time in history rather than end Bush tax cuts for the wealthiest of Americans.

ON THE ATTACK

But Republican operatives were not content with upsetting Obama's legislative applecart, because their opposition to Barack Obama was seldom based on differences in policy. From the beginning, it was largely personal, political, and mean-spirited. So Republicans set out to destroy Obama personally and politically, elaborating on many of the charges leveled against him during the presidential campaign of 2008—and adding a few new ones, just for bad measure.

During his brief political career as candidate and Illinois state senator, Obama had already faced and dealt with a slew of personal attacks, which critics somehow twisted out of both his unique life story and his network of friends and associates in Chicago. As we will see, and refute, in more detail later, those campaign charges included, but were not limited to, the following.

Because his grandfather was a Muslim, Obama was also a Muslim—and, as such, like all Muslims, was an Islamic extremist and follower of Osama bin Laden.

Because Obama attended Pastor Jeremiah Wright's church, he was not a true Christian. Not only that, he and his wife hated America, and hated white people.

Because Wright's church, Trinity United, had once presented an award to Nation of Islam leader Louis Farrakhan, Obama was a disciple of Farrakhan and a black separatist.

Because he once conducted a training session for the community activist organization ACORN, Obama was one of its top leaders and directly responsible for running fraudulent voter-registration drives across the country.

Because he lived in the same neighborhood and served on a foundation board with long-reformed Weatherman founder William Ayers, in the famous words of vice presidential candidate Sarah Palin, Obama "pals around with terrorists," meaning he was one.

Because he attracted large crowds at campaign rallies and spoke with passion, according to talk-radio host Mark Levin and others, he resembled another Hitler.

And, of course, because he was born in Hawaii—or Kenya? Indonesia? Iraq?—Obama wasn't even an American citizen and was therefore ineligible to run for or serve as president of the United States.

Yes, supposedly intelligent people actually said—and believed— all this stuff about candidate, and our forty-fourth president, Barack Obama! And they still say it today.

HAIL TO THE CHIEF

Once Obama took the oath of office, his political enemies, without even observing a temporary cease-fire, repeated, built upon, and enlarged the ridiculous slurs made against him—and disproven—during the campaign. And then, on top of those stale attacks, they leveled a whole new set of charges.

Because his father once wrote an article outlining how Kenya might escape from British colonial rule and achieve independence, Obama was charged with now applying those same principles to the United States. "What if Obama is so far outside our comprehension, that only if you understand Kenyan, anti-colonial behavior, can you begin to piece together his actions?" asked former House Speaker Newt Gingrich, a man smart enough to know better.

Because he told the truth on foreign soil—telling the French that the United States had in the past "shown arrogance" toward Europe; admitting to reporters in the Czech Republic that only the United States had "used a nuclear weapon" in wartime; and acknowledging to our Latin American partners that the United States has often failed to recognize "that our own progress is tied directly to progress throughout the Americas"—Obama was accused of embarking on an international "apology tour."

Because he followed through with a campaign pledge to give a major address in a Muslim nation during the first year of his presidency—having vowed to students at Cairo University in June 2009 to seek "a new beginning between the United States and Muslims"—Obama was accused by Sean Hannity and other conservative critics of "Blaming America First."

When Cairo erupted in revolution a year and a half later, these same talking heads accused Obama of ignoring the region. When the president joined our European allies in a military intervention to stop massacre in Libya and aid rebels in overthrowing the regime of Muammar Qaddafi, many of these same pundits spun around and argued Obama was doing too much in the region. Damned if you do, damned if you don't.

Because the president chose to follow the policies of George W. Bush and continue providing federal loans to Wall Street banks and U.S. auto manufacturers, saving them from collapse and preventing the economy from going into a tailspin, Obama was accused of being a "Communist dictator" whose goal was to nationalize all banks and manufacturers.

And even though he angered liberals by rejecting any consideration of a Canadian-style "single-payer" system as part of the debate on health-care reform—in the end, even dropping a public plan, or "public option"—Obama was nonetheless accused of being a "socialist" for engineering a government takeover of America's health-care system.

The phrase "government takeover of health care," in fact, was named the 2010 Lie of the Year by the highly respected blog PolitiFact, published by the *St. Petersburg Times*. The terminology was seized upon by Republicans on the advice of pollster Frank Luntz, who advised them, early in 2009, "Takeovers are like coups. They both lead to dictators and a loss of freedom."

Republicans then ran with that misrepresentation. And they stuck with it, even though it was proved patently false. The truth is, Obama's health-care plan (sadly) contained no expansion of public health care. Indeed, its key provision actually required 32 million Americans to purchase *private* health-care insurance, thereby granting insurance companies a Niagara of new customers—a requirement immediately challenged in court by several state attorneys general as unconstitutional.

Nevertheless, according to PolitiFact, in 2010 the phrase "government takeover" could be found more than ninety times on John Boehner's Web site, over two hundred times on the Republican National Committee's Web site, and eight times in the "Pledge to America" presented by House Republicans as their campaign

agenda in the midterm elections. It was also picked up and repeated by the media, appearing twenty-eight times in the *Washington Post,* seventy-seven times on Politico, and seventy-nine
times on CNN. In one appearance on NBC's *Meet the Press,*
Boehner used the phrase five times. No wonder people started to
believe it.

And no wonder so many Americans were confused. Exactly
who was Barack Obama? Was he a Communist, Bolshevik,
Muslim, socialist, Nazi, dictator, or imposter? For his political
enemies, any name but president would do.

THE PARTY OF NO

Name-calling was not the only line of attack President Obama
had to contend with. In his first two years in office, not one of
his legislative initiatives saw any Republican willing to cooper-
ate or compromise.

Not one Republican in the House or Senate, for example,
voted for the final health care–reform package. Nor did they put
forth their own proposal. And, of course, once Republicans took
control of the 112th Congress, their first move was to repeal
Obama's Affordable Care Act and replace it with . . . nothing.
And when that failed, they tried over and over again throughout
2011 to defund health-care reform instead.

Only three Senate Republicans—Arlen Specter of Pennsylvania (then still a Republican) and Olympia Snowe and Susan Collins of Maine—voted for the president's $787 billion American
Recovery and Reinvestment Act of 2009, aka the "stimulus" package. Not one Republican voted for it in the House, even though
many of them, including Minority Leader Boehner himself, later
showed up for ribbon-cutting ceremonies for new construction
projects in their own districts.

Only four Senate Republicans—Kit Bond of Missouri, Thad
Cochran of Mississippi, Susan Collins of Maine, and George

Voinovich of Ohio—voted to extend the extremely popular "cash for clunkers" program, credited by auto dealers with sales of 542,000 new cars at a time when many dealers were afraid they'd have to close their doors.

Then came the midterm elections and Republicans reaped the dividends of their obstructionism. With Republicans capturing sixty-three seats, and thereby control of the House of Representatives, President Obama said the clear message of the midterm elections was that voters wanted an end to partisan bickering. They wanted members of both parties to work together and get things done.

Indeed, there was a brief flurry of bipartisanship. Republicans, after two years of "just saying no," finally found something they could vote for: tax cuts for the superrich. One hundred and thirty-eight House Republicans joined 139 Democrats in approving the deal Obama cut with Senate Republican leader Mitch McConnell, which extended the Bush tax cuts in return for a one-year cut in the payroll tax. All but five Senate Republicans followed their leader McConnell in supporting the compromise.

When Obama signed the compromise bill on December 17, 2010, Republican minority leader Mitch McConnell stood by his side—the first time in two years McConnell had attended a bill signing. Just as significant, however, was the fact that Senate majority leader Harry Reid and House Speaker Nancy Pelosi were not present. Nor was John Boehner, the man who would soon succeed Pelosi as Speaker.

But even that promise of bipartisanship didn't last very long. Even though he voted for the compromise tax package, Boehner soon showed he had an entirely different view of what the midterm election results meant. For Boehner, the message was not more cooperation, but more entrenched opposition. He insisted to reporters that, by giving Republicans control of the House and additional seats in the Senate, voters were demanding a complete repudiation of the policies of the Obama administration—a repeal of the Recovery Act, or stimulus, of the Affordable Care Act, of the Dodd-Frank financial reforms—everything Obama and the Democrats had worked to accomplish. This, Boehner gleefully set out to deliver, even if it meant bringing the government to the brink of a shutdown to get his way.

PULLING THE STRINGS

For most Americans, watching from a distance, the political wrangling between President Obama and congressional Republicans was just politics as usual: a president of one political party dutifully challenged by members of Congress from the opposite political party. That's the way it always had been; that's the way it always would be.

Not true. Because, in the case of Barack Obama, it was not just members of Congress who were leading the opposition—and the hate barrage—against him. He was the target of a well-funded, carefully orchestrated, and relentless corporate-funded political campaign unlike any seen before in American politics.

As we will see in greater detail in chapter 5, even before he walked into the Oval Office, Obama was declared fair game for an all-out, carefully planned, take-no-prisoners attack campaign: one paid for and staged by some of the nation's wealthiest and most antigovernment corporate chieftains, led by brothers Charles and David Koch.

As already noted, Bill Clinton had been the target of a similar smear campaign, funded largely by Richard Mellon Scaife, who gave two million dollars to *The American Spectator* in 1993 for the express purpose of investigating and discrediting the Clintons.

The result was a series of "investigative reporting" articles, known collectively as "the Arkansas Project," which focused on a string of manufactured scandals: the death by suicide of top White House aide Vincent Foster; a real estate investment made by Bill and Hillary Clinton in a project called "Whitewater";

reports that Arkansas state troopers had arranged secret rendez-vous with women friends for Governor Clinton; and allegations that he had sexually harassed an Arkansas state employee named Paula Jones.

So far, the attacks on President Obama have been less lurid in nature—due, no doubt, not to any restraint on the part of his political enemies, but to the lack of opportunity and ammunition provided by the president. But the anti-Obama campaign has been no less intense—and far, far more generously funded. In fact, by comparison, the Koch Brothers make Richard Mellon Scaife look like a piker.

The Koch Brothers used a big block of their oil money to found and fuel a right-wing political machine so big, so wide-spread, and so influential that it's known in political circles as the "Kochtopus." In 2009 and 2010 alone, they provided much of the funding for Tea Party rallies nationwide, political and legal opposition to Obama's health care–reform and energy-reform leg-islation, rallies opposing Obama's $787 billion stimulus package, and efforts to overturn California's global-warming initiative, Proposition 23—as well as, of course, continued personal attacks on President Obama.

One could even argue that the entire Tea Party is nothing but a corporate political brand of the Koch family's empire. And their war on Obama continues.

THE ROLE OF THE MEDIA

Sadly, the Obama Hate Machine didn't just thrive on the vehe-mence of its attacks and the unbounded generosity of its corpo-rate backers. It also depended on, and benefited from, the willing cooperation by, and compliance of, the media.

To put it bluntly, in their coverage of the attacks leveled against Barack Obama, the media has, with far too few excep-tions, fallen down on the job. Rather than live up to their responsibility to dig for and report the truth, they have merely repeated false claims, spread lies, ignored the evidence, failed to challenge even the most absurd allegations, and thereby given credibility and long life to political charges that never should have been taken seriously in the first place.

To cite but one example for now: Barack Obama's relationship with Weather Underground founder William Ayers was sketchy at best.

Obama was eight years old and living in Indonesia with his mother and stepfather when Ayers and his Weathermen began planting bombs in banks and government buildings. He didn't meet Ayers until 1995.

That's the year Illinois state senator Alice Palmer decided she would not run for reelection and endorsed attorney and Hyde Park neighbor Barack Obama as her successor. So she gathered a group of political activists together to make the announcement and introduce them to Obama—at the home of her friends William Ayers and Bernardine Dohrn, both former members of the Weather Underground but now well-respected residents of Chicago's South Side. Ayers wrote Obama a check for two hundred dollars.

Later, Obama and Ayers also served together for three years on the board of Chicago's Woods Fund, an antipoverty organization. By that time, Ayers was a professor of education at the University of Illinois and former aide to Chicago mayor Richard M. Daley.

That's it! That's the extent of the connection between Senator Barack Obama and former Weatherman Bill Ayers. But if you believed the rhetoric of John McCain and Sarah Palin during the 2008 campaign and beyond, they were brother terrorists, still making bombs in their basements, and committed to the murder of innocent people and the violent overthrow of the U.S. government.

That accusation was unfounded and outrageous enough in

itself. But what made it even more irresponsible was the fact that it was repeated, broadcast, and spread—without ever being challenged—by the mainstream media. Later in the campaign, Sarah Palin came under more scrutiny and, indeed, became an embarrassment to the McCain campaign. But in the beginning, the media gave her a long honeymoon and a license to lie. Very few ever challenged her assertion that Barack Obama "pals around with terrorists." Instead, they provided her with the megaphone for broadcasting the charge.

At the same time, there was zero media coverage of the fact that, in the closing days of his presidency, Bill Clinton had commuted the sentences of two former members of the Weather Underground still in prison, Susan Rosenberg and Linda Sue Evans.

Neither set of circumstances proves that Obama or Bill Clinton had any connection to terrorism. But certainly you could stage an interesting debate over which was the more questionable action: accepting a two-hundred-dollar campaign contribution from a former terrorist or reducing the sentences of known terrorists already in prison. But since such research might have required too much effort on the part of the media, that debate never happened.

THE OBAMA HATE MACHINE

Ever since he first stepped onto the national political stage, all the necessary ingredients were in place for an intense and wholesale political assault on Barack Obama. The Koch Brothers and other corporate bigwigs wrote the checks. Republican politicians and Tea Party activists voiced the attacks. And cable television and newspapers provided a ready national platform. Together, they formed a vicious, well-funded, and amoral attack campaign virtually unprecedented in our history: an Obama Hate Machine.

It's been a wild and ugly ride. What's surprising is that the

Obama administration has weathered this historic storm—barely, and only so far.

I witnessed this barrage of personal attacks, and how Obama dealt with them, up close, from my position in Washington as a nationally syndicated radio talk-show host, television pundit, columnist, blogger, and member of the White House Press Corps. Here's the story as I observed it.

PRESIDENTS UNDER FIRE

Barack Obama, of course, is not the first president to have experienced withering personal attacks. They are as old as the presidency itself. In some ways, they are a tribute to our American experiment. Unlike forced allegiance to a monarch or tyrant, criticism of elected leaders is not only tolerated here; it is considered a necessary function of our democracy. And from the moment the first president took office, U.S. presidents have had to deal with sometimes-nasty attacks. In this day and age, all of us, Democrats, Republicans, and Tea Partiers alike, revere our Founding Fathers. We even put them on a pedestal. But that's not how they were treated in their own day. Not even Saint George Washington.

It was an open secret that Thomas Jefferson, as our first secretary of state, tried to undermine President Washington's declared policy of neutrality in the matter of war between France and Great Britain. From his position in the cabinet, Jefferson worked behind the scenes, helping orchestrate Republican opposition to Washington and trying to turn public opinion toward the position of siding with France.

Once Washington left the White House, our first president became an open target of abuse. He was publicly mocked and criticized as being weak and ineffective. Rumors resurfaced that he had enjoyed an affair with a young cleaning woman, whom he called "pretty little Kate, the Washer-woman's daughter." The Philadelphia *Aurora,* the chief Republican newspaper, heavily influenced by Jefferson, described Washington's farewell address as "the loathings of a sick mind." Its publisher, Benjamin Franklin Bache, revived charges that Washington had assassinated an unarmed officer during the French and Indian War and accused Washington of offering America nothing better than a "despotic counterfeit of the English Georges."

Writing in the *Aurora,* the one and only Thomas Paine even questioned Washington's leadership of the Revolutionary army, deeming him worse than a sunshine patriot. "You slept away your time in the field till the finances of the country were completely exhausted," he charged, "and you have but little share in the glory of the event." Paine demanded that Washington ask himself "whether you are an apostate or an imposter, whether you have abandoned good principles, or whether you ever had any."

Ouch! Watching from a distance, Abigail Adams was appalled by the attacks on our first president. It just proved, she wrote her husband, Vice President John Adams, "that the most virtuous and unblemished Characters are liable to the Malice and venom of unprincipald [*sic*] Wretches." And, of course, she was afraid of what level of attacks might fall on her husband, who enjoyed nowhere near the popularity of the haloed Washington. She later warned Adams that, as president, he might well find himself "being fastned [*sic*] up Hand and foot and Tongue to be shot at as our Quincy Lads do at the poor Geese and Turkies." And, indeed, he was.

Adams was no fool. He knew he would be in for a rough time. As he wrote Abigail of the departing George Washington after his inauguration, "He seemed to enjoy a triumph over me. Methought

I heard him think, 'Ay! I am fairly out and you are fairly in! See which of us will be the happiest!' "

As vice president, Adams had already endured his share of ridicule, some of which he brought on himself. After suggesting to Congress that Washington be called "Your Highness," rather than the populist "Mr. President," Adams was henceforth called "The Duke of Braintree," or simply "His Rotundity." Privately, Senator William Maclay of Pennsylvania dismissed Adams as "a monkey just put into breeches."

After eight years of running interference for President Washington against Secretary of State Thomas Jefferson, the last thing John Adams needed when he himself assumed the presidency was having to put up with Jefferson as vice president. But that's what the electoral vote delivered, after a noncontested and practically nonexistent presidential campaign. Still trying to figure out the proper way to choose leaders in the new republic, neither Adams nor Jefferson declared their candidacy or campaigned for the office. Once their new roles were decided, however, the two leaders, from different political parties and with separate agendas, were bound to clash—and did.

At first, heeding his wife Abigail's advice, Adams held forth an olive branch to Jefferson, offering him cabinet status, a major voice in foreign policy, and designation of him or his ally James Madison as the new American envoy to France. But Jefferson rejected all three, choosing to pursue his Republican party agenda instead.

As Joseph Ellis reports in *First Family,* Jefferson was, in fact, already in clandestine conversations with the French consul in Philadelphia, urging him to ignore any peace initiatives from the new president—since, according to Jefferson, Adams did not speak for the true interests of the American people. Just imagine! Today, this act would be considered treason.

There followed a rocky four years, during which Adams was

constantly fighting rear-guard actions by his disloyal vice president, who was busy plotting with the French, and by his own cabinet (he had mistakenly retained all appointees of Washington, believing the cabinet should be a permanent body). It was all too much for First Lady Abigail Adams, who lamented the steady stream of "Lies, falsehoods, calamities and bitterness" and denounced Philadelphia as "a city that seems devoted to Calamity."

And it led, inevitably, to the first contested election for president, in 1800, and one of the ugliest presidential campaigns ever.

For the incumbent vice president to challenge the incumbent president for reelection was, in itself, a direct personal attack. It'd be as if Dick Cheney had dared to run against George W. Bush in 2004. Today, that would never happen. It would be considered inappropriate, in bad taste, even treacherous. But back then, the country was new, and people were still feeling their way around the political process.

Even before the campaign, intrigue began. Adams first had to defend himself from a scurrilous attack by fellow Federalist Alexander Hamilton that he had, in effect, begun to lose his mind. Adams's "ungovernable temper," matched by his "disgusting egotism" and "distempered jealousy," Hamilton charged in his *Letter from Alexander Hamilton, Concerning the Public Conduct and Character of John Adams, Esq. President of the United States*, were characteristics that "unfit him for the office of chief magistrate."

But his strongest challenge came from Vice President Thomas Jefferson and Republicans. Determined to weaken, if not destroy, Adams's reputation ahead of any actual campaigning, Jefferson commissioned fiery pamphleteer James Callender to wield the political ax.

As I noted in my first book, *Spin This!*, Callender—who would later turn on Jefferson and charge him with sexual abuse of slave Sally Hemings—published *The Prospect Before Us*, in which he accused Adams of corruption and secretly attempting to lead the United States into war, which was the exact opposite of what Adams was fighting for. In his private life, charged Callender, Adams was "one of the most egregious fools upon the continent." Then, in typical Callender style, he vilified the president as "a repulsive pedant, . . . a gross hypocrite, . . . a wretch that has neither the science of a magistrate, the politeness of a courtier, nor the courage of a man."

With that, the stage was set. And once the Adams-Jefferson campaign got under way, neither side held back. Because of his known aversion to any established religion—he was a Deist—Jefferson was accused of being an atheist. Not to mention a Francophile (guilty), a revolutionist, and a man devoid of morals, whose election would deliver the country to licentiousness and debauchery and who, if elected, would immediately order the confiscation of Bibles and the burning of churches. Almost in anticipation of the questions raised about Barack Obama's birth certificate, Adams supporters called Jefferson "a mean-spirited, low-lived fellow, the son of a half-breed Indian squaw, sired by a Virginia mulatto father." George Washington stayed above the fray, but not Martha. She couldn't resist jumping on the bandwagon, telling a clergyman that Jefferson was "one of the most detestable of mankind."

The Jefferson camp, meanwhile, responded in kind, accusing President Adams of being unpatriotic because he opposed joining France in another war with Great Britain and, here at home, wanted to maintain a standing army. He was also charged with wanting to turn the presidency into a monarchy and with planning to marry one of his sons to a daughter of George III, thus starting an American dynasty that would reunite the country with Great Britain.

As the great historian Page Smith relates in his magnificent two-volume life of Adams, another rumor more amused than annoyed him. Republicans accused Adams of sending Gen. Charles Pinckney to England in a United States frigate to procure four pretty girls as mistresses, two for the general and two for himself. "I do declare upon my honor," Adams responded, "if this be true General Pinckney has kept them all for himself and cheated me out of two."

At the same time, Jefferson's backers also questioned Adams's sexuality. Campaign brochures repeated James Callender's description of Adams as being of "hideous hermaphroditical character, which has neither the force and firmness of a man, nor the gentleness and sensibility of a woman."

Jefferson, of course, won that round and became our third president. A bitter Adams didn't wait around for his archenemy to take the oath of office. On Inauguration Day, 1801, he left early in the morning to return to Massachusetts.

Once in the White House, Jefferson had his own political enemies to deal with, and few more lethal than the beast he created, notorious once and future mudslinger James Callender. When refused a presidential appointment, Callender turned on the man who had once paid him to smear John Adams, accusing the refined "gentleman" of Monticello of having sexual relations with his slave Sally Hemings and fathering her children. Which, of course, was true. For Abigail Adams, this was the revenge she'd been looking for. "The serpent you cherished and warmed," she wrote much later to Jefferson, "bit the hand that nourished him."

GETTING PHYSICAL

The point is, over-the-top political invective was here from the beginning, directed against, and even exercised by, some of the most revered figures in the American political pantheon. And it wasn't always just verbal. Too often, it got physical. Not yet in the White House, perhaps, but, from its earliest days, on the floor of the United States Congress. Norm Ornstein, who follows Congress from his perch at the American Enterprise Institute,

has documented many cases where debate over issues degener-
ated into acts of physical violence between members of Congress. Among the more colorful and memorable are:

- Lyon v. Griswold. On January 30, 1798, debate over whether
  the United States should enter the ongoing war between
  France and England on the side of France escalated into a
  shouting match between Matthew Lyon, Republican of Vermont, and Roger Griswold, Federalist from Connecticut. At
  one point, Lyon, a tobacco chewer, like many other members
  of Congress, spit tobacco in Griswold's face. Two weeks later,
  on February 15, Griswold responded by attacking Lyon with
  a hickory cane. At which point, Lyon picked up a pair of fire-
  place tongs and struck back. Neither one was expelled from
  Congress.
- Black v. Giddings, 1845. We only know about this incident
  thanks to John Quincy Adams, who recorded it in his diary.
  As Representative Joshua R. Giddings, an Ohio Whig, was
  speaking on the floor, Representative Edward J. Black, a Democrat from Georgia, "crossed over from his seat . . . and, coming within the bar behind Giddings as he was speaking, made
  a pass at the back of his head with a cane." Adams reported
  that Representative William H. Hammett of Mississippi then
  "threw his arms round [Black] and bore him off as he would
  a woman from a fire."
- Brooks v. Sumner, 1856. This is the most notorious incident
  of congressional violence in our history. Pro-slavery senator
  Andrew Butler of South Carolina was the subject of strong
  verbal attacks from abolitionist senator Charles Sumner of
  Massachusetts. Over the course of a fiery three-hour speech,
  Sumner argued that Butler had taken "a mistress who, though
  ugly to others, is always lovely to him; though polluted in the
  sight of the world, is chaste in his sight—I mean, the harlot,
  Slavery."

Butler's relative, Representative Preston Brooks of South Carolina, rallied to his defense. Brooks walked from the House to the Senate floor and beat Sumner senseless with his gutta-percha walking cane. When other senators tried to come to Sumner's defense, they were stopped by Representative Laurence Keitt, also of South Carolina, who pulled out his pistol and kept them away. After an attempt to expel Brooks from the House failed, he nevertheless resigned his seat, but he ran again and was reelected the following November. Indeed, Brooks subsequently received dozens of canes in the mail from admiring southerners.

For his part, Sumner could not return to the Senate for three years due to his injuries, but he was reelected in 1856 regardless by an equally angry Massachusetts state legislature.

- Tilman v. McLaurin, 1902. South Carolina strikes again. This time, violence between two Democrats from South Carolina. On the Senate floor, Senator John McLaurin accused a fellow South Carolinian, Senator Benjamin Tillman, of telling a "willful, malicious and deliberate lie." Tillman, known as "Pitchfork Ben," hauled off and punched McLaurin in the face.
- Thurmond v. Yarborough, 1964. One of the strangest of all physical encounters between members of Congress was a wrestling match between segregationist Strom Thurmond of South Carolina (again!) and Ralph Yarborough of Texas. Thurmond was so determined to prevent the confirmation of LeRoy Collins as President Johnson's head of the Community Relations Service that he stood outside the door to the Commerce Committee hearing room, blocking other senators from entering. When Yarborough tried to get around him, Thurmond threw Yarborough to the floor. At which point, Chairman Warren Magnuson came to the door and broke up the scuffle. Thurmond won the wrestling match but lost the vote, sixteen to one.

There were many other times, of course, when members of Congress engaged in angry debate. But, perhaps mindful of losing their seats, they stopped just short of coming to blows. In 2003, all but one Democrat on the House Ways and Means Committee walked out to protest Chairman Bill Thomas's lack of notice about markup of a pension bill. Pete Stark of California was left behind to observe the proceedings and report back to his fellow Democrats. When Stark attempted to speak, Congressman Scott McInnis of Colorado told him to "shut up." At which point, Stark, known for his temper, shouted back, "You think you are big enough to make me, you little wimp? Come on. Come over here and make me, I dare you. You little fruitcake." In earlier days, that could easily have led to blows with a hickory cane, or worse.

Senator Patrick Leahy showed similar restraint in his famous contretemps with Vice President Dick Cheney in 2004. After a heated exchange over Cheney's ties to his old firm, Halliburton, and President Bush's judicial nominees, the veep ended the debate by telling Leahy to "go fuck yourself" and walked away. Cheney later said, "That's sort of the best thing I ever did." Leahy did not return fire, which was probably for the best, given that Cheney later shot hunting partner Harry Whittington in the face.

MEET YOU IN BLADENSBURG

These are just the fisticuffs that happened in the halls of Congress. Too often in our early history, political disagreements escalated from the verbal to the physical—all the way to the fatal.

By the late 1700s, in fact, settling disputes with a duel had become an accepted part of the culture, especially in the South, as a way of finally deciding an argument. Like many other features of American politics, the practice was introduced from Europe, where the *codo duello* contained twenty-six rules governing proper etiquette between dueling partners.

Most duels were usually conducted in a remote location, with just the principals and their seconds present. But duels among politicians were often widely publicized in advance. For members of Congress, the preferred location was Bladensburg, Maryland, only eight miles from Washington, favored both for its isolation and its proximity to the Capitol, where dueling was already banned.

As the century turned, public opinion began to turn against dueling in state after state. But not before several members of Congress had fallen victims to it. In *The Almanac of Political Corruption, Scandals, & Dirty Politics*, Kim Long documents some of the more famous cases.

- July 31, 1802. In the middle of a heated reelection campaign, Senator DeWitt Clinton of New York challenged his political opponent, John Swartwout, to a duel. Neither was apparently a good marksman, because both men survived the exchange of five rounds. But Swartwout was hit twice in the leg—and went on to lose the election.

- September 5, 1802. Nearing the end of a nasty reelection campaign, North Carolina congressman Richard Dobbs Spaight complained about his opponent, John Stanly: "I must now gentlemen, declare to you, that in my opinion, Mr. Stanley [sic] is both a lyar and a scoundrel." To which Stanly responded with the classic challenge to a duel: "To your disappointment, this letter informs you, that humiliating as it is to my feelings, to fight a man who can descend to the filth contained in your handbill, I shall expect that *you will meet me* as soon as may be convenient." But first came the vote. Spaight lost. The next day came the duel. Spaight lost that one, too. He was wounded, and died the following day.

- March 2, 1808. Angry over comments made on the House floor during debate over an embargo on trade with Great Britain, New York congressman Barent Gardenier threw the gauntlet down to Tennessee congressman George Washington Campbell. They met with their pistols on the field in Bladensburg. Both survived.

- December 4, 1809. Once again, debate on the floor led to the dueling grounds. This time, debate over negotiations with Spain over the so-called Yazoo lands. John George Jackson, Republican congressman from Virginia, challenged Joseph Pearson, Federalist congressman from North Carolina, to settle their differences at gunpoint. On the second shot, Pearson was seriously wounded; Jackson was permanently crippled from a shot to the hip, and he resigned from Congress.

- February 16, 1819. If at first you don't succeed . . . During his campaign, Armistead Thomson Mason, Democratic-Republican Senator from Virginia, had so many angry exchanges with his opponent, John Mason McCarty, that they challenged each other to, and carried out, several duels. In their final exchange, held in Bladensburg, Mason was killed by McCarty, who was also his brother-in-law. Go figure.

- April 8, 1826. Another debate prompted by heated words on the floor of the House of Representatives. After President John Quincy Adams and Secretary of State Henry Clay proposed that representatives of the United States participate in a Pan-American conference in Panama called by Venezuelan leader Simón Bolívar, Virginia representative John Randolph let fly a colorful condemnation of Clay: "Like a rotten mackerel by moonlight, [Clay] shined and stunk." Clay challenged; Randolph accepted. Both first round shots missed their target. Clay's second shot also missed, whereupon Randolph fired his second shot into the air—and the duel was over.

The most notorious duel in American history took place early on the morning of July 11, 1804, in Weehawken, New Jersey, between the former secretary of the treasury and the sitting vice president of the United States. Alexander Hamilton and Aaron Burr were hotheaded political activists and longtime rivals, and both men had been involved in duels in the past. This fatal encounter stemmed from comments Hamilton had allegedly made about the vice president at a dinner party. Those comments were relayed by Charles D. Cooper in a letter to Hamilton's father-in-law, Philip Schuyler—which letter was somehow leaked and then reprinted in the *Albany Register.* Burr demanded an apology. Having received none, he challenged Hamilton, and Hamilton accepted.

Because dueling had been outlawed in New York, the participants were rowed across the Hudson from Manhattan to Weehawken, where Hamilton, as challenged, chose to fire first. He fired into the air. Historians will forever debate whether that was his intention, expressed in writing the night before, or whether he just fired wide. At any rate, Burr had no intention of missing. And he didn't. Hamilton was mortally wounded and taken back to Manhattan, where he died the next day.

What's still remarkable is that such a prominent political figure was shot and killed and yet nothing happened. The vice president of the United States committed a very public act of murder—and got away with it. Burr was charged with murder in New York and New Jersey, but neither case ever reached trial. After fleeing to South Carolina to hide out with his daughter, he returned to Washington and completed his term as vice president, presiding over the United States Senate.

By the time of the Civil War, dueling was on its way out—now seen not as an honorable way to resolve a dispute, but as cold-blooded murder.

Words became the new weapon of choice. More and more ugly words were directed against elected officials. Every president, Republican and Democrat, has suffered the slings and arrows of public abuse. But before Barack Obama, three presidents in particular experienced the worst verbal attacks: Abraham Lincoln, Franklin Roosevelt, and Bill Clinton.

PRESIDENT ABRAHAM LINCOLN

The Lincoln Memorial, at the western end of the Washington Mall, is the closest thing we Americans have to a national religious shrine. Some would argue, in fact, that it's our only national shrine.

Indeed, no matter how many times you've been there, there's an out-of-this-world thrill to climbing the steps of the Lincoln Memorial and approaching the magnificent nineteen-foot-high Daniel Chester French sculpture of our sixteenth president, seated and gazing solemnly up the Mall, across the reflecting pool, and, past the Washington Monument, to the U.S. Capitol.

To Lincoln's right, etched into the memorial's walls, is the iconic Gettysburg Address. To his left, on the north side of the chamber, are enshrined the words of what Lincoln himself considered his greatest speech: The second inaugural address, the closest we Americans have ever come to the delineation of a national theology, with its admonition to go forward "with malice toward none; with charity for all."

There are no signs telling visitors to speak softly. But they do so anyway, automatically, somehow sensing the almost-holy nature of the place. They take time to read every word of the sacred American scripture on the walls. They stand in awe before the Great Emancipator, holding young children in their arms for a close look, gazing up at him with the same hushed reverence tourists show Michelangelo's *Pietà* in St. Peter's Basilica.

There's a reason why. It is a place that resonates with all that is best in our American democracy. On Saturday morning, April 9, 2011, when President Obama wanted to remind the American people that Congress had failed to shut down the government and that the people's government was still open for business, he went to the Lincoln Memorial.

Yet surely Abraham Lincoln, with his wonderful sense of humor, would appreciate the irony behind every visitor's presence were he alive today. If only they knew what a remarkable contrast they represent. How we revere Abraham Lincoln today. But how reviled he was during his own lifetime.

The Lincoln literature is full of examples of the personal attacks directed against our sixteenth president. Larry Tagg, author of *The Unpopular Mr. Lincoln*, even calls him "America's most reviled president." In Tagg's reading of history, the weeks surrounding Lincoln's inaugural—due to both the frightening secession of southern states and the widespread condemnation of the way he was secretly whisked into the capital wearing a disguise—mark "the historical nadir of presidential prestige in the United States."

Criticism began with his physical appearance. Later, cartoonists had fun with Nixon's nose, Jimmy Carter's teeth, and Barack Obama's ears. But nothing compared to the personal attacks on Lincoln.

British journalist Edward Dicey reported in 1862, "To say he is ugly is nothing; to add that his figure is grotesque is to convey no adequate impression. Fancy a man almost six feet high, and thin out of proportion, with long bony arms and legs, which somehow seem to be always in the way." As if that weren't enough, Dicey continued: "Add to this figure a head, cocoanut shaped, and somewhat too small for such a stature, covered with rough, uncombed hair, that stands out in every direction at once; a face, furrowed, wrinkled, and indented as though it had been scarred by vitriol."

Lincoln's political enemies welcomed him to Washington with a mock biography: "Mr. Lincoln stands six feet tall in his socks, which he changes once every ten days. His anatomy is composed mostly of bones, and when walking he resembles the offspring of a happy marriage between a derrick and a windmill. . . . His head is shaped something like a rutabaga, and his complexion is that of a Saratoga trunk. . . . He can hardly be called handsome, though he is certainly much better looking since he had the small-pox."

Authentic American journals of the time treated him no more kindly. Here's how readers of the *Kentucky Statesman* were introduced to their new president: "Abraham Lincoln is a man above the medium height. He passes the six foot mark by an inch or two. He is raw-boned, shamble-gaited, bow-legged, knock-kneed, pigeon-toed, slob-sided, a shapeless skeleton in a very tough, very dirty, unwholesome skin. . . . His lips protrude beyond the natural level of the face, but are pale and smeared with tobacco juice. His teeth are filthy."

Gen. George B. McClellan, Lincoln's chosen head of the Army of the Potomac and later his opponent in 1864, didn't need that many words. He simply called him "the Gorilla." And according to Virginian congressman Sherrard Clemens, who met him days before the inauguration, Lincoln carried himself like "a cross between a sandhill crane and an Andalusian jackass."

By the time he faced reelection, Lincoln had a record, including an ongoing, bloody, and unpopular Civil War and an Emancipation Proclamation, to defend. All of which provided his political enemies with more ammunition and more targets to attack.

Even some Republicans, fearful of defeat, turned on Lincoln. In what became known as the Wade-Davis Manifesto, Radical Republicans Ben Wade and Henry Winter Davis charged Lincoln with "grave Executive usurpation" and "a studied outrage on the legislative authority." They further accused him of "personal ambition" and "sinister motives," and urged the Republican party either to impeach him or dump him as their candidate. Tagg calls it "the fiercest, most public challenge to Lincoln's—or, for that matter, any president's—authority ever issued by members of his own party."

Once the campaign got under way, the Democratic press was

equally vicious. "The most powerful monarchy in Europe would not dare commit the outrages which have been put upon us by the Lincoln administration," declared the *Illinois State Register.*

Cried the *Newark Evening Journal,* "We have no honeyed words for such a ruler as Abraham Lincoln who is a perjured traitor, who has betrayed his country and caused the butchery of hundreds of thousands of the people of the United States in order to accomplish either his own selfish purpose, or to put in force a fanatical, impracticable idea."

From Wisconsin, the *Lacrosse Democrat* prayed, "May God forbid that we are to have two terms of the rottenest, most stinking ruin-working small pox ever conceived by friends or mortals."

Those savage comments from the American press were echoed by their influential British counterparts. The London *Evening Standard* blasted Lincoln as a "foul-tongued and ribald punster," and also as "the most despicable tyrant of modern days," while the *Leeds Intelligencer* portrayed him as "that concentrated quintessence of evil, that Nero in the most shrunken and detestable form of idolatry, that flatulent and indecent jester."

In the end, a sympathetic but exasperated *Harper's Weekly* took upon itself the obligation to sum up all the names President Lincoln was called by his political enemies: "Filthy Story-Teller, Ignoramus Abe, Despot, Old Scoundrel, Big Secessionist, Perjurer, Liar, Robber, Thief, Swindler, Braggart, Tyrant, Buffoon, Fiend, Usurper, Butcher, Monster, Land-Pirate, A Long, Lean, Lank, Lantern-Jawed, High-Cheek-Boned, Spavined, Rail-Splitting Stallion." And that was just a warm-up for what would be leveled against Barack Obama.

Lincoln, of course, won reelection with 55 percent of the vote and overwhelmingly carried the Electoral College, 212–21. This news was greeted with bitterness by the *Richmond Dispatch*: "Yesterday . . . the freest people on earth . . . made a formal surrender of their liberties . . . to a vulgar tyrant . . . whose personal qualities are those of a low buffoon."

But within five months, on April 9, it was the South that surrendered. Then, just five days later, Lincoln lay dying from an assassin's bullet, and public opinion turned completely around. In the words of historian Larry Tagg, the most hated man in America became a "sudden saint."

The previous May, for example, the *New York Times* had lamented in an editorial, "No living man was ever charged with political crimes of such multiplicity and such enormity as Abraham Lincoln. He has been denounced without end as a perjurer, a usurper, a tyrant, a subverter of the Constitution, a destroyer of the liberties of his country, a reckless desperado, a heartless trifler over the last agonies of an expiring nation."

But no longer. Fellow Republican and onetime political opponent Senator James W. Grimes of Iowa spoke for all his former detractors: "Mr. Lincoln is to be hereafter regarded as a saint. All his foibles, and faults, and shortcomings, will be forgotten, and he will be looked upon as the Moses who led the nation through a four years' bloody war, and died in sight of peace." And he has been.

In an interesting twist of history, it would take another president from Illinois to match the record of Abraham Lincoln for political opprobrium directed against him. Perhaps Barack Obama realized that on February 10, 2007, when he chose the Old State Capital in Springfield, Illinois, Lincoln's original political stomping grounds, to announce he was running for president. Obama was steeling himself for the onslaught that lay ahead.

FRANKLIN DELANO ROOSEVELT

There are many reputable historians who insist that history never repeats itself. Barack Obama and Franklin Roosevelt have proved them wrong. The challenges FDR faced as president, the actions he took, and the opposition he met are uncannily similar to Obama's situation. Like Obama, FDR came into office with the economy in ruins. And, like Obama, he was denounced as both a socialist and a Communist for trying to use the resources of the federal government to prevent complete collapse and get the economy back on track. Even today, FDR is still called thus. In April 2011, Republican congressman Paul Broun of Georgia argued on the House floor that Roosevelt held "socialist beliefs" and had mimicked Stalin to replicate Russian communism in America.

Like Obama, FDR faced a so-called "grassroots" opposition that was, in fact, funded by a team of brothers and their corporate fat-cat friends. For Obama, it's the Koch Brothers and the Tea Party. For FDR, it was the du Pont Brothers and the American Liberty League.

Like Obama, FDR also encountered serious criticism and opposition from members of his own party, who slammed him for not doing enough to help poor and middle-class Americans. Huey Long, the "Kingfish," was FDR's equivalent of Obama's modern-day critics on the "professional left," as former press secretary Robert Gibbs deemed them.

And, like Obama, FDR suffered from the relentless attacks of a popular talk-radio host. As I related in my last book, *Toxic Talk,* Father Charles Coughlin, the "Radio Priest," was the prototype for Rush Limbaugh and Glenn Beck today.

There are differences, of course. And they are real. FDR was much more bold and daring in his use of executive power. And neither the Liberty League nor Huey Long ever achieved the electoral clout of the Tea Party. But the parallel challenges of FDR and Barack Obama are still strikingly similar.

When FDR was elected in 1932, the nation was still reeling from our longest, most widespread, and deepest economic downturn ever. Taking the oath of office on March 4, 1933, he in effect declared war on the Depression. If Congress did not act decisively, he warned, he was ready to ask for "broad emergency powers to wage war against the emergency, as great as the power that would be given to me if we were in fact invaded by a foreign foe."

And Congress, goaded by him and a long-suffering public, rose to the occasion. As documented by Anthony Badger in his valuable study of the period, *FDR: The First Hundred Days,* by June 16, after only one hundred days, "sixteen pieces of major legislation gave the federal government the power to decide which banks should or should not reopen, to regulate the Stock Exchange, to determine the gold value of the dollar, to prescribe minimum wages and prices, to pay farmers not to produce, to pay money to the unemployed, to plan and regenerate a whole river basin across six states, to spend billions of dollars on public works, and to underwrite credit for bankers, homeowners, and farmers."

At first, leaders of the hard-hit business community supported FDR. But within a year, his expansion of government powers had stirred up great resistance among many of them, who accused Roosevelt of manufacturing an artificial crisis in order to justify an unprecedented expansion of federal power and regulation. Sound familiar?

Leading his newly avowed political enemies were scions of one of the wealthiest families in the nation: Delaware's three du Pont brothers—Pierre, Irénée, and Lammot. Irénée complained about efforts by the newly created Securities and Exchange Commission to regulate free market activity. Pierre feared the National Labor Board's support for the workers' right to strike. Irénée summed up their opposition in a letter to a friend: "It must now have become clear to every thinking man that the so-called 'New Deal,' advocated by the Administration, is nothing more or less than the Socialistic doctrine called by another name." Creeping socialism. Again, sound familiar?

The reality is that FDR's New Deal did not kill capitalism. It saved capitalism. The president refused to nationalize the banks, for example, as many on the Left demanded, then and now.

Instead, banks emerged from the crisis stronger and more stable than ever. So did Wall Street's financial institutions, able to attract new investors only because of their confidence in the new regulations in place.

We saw the same overreaction to actions taken by President Obama to rescue the economy from the collapse of October 2008. He, too, was accused of using a crisis to grab unprecedented federal government powers. Yet he didn't seize control of the banks or auto companies. He loaned them money so that they might weather the crisis and get back on their feet. They are now both back, stronger than ever, and have paid back their loans—with interest! And corporate profits jumped to a record high. Like FDR, Obama, too, saved capitalism.

But as we will see, that didn't silence his critics. Nor did it FDR's. In an eerie preview of what we would see from Obama's corporate enemies and the Tea Party, the du Pont Brothers invited their fellow corporate chieftains to meetings at the Empire State Building and the General Motors headquarters in Detroit. They banded together to disseminate information about the "danger to investors" presented by the New Deal. Their goal was to "combat radicalism, preserve property rights, uphold and defend the Constitution." They pledged to form alliances with other defenders of the Constitution, including the American Legion and "even the Ku Klux Klan." And they called it the American Liberty League.

In short, the Liberty League of FDR's time was the Tea Party of today. Only the players are different. Otherwise, they are exactly the same: a big business political attack squad masquerading as a grassroots organization, and hiding behind an oft-professed reverence for the Constitution.

And, like the Tea Party, the Liberty League eventually attracted the support of many working-class Americans, blissfully ignorant of the fact that they were merely being used as political pawns by big corporations that were, in fact, their worst enemies. FDR himself sardonically noted that the Liberty League's stated mission was notably silent "about the protection of the individual against elements in the community that seek to enrich themselves at the expense of their fellow citizens."

Then, like today, big business eagerly bellied up to the bar. At the request of the du Pont brothers, CEOs not only kicked in corporate funds; they even wrote letters to their shareholders, asking them to contribute. As documented by historian Kim Phillips-Fein in *Invisible Hands,* this was the foundation of the corporate-funded conservative movement of today. In 1935, more than half the Liberty League's funds came from fewer than two dozen bankers, industrialists, and businessmen. Members of the du Pont family contributed 30 percent of the total.

The League jumped into the 1936 presidential campaign, supporting Republican Alf Landon. They set up headquarters in the National Press Building in Washington, with branches in all fifty states, and hired fifty staffers. And they amassed what was then a new record of $1.5 million in corporate contributions.

With those funds, the Liberty League launched a no-holds-barred attack to deny FDR a second term. They called the New Deal a "monstrous usurpation of power." They warned about a "totalitarian" centralization of power. They blasted the Roosevelt administration for "spreading its tentacles over the business and private life of the citizens of the country." They accused FDR of trying to "redistribute the wealth," and opposed Social Security as a "gigantic fraud" and an unlawful taking of property from employers. They called the president a socialist and a Communist. In his newspapers, publisher William Randolph Hearst reported that FDR was supported by "the Karl Marx Socialists, the Frankfurter radicals, communists and anarchists, the Tugwell Bolsheviks, the Richberg revolutionists," and other "enemies of the American system of government."

But Roosevelt and his political allies didn't wilt under fire. They fought back with equal verbal vigor. Democrats ridiculed the Liberty League as a "millionaire's union." The Democratic party chairman suggested it should actually be called "the American Cellophane League" because, "first it's a Du Pont product and second, you can see right through it." And in a historic campaign rally at Madison Square Garden, FDR let loose with his own brand of political bombast.

He identified his corporate foes by name and gloried in their opposition: "Never before in all our history have these forces been so united against one candidate as they stand today. They are unanimous in their hate for me—and I welcome their hatred." Big business was willing to spend anything, he charged, to take over the reins of government. But he hastened to warn: "We know now that Government by organized money is just as dangerous as Government by organized mob."

Then the president defiantly promised an end to the rule of those his cousin Teddy Roosevelt called the "malefactors of great wealth." "I should like to have it said of my first Administration that in it the forces of selfishness and lust for power met their match," FDR declared. "I should like to have it said of my second Administration that in it these forces met their master."

When the votes were counted, the du Pont brothers and their American Liberty League certainly had met their master. Franklin Roosevelt won 98.5 percent of the electoral vote, the highest percentage since 1820. He also won the largest number of electoral votes ever recorded at the time, 593 to Alf Landon's 8. And he won 60.8 percent of the national popular vote.

With FDR's overwhelming election victory, the American Liberty League was, for all practical purposes, dead. It limped along for another four years, until founder Pierre du Pont finally pulled the plug in 1940, lamenting to its few supporters left, "Perhaps, we were born too soon." Perhaps they were, indeed.

But FDR didn't just face a challenge from the Right. For a couple of years, he had to fight off equally vigorous opposition from the Left, in the person of the Kingfish—Louisiana's populist senator Huey Long. Like the du Ponts, Long had supported Roosevelt for president in 1932, but he soon soured on him—not because Roosevelt exercised too much government power, but because he didn't exercise enough. In Long's view, banks were still too powerful, unemployment was still too high, wealth was still concentrated in too few hands, and average Americans were still scraping bottom.

Instead of FDR's New Deal, the Kingfish proposed a "Share Our Wealth" platform, guaranteeing every American a homestead worth five thousand dollars and a minimum annual income of half that amount—all paid for by higher income, business, and inheritance taxes. It was a popular message in a country still hard-hit by the Depression. Soon there were 27,000 Share Our Wealth chapters, with over eight million members nationally—enough to scare FDR and his political advisers into preparing for a serious threat from the Left: a threat cut abruptly short by the assassination of Huey Long in the Louisiana State Capitol in 1935.

Even before Franklin Roosevelt was in the White House, Huey Long had pioneered the use of regular radio addresses, as governor of Louisiana, to get his message out. He continued the practice, keeping pace with FDR, as head of his own Share Our Wealth movement. So it was only fitting that FDR's other big populist nemesis was a professional radio broadcaster: Father Charles Coughlin.

As I documented in *Toxic Talk*, Coughlin was one of the pioneers of today's right-wing talk radio and, in his day, attracted an audience far exceeding that of any talk-show host today, including Rush Limbaugh. More than forty million people, one-third of the nation at the time, tuned into his weekly broadcasts from the Shrine of the Little Flower in Royal Oak, Michigan. "The Radio Priest" started out a strong supporter of Franklin Roosevelt and the New Deal. In 1933, he exhorted Americans to believe in "Roosevelt or Ruin!" and argued that "The New Deal is Christ's Deal!" The following year, he called FDR "the answer to many prayers that were sent up last year."

Eventually, however, the Radio Priest, apparently believing his having a national listenership was tantamount to elected office, felt frozen out of policy decisions that had never been his to make in the first place. He had come to believe that remonetizing silver would be a cure-all for the American economy, and he spoke often about it to his audience. But when Roosevelt cheerfully ignored his silvery prescription for ending the Depression, Coughlin grew embittered. "We were supposed to be partners," complained Coughlin. "He said he would rely on me. That I would be an important adviser. But he was a liar."

In 1936, while the du Pont brothers were organizing the American Liberty League behind the candidacy of Alf Landon, Father Coughlin started his own organization, the National Union for Social Justice, and his own political party, the National Union party, to support his candidate for president, North Dakota congressman William Lemke. But, despite his radio appeal, Coughlin's political debut failed. Lemke did even worse than Landon, garnering only 900,000 popular votes—and no electoral votes.

After this defeat, Coughlin began to unleash his full fury against Roosevelt, calling him "a dangerous citizen of the Republic." He also spoke harshly of President Roosevelt's pro-Allied foreign policy leading up to World War II: "He has consorted with the enemies of civilization. . . . He has deceived the citizens of the United States. . . . He has transcended the bounds of his Executive position. . . . He stands revealed as the world's chief war-monger."

Unlike today's radio talk-show hosts, Coughlin did not call the president of the United States a Nazi. But he did compare him to Hitler—unfavorably! As war in Europe drew closer, Coughlin praised Germany's Adolf Hitler and Italy's Benito Mussolini. He even adopted their anti-Semitic language, blaming the Great Depression on an "international conspiracy of Jewish bankers" and arguing that the Russian Revolution "was launched and fomented by distinctively Jewish influence."

Even as news of Nazi atrocities against Jews reached the United States, Coughlin dismissed them or tried to explain them away. "Jewish persecution only followed after Christians first were persecuted," he insisted. Like his modern-day successor, Glenn Beck, Coughlin started to lose listeners the crazier his anti-Roosevelt, pro-Germany screeds got. And so, with the outbreak of World War II, and most of his listeners gone, Catholic Church authorities finally forced him to give up his radio broadcasts.

FDR outlived and outfought his political enemies, serving twelve years as president—longer than any president before or since. As late as 1944, he was still a happy warrior, fighting back against his political enemies with wit and verve. When Republicans tried to rewrite the history books by claiming the Depression was a Democratic creation, FDR told America that "there is an old and somewhat lugubrious adage which says: 'Never speak of rope in the house of a man who has been hanged.' In the same way, if I were a Republican leader speaking to a mixed audience, the last word in the whole dictionary that I think I would use is that word 'depression.'" Similarly, when Republicans claimed a dictatorial Roosevelt had sent a destroyer overseas to pick up his dog, Fala, FDR wryly returned fire:

These Republican leaders have not been content with attacks on me, or my wife, or on my sons. No, not content with that, they now include my little dog, Fala. Well, of course, I don't resent attacks, and my family doesn't resent attacks, but Fala does resent them. You know, Fala is Scotch, and being a Scottie, as soon as he learned that the Republican fiction writers in Congress had gone out and concocted a story that I had left him behind on the Aleutian Islands and had sent a destroyer back to find him—at a cost to the taxpayers of two or three, or eight or twenty million dollars—his Scotch soul was furious. He has not been the same dog since. I am accustomed to hearing malicious falsehoods about myself—such as that old, worm-eaten chestnut that I have represented myself as indispensable. But I think I have a right to resent, to object to libelous statements about my dog.

Roosevelt was too much for the right-wing onslaught that tried to destroy his New Deal. But this was not the last time an American president would be forced to confront a hate campaign orchestrated by the combined forces of conservative corporate chieftains and extreme right-wing radio hosts. As the right wing gained strength, and as unfettered money obtained more of a foothold in our politics, the corporate-funded hate machine first road tested under Roosevelt grew ever stronger.

WILLIAM JEFFERSON CLINTON

As we have seen, politicians and newspapers alike jumped all over Abraham Lincoln. Big business and talk radio were added to the opposition mix under Franklin Roosevelt. And all four pillars of the right-wing message machine piled on in full force against the presidency of William Jefferson Clinton. The nineties saw a nonstop eight-year fusillade of political invective that foreshadowed what lay in store for Barack Obama. I know many of you remember it well. For those who don't, the corporate-sponsored blitzkrieg against Clinton has been carefully documented by Joe Conason and Gene Lyons in their definitive *The Hunting of the President*. As they show, attacks on Clinton were personal from the beginning. They began while he was still governor of Arkansas and running for reelection, but already thinking about running for president in 1992.

Looking over the potential Democratic field, the Republican

National Committee chairman, Lee Atwater, whose job was to re-elect George H. W. Bush, knew he did not have to worry about Mario Cuomo, Bill Bradley, or any other liberal from the Northeast. He feared only a moderate Democratic candidate from the South. And the most dangerous of them all was Governor Clinton.

So Atwater decided to take Clinton down before he could even emerge as a presidential candidate. He recruited Democratic congressman Tommy Robinson to switch political parties and run for governor as a Republican, against his former Democratic ally. He took the unusual position of endorsing Robinson in a contested Republican primary. And he used Robinson as his battering ram against Clinton.

"You boys have to remember, I don't give a fuck who the governor of Arkansas is," he told a couple of political operatives from Arkansas who were meeting in his Washington office. "My only job as chairman of the Republican National Committee is to get George Bush reelected." And then he outlined his plan: "We're going to take Tommy Robinson and use him to throw everything we can think of at Clinton—drugs, women, whatever works. We may or may not win, but we'll bust him up so bad he won't be able to run again for years."

And so it began. But Atwater overestimated the damage Robinson could do—and underestimated Bill Clinton's political drive. Having failed to stop Clinton, or even slow him down, Atwater next focused on attempting to prevent him from becoming the Democratic nominee—using all the rumors, innuendos, and slime he and his cohorts had dug up against Clinton in Arkansas, mostly about women, including a Little Rock torch singer named Gennifer Flowers.

With the prodding of Atwater's agents, plus the enticement of a check for $150,000 from the tabloid newspaper the *Star*, Flowers popped up on the national scene just before Clinton was widely expected to win the New Hampshire primary. She claimed that she and the governor of Arkansas had conducted a twelve-year-long love affair. A few days later, she followed up with edited audiotapes of telephone conversations with Clinton she'd secretly recorded.

But Clinton refused to be counted out. And, most important, he had a wife who was willing to fight by his side. Bill and Hillary appeared together on an extraordinary *60 Minutes* interview with Steve Kroft, in which Clinton acknowledged having caused pain in their marriage but denied the allegation made by Flowers of a twelve-year affair. Two days later, he came in second in New Hampshire, dubbed himself "the Comeback Kid," and went on to win the Democratic nomination.

But, while unsuccessful in derailing Clinton, the Flowers incident proved that there was some "pain" to be unearthed, and that there were plenty of people willing to pay big money to anyone with information that could destroy or damage his political career. Gennifer Flowers was paid over $500,000 by the *Star* and *Penthouse* magazine. Others would pay much more for dirt on Clinton.

First up was Chicago investment banker Peter Smith, a major contributor to Newt Gingrich's political action committee, GOPAC, who feared Clinton was about to make Bush 41 a one-term president. At the time, Arkansas newspapers and the tabloids were exploding with allegations about Clinton's sexual misadventures, including one headline in the *Globe*, BILL CLINTON'S FOUR-IN-A-BED SEX ORGIES WITH BLACK HOOKERS, and a report that he had fathered an illegitimate child with a black prostitute, Bobbie Ann Williams. Smith reportedly put up eighty thousand dollars to get those stories in the mainstream media.

Among those he approached was David Brock, then an investigative reporter for *The American Spectator* and later the founder of the liberal media watchdog Web site Media Matters for America. Brock looked into the charges but found no evidence—no

Bobbie Ann Williams, no illegitimate son—and soon concluded the entire story was a hoax.

Clinton's enemies then dredged up a wild story that he had raped businesswoman Juanita Broaddrick during a 1978 nursing home convention in Little Rock. Especially coming so close to the 1992 election, it was still an explosive charge. But as Broaddrick kept changing her story, skeptical reporters dismissed the possibility of any criminal activity on Clinton's part as inconclusive at best.

By this time, there was no stopping Bill Clinton. With the help of mercurial Texas billionaire Ross Perot, he defeated George H. W. Bush and, like FDR before him, assumed the office of president of the United States after twelve years of Republican rule. But that didn't deter his political enemies. Knowing they could not defeat Clinton on the policy level, they redoubled their efforts to destroy him personally—and wealthy Republicans, led by banker Peter Smith, once again called on David Brock.

Flash forward to August 1993. Brock had already published a conservative bestseller, *The Real Anita Hill,* and was considered the go-to guy for political smear campaigns when Smith approached him and offered to fund a whole new line of attack: reports that four of Clinton's former Arkansas state trooper body guards had procured countless women to have sex with him while he was still governor—and that they were willing to talk about it.

The result was Brock's so-called Troopergate article ("Living with the Clintons") in *The American Spectator,* and the beginning of a series of right wing–funded scandals that plagued Clinton until the day he left the White House—largely financed by a man far wealthier than Peter Smith.

The *Spectator* itself was another rich man's playpen, founded in 1967 by conservative trust fund baby R. Emmett Tyrrell, Jr. Thanks largely to Brock, it had become what Conason and Lyons call "the premier venue for right-wing muckraking" by the time Clinton had reached the White House. But Tyrell's resources were limited. In order to continue, lead, and expand the personal assault on Clinton, he needed bigger bucks. Enter reclusive Pittsburgh billionaire Richard Mellon Scaife.

Heir to the Mellon family banking, oil, and steel fortune, Scaife had, through his foundations, already spent some $300 million to help build a powerful conservative movement when he was approached by Tyrell's agents to fund a secret special operation at the *Spectator*—known, inside the magazine, as "the Arkansas Project." Already an early supporter of the magazine and a self-professed political enemy of Clinton's, Scaife readily signed on. Over the next four years, he pumped $2.4 million into this *Spectator*-based conspiracy to ruin the president of the United States. As he told friends, his goal was simple: "to get that goddamn guy out of the White House."

Scaife, of course, failed in his long-term goal. But, in the short term, he succeeded in making Clinton's presidency hell. It all started with charges by Little Rock businessman David Hale, duly reported in the *Spectator,* that Clinton had "pressured" him into making an illegal $300,000 loan to Jim and Susan McDougal to cover Bill and Hillary's investment in a vacation-home development called "Whitewater Estates."

Little did Scaife realize what an avalanche of events, ending in Clinton's impeachment, he had triggered.

- Republicans demanded that Attorney General Janet Reno appoint a "special prosecutor" to investigate Whitewater—even though they had voted two years earlier to abolish the position of independent counsel.
- Confident of his innocence in the matter, President Clinton overrode his attorney general and ordered her to name a Whitewater special counsel. Reno named former New York U.S. attorney Robert Fiske.

- On February 11, 1994, Paula Jones, one of the women mentioned in the *Spectator*'s "Troopergate" article, made her national debut at a meeting of the Conservative Political Action Committee in Washington, charging then-governor Bill Clinton with forcing sex on her during a "job interview" in his room at the Excelsior Hotel in Little Rock. Now represented by the Landmark Legal Foundation, another Scaife-funded conservative organization, she announced plans to file a lawsuit against the president of the United States.

- As if sealing his own fate, President Clinton made the mistake of signing legislation that returned the power to select an independent counsel to the Special Division of the Justice Department, a panel of three federal judges named by the chief justice of the Supreme Court, at this time William Rehnquist. On August 5, at the urging of Senate Republicans, the newly appointed panel voted to fire Robert Fiske and replace him with former solicitor general Kenneth W. Starr, who had earlier spoken out publicly in support of Paula Jones's legal right to take the president to court.

- Ken Starr launched his investigation into alleged financial improprieties surrounding Bill and Hillary Clinton's investment in Whitewater, but he soon expanded his probe by starting to interview Bill Clinton's former state trooper bodyguards about their totally unrelated charges of his sexual misconduct. And that questioning, of course, led to Paula Jones, whose right to challenge the president was now before the Supreme Court.

- Criticized by the media for his "sexual prurience" and for exceeding the bounds of what he was supposed to be investigating, Starr suddenly resigned his post to accept a teaching position in Pepperdine University's School of Public Policy. Two days later, he announced he'd changed his mind—apparently embarrassed by media reports that the single most generous donor to the Public Policy School was none other than lifetime

Pepperdine regent Richard Mellon Scaife himself. Starr eventually went to Pepperdine, on Scaife's ticket, after his investigation
was complete.

- Back on the job, Starr joined forces with Paula Jones's attorneys. While preparing to depose the president about his con-
tacts with Jones, they were contacted by Linda Tripp, who
said she had another story they might be interested in. As has
been exhaustively reported, Starr's lawyers then went after
Monica Lewinsky, lured her into a meeting at the Pentagon
City Ritz-Carlton, and threatened her with twenty-seven years
in prison unless she'd consent to wear a body wire for record-
ing her conversations with President Clinton. Showing good
judgment (this time), Lewinsky insisted on calling her lawyer
first.

- The very next day, in the downtown Washington law offices
of Skadden, Arps, President Clinton spent six hours under
deposition in the Paula Jones case. He denied the allegations
made by Paula Jones. And then he denied ever having had
sexual relations, as defined, with Monica Lewinsky. Only on
the strictest reading of the judge's definition—"contact with
the genitalia, anus, groin, breast, inner thigh, or buttocks of any
person with an intent to arouse or gratify the sexual desire
of any person"—was he telling the truth. But nobody else
bought it.

- Starr issued his final report, basically exonerating the Clintons of any fault in the Whitewater matter but accusing President Clinton of lying under oath about his relationship with
Lewinsky. This, of course, led to House Judiciary Committee
hearings, Clinton's impeachment, and his acquittal by the
Senate.

By now, Scaife thought he saw his investment coming to frui-
tion. As a result of the millions he had personally and singularly
donated to fuel the campaign against Clinton, Whitewater led to

Troopergate, Troopergate led to Paula Jones, Paula Jones led to Monica Lewinsky, and Monica Lewinsky led to impeachment.

And yet, as the impeachment fiasco raged, President Bill Clinton only become more popular, enjoying some of the highest poll ratings of his presidency at the very moment Republicans were trying to destroy him. Americans knew a railroading when they saw one.

Still, for Richard Mellon Scaife, it was money well spent. He got a lot more for his investment than the du Ponts ever did in their war against FDR. And the Scaife machine provided the blueprint for a similar corporate-funded campaign of personal attacks against future Democratic candidates. The only difference is that future campaigns were even more vicious and much better funded. By all accounts, Charles and David Koch would make Scaife look like a cheapskate. And by the time a new political star was born in Barack Obama of Illinois, the right-wing attack machine was sleek, well oiled, and already grinding away.

2

THE "OTHERING" OF CANDIDATE OBAMA

For Democrats, 2004 was a depressing year. That summer saw hopes rise that Massachusetts senator and Vietnam War hero John Kerry would unseat the increasingly unpopular George W. Bush. Then came the Swift Boat lies, Kerry's failure to respond quickly and strongly enough, and a close loss in November which ended up being decided by the swing state of Ohio.

Only one ray of light shone through for Democrats that year: the discovery of a young and dynamic Senate candidate from Illinois named Barack Obama. Four years earlier, this young lawyer was fresh off a primary defeat against Congressman Bobby Rush, and he could not even get a floor credential at the Democratic National Convention that summer. But in 2004, Obama walked into the Boston convention a total unknown and walked out the star of the show. Forget the Senate. For him, that was already considered a lock. The buzz was about Obama as the Democratic nominee for president four years hence, in the event Kerry didn't succeed.

Obama's enemies saw the threat. They didn't wait until this new Democratic hopeful was a candidate for president, or in the White House, to attack him personally. They started from the moment he entered public life. And, from the beginning, it was distinctly personal.

We all remember the 2008 election. The campaign against Obama wasn't built on the usual premises that Republicans use against Democrats—that Obama was pro-gun control, pro-choice, pro-taxes, or antiwar. In fact, it had nothing to do with the issues at all. It was focused almost entirely on implications and insinuations about Obama the man, drawn from his unusual personal story.

It was all summed up in the question John McCain deliberately and diabolically used to stir up his supporters at every campaign event: "Who is the real Barack Obama?" The question implied that Obama was hiding something, as if he were not the man they saw, a young freshman senator from Illinois. Republicans tried to portray Obama, instead, as so unlike the rest of us that he couldn't be trusted. And, in a sense, he provided them plenty of opportunity.

Barack Obama described himself as "a skinny kid with a funny name." And, indeed, in many ways, he was different from your average candidate for president. Not only because he was black but also because he had a black Kenyan father, a white Kansan mother, had been raised in Hawaii and Indonesia, and had gone to Columbia and Harvard. How strange is that? On top of that, his middle name was Hussein and his last name rhymed with Osama.

All of which gave those intent on destroying Obama lots of ammunition. And they didn't hesitate to twist it to portray him as dangerously different. By the time he announced his candidacy for president, the right-wing agitprop machine had already spent years painting him as a foreign, un-American leftist.

Because he had a Muslim father, he obviously was a Muslim.

Because he had gone to school in Indonesia, he must have attended a madrassa and been taught to hate America.

Because he had worked as a community organizer, he was undoubtedly a socialist.

Because he had worked in poor black neighborhoods, he was a stealth Black Nationalist.

Because he attended Pastor Jeremiah Wright's Trinity United Church of Christ, he was a black separatist.

Because, as a state senate candidate, he had once attended a coffee klatch in the home of former Weatherman William Ayers, he was a terrorist sympathizer.

In fact, many Republicans argued, he might not even be an American citizen, and therefore ineligible to run for president. After all, how do we *really* know he was born in Hawaii? I mean, does he look American to you? (Wink, wink.) Not even the online publication of his birth certificate, supplied by the Hawaii Department of Health and posted by the Obama campaign in June 2008, was sufficient evidence to kill that rumor.

As a candidate for president, Obama also had to deal with charges of an illegal land deal with developer Tony Rezko. At Sarah Palin rallies, her supporters called him a "traitor." Republicans also questioned the patriotism of his wife, Michelle. They even compared Obama to Hitler.

Looking back on the sheer number and ferocity of personal attacks he had to overcome, it's a wonder Obama survived the Democratic primary, let alone won his bid for the presidency. Those attacks began early and they were repeated often.

MADRASSA

The very day after Obama announced the formation of his presidential exploratory committee, the conservative Web site Insight Mag.com reported that according to "sources close to a background check" allegedly conducted by the Hillary Clinton campaign, Obama "had spent at least four years in a so-called Madrassa, or

Muslim seminary, in Indonesia." The same report also speculated that the madrassa he attended might have taught "a Wahhabi doctrine that denies the rights of non-Muslims."

CNN, AP, and ABC quickly investigated and debunked the charge. Yes, Obama had attended a Muslim public school while living in a Muslim country. But he had *not* attended a radical religious school, or madrassa. Nonetheless, Fox News and other conservative outlets continued to repeat that charge throughout the primary and general campaigns. Some still do so today.

Among the many madrassa voices were these:

As early as January 2007, *Fox & Friends* cohost Steve Doocy, accepting as fact the rumor that Obama had attended a madrassa, pointed out that madrassas are "financed by Saudis" and "teach this Wahhabism which pretty much hates us." The only question remaining, Doocy insisted, was this: "Was that on the curriculum back then?"

Newsmax.com columnist Lowell Ponte jumped in a year later: Senator Barack Obama could "become the first American president whose thinking was shaped by childhood in a Muslim madrassa in Islamic Indonesia."

Or as radio talk-show host Michael Savage said in April 2008, well after he should have known better, "Now we have an unknown stealth candidate who went to a madrassa in Indonesia and, in fact, was a Muslim."

In the same breath, conservatives accused Obama of lying about his early education and study of the Koran. This was manifestly not true. In his first book, *Dreams from My Father,* Obama was upfront about his early schooling and Koran studies in Indonesia, where he had moved with his mother and stepfather: "In Indonesia, I had spent two years at a Muslim school, two years at a Catholic school. In the Muslim school, the teacher wrote to tell my mother that I made faces during Koranic studies. My mother wasn't overly concerned. 'Be respectful,' she'd said."

MUSLIM, LIKE HIS FATHER

Aha! So Obama *had* attended a Muslim school. He grew up in a Muslim country. His father and grandfather were Muslims. His stepfather was a Muslim. Therefore, Barack Obama must be a Muslim. Or so said an unending chorus of right-wingers. And, of course, to them, then and now, the implication was that being a Muslim was the same as being a terrorist.

Among instant self-anointed experts on Islam was conservative blogger Debbie Schlussel: "I decided to look further into Obama's background. His full name—as by now you have probably heard—is Barack Hussein Obama, Jr. Hussein is a Muslim name, which comes from the name of Ali's son—Hussein Ibn Ali. And Obama is named after his late Kenyan father, the late Barack Hussein Obama, Sr., apparently a Muslim. And while Obama may not identify as a Muslim, that's not how the Arab and Muslim Streets see it. In Arab culture and under Islamic law, if your father is a Muslim, so are you. And once a Muslim, always a Muslim. You cannot go back. In Islamic eyes, Obama is certainly a Muslim. He may think he's a Christian, but they do not."

For Michael Savage, the question was not whether Obama was a Muslim but what kind of Muslim he was. "We have a right to know if he's a so-called friendly Muslim or one who aspires to more radical teachings." Again, the truth on the ground was just the opposite. Yes, the elder Barack Hussein Obama was a Muslim, but he was never a practicing one and, by the time he was an adult, he'd become an atheist. Obama's mother was, technically, a Christian. But she didn't attend church regularly, and didn't provide her son with any formal religious upbringing. Nevertheless, Obama credits her for planting the seeds that eventually led him to embrace Christianity.

"My mother, whose parents were Baptist and Methodist, grew up with a certain skepticism about organized religion, and so she usually only took me to church on Easter and Christmas—

sometimes," Obama told the National Prayer Breakfast on February 3, 2011. "And yet my mother was also one of the most spiritual people that I ever knew."

He went on to say, "And it's because of her example and guidance that despite the absence of a formal religious upbringing my earliest inspirations for a life of service ended up being the faith leaders of the civil rights movement. . . . Their call to fix what was broken in our world, a call rooted in faith, is what led me just a few years out of college to sign up as a community organizer for a group of churches on the Southside of Chicago. And it was through that experience working with pastors and laypeople trying to heal the wounds of hurting neighborhoods that I came to know Jesus Christ for myself and embrace Him as my lord and savior."

In Chicago, Obama joined a Christian church, where he worshiped for twenty years. (That, too, would become a problem for Obama, as we shall see.) As president, he continues to attend Christian church services and has assembled a small group of Christian pastors as his spiritual advisers. Barack Obama is, indeed, a Christian. He is not a Muslim. Although, as former secretary of state Colin Powell correctly observed, "What if he is? Is there something wrong with being a Muslim? No, that's not America."

BLACK OR WHITE?

Barack Obama was the first black president of the *Harvard Law Review*. He was only the fifth black man ever elected to the U.S. Senate. And, obviously, he is the first black president of the United States. But the fact that he's the child of a black man and a white woman still leads many critics to question his "real" ethnicity. For them, he's neither black enough nor white enough.

Refusing to accept either alternative, at first, former Fox superstar Glenn Beck actually called Obama "colorless." Speaking of his own first impressions, Beck added, "As a white guy, you don't notice that he is black. So he might as well be white."

Conservative talk-show king Rush Limbaugh also weighed in, calling Obama a "Halfrican" and dismissing him as only a "half-minority."

Brian Sussman, right-wing talk-show host on San Francisco's KSFO, decided that he, a white man, could decide who was qualified to speak for black Americans and who was not. Obama, Sussman argued, was not. "I have nothing against mixed-race people," Sussman told his listeners, "but when this guy stands in front of a black audience, pretending like he was born and raised in the hood, and he can identify with their problems, he doesn't allow—he is not, in my opinion—'cause my opinion is your average white guy—he is not allowed to wear the African-American badge because his family are not the descendants of slaves, OK? He can't identify with the discrimination and the slavery and all of that that's gone into these black families for generations, he's a kid who was raised with a silver spoon in his mouth in a white family in Hawaii."

And conservative columnist Steve Sailer, who had previously written that blacks "tend to possess poorer native judgment than members of better-educated groups," insisted that Obama was more properly referred to as a "wigger." In case you're not familiar with that term, check the Wikipedia entry: "Wigger is a pejorative slang term for a white person who emulates mannerism, language, and fashions associated with African-American culture, particularly hip hop . . ." Obama, in other words, was nothing more than the member of a twenty-first-century minstrel troupe.

BLACK RADICAL

Ironically, many of the same voices that first questioned the authenticity of Obama's race did not hesitate to play the race card against him later on.

Republicans were often quick to throw every ugly stereotype about blacks his way. Karl Rove repeatedly called Obama "lazy." Congressman Lynn Westmoreland of Georgia said both Barack and Michele Obama were "uppity." Congressman Geoff Davis of Kentucky feared Obama's use of nuclear power: "I'm going to tell you something: That boy's finger doesn't need to be on the button." Really? "That boy"?

Obama was such a dangerous black man, his political enemies couldn't even agree on whether it was better if he won or lost. "You want to ask me what I fear," Michael Savage told listeners. "I think Obama will empower the racists in this country and stir up a race war in order to seize absolute power." On the other hand, Cincinnati talk-show host Bill Cunningham remarked, "I think there will be 100 cities burning if Barack loses."

In the end, according to his race-obsessed critics, it was the very fact that Barack Obama was a black man, dangerous or not, that assured his election as president. According to Rush Limbaugh, nothing else could explain it—and it started when he was a U.S. senator. "I kind of like that analogy that he's the Donovan McNabb of the U.S. Senate . . . in the sense that he is being propped up . . . because they want to see him do well."

As I reported in *Toxic Talk,* Limbaugh had earlier been forced to resign as a football color commentator for ESPN in 2003 for making almost a word-for-word argument about all the positive publicity surrounding Eagles quarterback Donovan McNabb: "The media has been very desirous that a black quarterback do well."

You'd think that, having stepped in it once, Limbaugh would have thought twice about jumping in headfirst once again. But, obviously, Rush never learns. And the race card has long been one of the only cards in his deck.

He played it with glee when Obama's campaign took off, chalking his success up to one factor alone: not the appeal of his message or the skill of his candidacy, but the color of his skin.

"If Barack Obama were Caucasian, they would have taken this guy out on the basis of pure ignorance long ago," he declared in May 2008. And, according to Rush, that ultimately presented an insurmountable problem to John McCain: "It's—you know, it's just—it's just we can't hit the girl. I don't care how far feminism's saying, you can't hit the girl, and you can't—you can't criticize the little black man-child. You just can't do it, 'cause it's not right. It's not fair. He's such a victim."

For Limbaugh and others, that summed up how Obama won the Democratic nomination and, later, the presidency. After Obama's acceptance speech in Denver, Limbaugh lamented, "It is striking how unqualified Obama is, and how this whole thing came about with, within the Democrat [sic] Party. I think it really goes back to the fact that nobody had the guts to stand up and say no to a black guy."

Imagine that! All this time, we thought it would be difficult for a black man to be elected president. Guess we had it wrong. In Rush Limbaugh's parallel universe, it's impossible for a black man *not* to be elected president! Even if he's not a true American.

LOVE OF COUNTRY

Behind most of the campaign attacks on Barack Obama were the underlying, but unspoken, questions: Is he, in fact, an American? If so, does he even love his country? Is he a true patriotic American?

Those questions might have remained unspoken for a while, but not for long. Challenging Obama's patriotism soon became the favorite sport of the right-wing hate machine. Again, maybe Sarah Palin summed it up best by asserting that Barack Obama "is not a man who sees America as you and I see America."

Obama haters first pounced when he refused to play silly political games over wearing a flag pin in his lapel—as if that were the true test of patriotism. Like almost everyone else, Obama said, he wore a lapel pin right after 9/11, but he stopped doing so when he noticed that the pin had become "a substitute for real patriotism." Which he correctly went on to define: "You show your patriotism by how you treat your fellow Americans, especially those who serve. And you show your patriotism by being true to your values and ideals. And that's what we have to lead with, our values and ideals."

Judging from the reaction on Fox News, you might have thought Obama had burned a flag in front of his campaign headquarters. Legal commentator Andrew Napolitano accused him of "disrespecting the American flag." *Fox & Friends* cohost Brian Kilmeade described him as "anti-Betsy Ross." Host E. D. Hill equated "I won't wear that pin!" (which Obama did not say) with "I did not have sex with that woman!" (which Bill Clinton did). And Karl Rove simply turned Obama's comments on their head, by misquoting him as saying, "If you wear a flag lapel pin, you're not a true patriot."

Twisting his words was another trick the Foxers used to cast a negative glow on Obama's love of country. Sean Hannity even turned Obama's call for more troops in Afghanistan—which he promised as a candidate and delivered as president—into an *attack* on our troops. That's a strange antiwar stance coming from Fox News.

Already in August 2007, Obama argued that we had to pay more attention to Afghanistan. "We've got to get the job done there," he said on August 13. "And that requires us to have enough troops so that we're not just air-raiding villages and killing civilians." Which is exactly what our generals on the ground were saying, after arguing for years for more troops. But for Hannity and others, that was tantamount to treason. Hannity accused Obama of "slamming the troops" and attacking "our troops as murderers."

From there, the question became whether we could trust Obama to defend America in time of war or against another terrorist attack. "Now, are you going to tell me that Obama, Hussein Barack Obama, is going to take our side should there be some kind of catastrophic attack on America?" Michael Savage asked his radio audience in January 2007. "I don't think so."

Not only was Obama on the side of the terrorists, others claimed; they were on his side. Republican Iowa congressman Steve King predicted a celebration among Islamic fundamentalists should Obama win the presidency: "I will tell you that, if he is elected president, then the radical Islamists, the al-Qaida, the radical Islamists and their supporters, will be dancing in the streets in greater numbers than they did on September 11 because they will declare victory in this War on Terror."

Actually, response in the Arab world to Obama's election, while positive, was fairly muted. We didn't see dancing in the streets of the Middle East until the people of Egypt, with Obama's not so hidden approval, toppled dictator Hosni Mubarak and began to build the democratic reforms in Egypt that President Obama himself had called for in his speech at the University of Cairo on June 4, 2009.

Still others went further on terrorism, going so far as to suggest that Obama might actually be the terrorists' handpicked candidate. Yes, Michael Savage may be a clinical paranoid, only his psychiatrist knows for sure. However, far too many Americans believe him when he says, "I think he was hand-picked by some very powerful forces both within and outside the United States of America to drag this country into a hell that it has not seen since the Civil War of the middle of the 19th century." Fox News regular Dick Morris, the most amoral and least talented man in American politics, added that "the determinant in the election will be whether we believe that Barack Obama is what he appears to be, or is he somebody who's sort of a sleeper agent who really doesn't believe in our system . . . ?" Conservatives rarely, if ever, made a serious attempt to document their charges against Barack Obama. They were not, after all, trying to win a debate. They were simply trying to scare their base into believing that Obama was so, so dangerous that they'd better not dare consider voting for him, no matter how unenthusiastic they might be about John McCain and Sarah Palin—who, by the end of the campaign, weren't even speaking to each other.

So, more and more, leaders of the Obama Hate Machine simply abandoned all arguments and resorted to name-calling.

Michael Savage: "He's an Afro-Leninist, and I know he's dangerous."

Glenn Beck: "This guy really is a Marxist. He believes in the redistribution of wealth."

Former House majority leader Tom DeLay: "He's a Marxist, but a very smart one—he doesn't let anyone know it."

Former Delaware Republican Senate candidate Christine O'Donnell: "He's anti-American. He did not vote for English as the official language."

And for commentators Mark Levin, Ann Coulter, Bill Cunningham, Jonah Goldberg, and others, Obama—mainly because of his capacity to attract large, enthusiastic crowds—was the second coming of Adolf Hitler. Ben Stein spoke for all of them when he denounced Obama's plan to accept the Democratic nomination in Denver's Invesco Field: "Seventy-five thousand people at an outdoor sports palace, well, that's something the Fuehrer would have done." Stein, of course, didn't mention that John F. Kennedy was the first presidential candidate to make his acceptance speech at an "outdoor sports palace"—the Los Angeles Coliseum, in 1960.

In so many ways, through so many lies, what they were all trying to say was, Barack Obama is not like you. He's black. He's dangerous, and he hates America.

That's what it boiled down to. Not that he was wrong on health care. Not that he might raise taxes or bring back the estate tax. No, no, no. The hate Obama campaign had nothing to do with the issues. It was all about painting Obama as different, evil, and dangerous: a man who hates America.

Here's the big lie in its purest form, from the master propagandist himself, Rush Limbaugh, on July 21, 2008: "It's a form of self-loathing, ladies and gentlemen—not of himself, of course, 'cause he's the Messiah—but in the aggregate self-loathing of nation, the kind of self-loathing of America that the left here and in Europe embraces. And that's why they love Obama—because he loathes America. He blames America. America's responsible for all that's wrong in the world."

And for a lot of his opponents, it wasn't hard to believe that Obama hated America—because, to them, he wasn't even born here!

MY COUNTRY, 'TIS OF THEE . . .

I'll never forget the White House briefing of July 27, 2009, one of the first I ever attended as a radio talk-show host. Not assigned a regular seat, I was one of several reporters crowded together, standing alongside the south wall, when I managed to get the attention of the press secretary at the time, Robert Gibbs. "Robert," I said, "I hate to ask this, but I guess somebody has to." (You could see Gibbs brace himself.) "Is there anything you could say that would make the Birthers go away?"

"No," replied Gibbs, shaking his head in frustration. "I mean, the God's honest truth is no." He explained that this was because "nothing will assuage" those who continue to pursue what he called "made-up, fictional nonsense." And then he went into a tirade about what lengths he had gone to during the campaign to shoot down the absurd rumor—which soon became right-wing gospel—that Barack Obama was not an American citizen because he had not been born in the United States.

At first, the campaign noted that Hawaii was, in fact, the newest of the fifty states—and became a state on August 21, 1959, almost two years before Obama was born, on August 4, 1961.

When that didn't satisfy the mob, Gibbs persuaded Hawaii health officials to provide him with an electronic copy of Obama's actual birth certificate, which he then posted on the campaign Web site. But that didn't fly, either. How do we know that's for real? Where's the "long form"? the naysayers asked.

The campaign then put forward one more solid piece of evidence: notices published in two Honolulu newspapers announcing the birth of Barack Hussein Obama at Kapi'olani Maternity and Gynological Hospital in Honolulu to parents Barack Hussein Obama and Stanley Ann Dunham.

As Gibbs noted a week later, at his August 6 briefing, the idea that these newspaper announcements were part of a wider conspiracy was "totally crazy." As he summed it up: "A pregnant woman leaves her home to go overseas to have a child—who there's not a passport for—so is in cahoots with someone . . . to smuggle that child, that previously doesn't exist on a government roll somewhere back into the country and has the amazing foresight to place birth announcements in the Hawaii newspapers? All while this is transpiring in cahoots with those in the border, all so some kid named Barack Obama could run for president 46 and a half years later."

Totally crazy indeed. The campaign might also have pointed out that it didn't really matter where Obama had been born. As the son of an American mother, he would automatically be an American citizen himself—much as John McCain, born in the Panama Canal Zone, was nonetheless accepted by everyone as an American.

But by this time, nothing would quiet those who had earned the derisive nickname "the Birthers," not even the fact that the conservative John Roberts Supreme Court refused to consider their challenge to Obama—three times! Questions about Obama's birthplace—and therefore his credentials to run for, or serve as, president—persisted during the campaign and even, as we shall see, into the Obama White House—all fueled by the flames of right-wing talk radio and the Obama Hate Machine.

From that time on, the charge that Barack Obama was actually born in parts unknown and even un-American has continued to compromise the third leg of American conspiracy theories held by people on the fringe, together with their distorted beliefs that the 1969 moon landing was fake and that September 11 was an inside job, planned by George Bush and Dick Cheney. Nothing will ever convince the Birthers that they might be wrong.

Just as nothing will convince them that Obama doesn't hate America, like his former pastor too often appeared to.

BLACK LIBERATION THEOLOGY

It wasn't long into the Democratic primary before the focus expanded from the exotic man Barack Obama was purported to be to the allegedly shady characters he hung out with. Of whom, by far the most explosive was his preacher, mentor, friend, and the man who married him and baptized his children, the Reverend Jeremiah Wright, pastor of Chicago's Trinity United Church of Christ.

Wright was one of America's foremost black religious leaders. After serving in the Marine Corps, he studied for the ministry and was named pastor of Trinity in 1972, when it counted only ninety souls. Under his dynamic leadership, it grew into a megachurch of over six thousand members. And its pastor, a leader in recruiting and training young black ministers and a leading proponent of black liberation theology, was a frequent guest at the White House.

But nobody outside Trinity had paid much attention to some of the things Wright had said inside Trinity, until ABC's chief investigative correspondent, Brian Ross, played video excerpts from his sermons on the evening news in early March 2008. The explosive nature of what Americans saw shook the political scene—and the Obama campaign—to its core.

Here was the Reverend Wright, Obama's pastor, blaming the United States for what happened on September 11. "We bombed Hiroshima, we bombed Nagasaki, and we nuked far more than the thousands in New York and the Pentagon, and we never batted an eye," he said in a sermon on September 16, 2001. "We have supported state terrorism against the Palestinians and black South Africans, and now we are indignant because the stuff we have done overseas is now brought right back to our own front yards. America's chickens are coming home to roost."

And here was the Reverend Wright, asking God's condemnation on America. "The government gives them the drugs, builds bigger prisons, passes a three-strike law and then wants us to sing 'God Bless America.' No, no, no, God damn America, that's in the Bible for killing innocent people," he said in a 2003 sermon. "God damn America for treating our citizens as less than human. God damn America for as long as she acts like she is God and she is supreme."

At first, Obama tried to shrug off Wright's remarks, noting he had not been present during some of the pastor's more incendiary sermons. "I don't think my church is actually particularly controversial," he stated. As for Wright, he's "like an old uncle who says things I don't always agree with," contended Obama, adding that everybody has somebody like that in their own family.

The controversy over Wright prompted Obama to give a speech on racism in Philadelphia on March 18. But even there, he went out of his way not to disassociate himself from his pastor. Acknowledging that what Wright had said was "wrong," "divisive," and "racially charged," Obama still said, "I can no more disown him than I can disown the black community. I can no more disown him than I can disown my white grandmother."

But, of course, that combination of outrage and compassion

did not silence Obama's critics. Ann Coulter, missing the point, as usual, deemed his speech "Throw Grandma under the bus." If he was a member of Wright's church, figured vice presidential candidate Sarah Palin, then Obama must agree with everything Wright said. "I don't know why that association isn't discussed more," she told the *New York Times,* "because those were appalling things that that pastor had said about our great country, and to have sat in the pews for 20 years and listened to that—with, I don't know, a sense of condoning it, I guess, because he didn't get up and leave—to me, that does say something about character."

Seton Motley, director of Communications at the right-wing Media Research Center, argued that because Trinity United was predominantly African-American, Obama's membership "seems to stand in diametric opposition to . . . the oath to faithfully execute the office of President of the United States."

And even Chris Matthews, who once admitted that "I felt this thrill going up my leg" while listening to an Obama speech, said it was impossible to distinguish Obama from Wright. The two of them were like "Dr. Jekyll and Mr. Hyde," observed Matthews. "Every time you have a problem with Barack, because you don't really know him and he seems a little foreign to you, you think of—you think of him as both these guys. They're different faces of the same guy. Jeremiah Wright, to a lot of people, is Barack Obama."

For Matthews, by the way, the transformation could go both ways. After Obama's well-received 2010 State of the Union address, Matthews told America on MSNBC, "He is post-racial, by all appearances. . . . I forgot he was black tonight for an hour."

As if they needed anything else, Obama's critics now had new license to label him as a dangerous, if not diabolical, Communist agitator and a black hater of America. Because of his association with Wright, Obama was no longer just a black man; he was a *scary* black man. "All the sudden you've got two dots, and two dots make a line," explained a gleeful Alex Castellanos, Republican media strategist. "You start getting some sense of who he is, and it's not the Obama you thought. He's not the Tiger Woods of politics." No, for right-wingers, he could now be painted as the Malcolm X of politics.

The problem for Barack Obama, of course, was that the Reverend Wright wasn't content with the endless recycling of his old sermons. He insisted on throwing more gasoline on the flames. He appeared before the National Press Club, where he defended and repeated his claims that the United States was responsible for terrorism and had invented AIDS to kill black Americans. And he accused Obama of political expediency: "He had to distance himself because he's a politician. . . . Whether he gets elected or not, I'm still going to have to be answerable to God."

The next day, campaigning in North Carolina, Obama again denounced Wright's remarks and finally severed his ties with his former pastor: "The person I saw yesterday was not the person that I met 20 years ago." With that disavowal, the issue of guilt by association with Jeremiah Wright moved to the back burner for a while—just in time to be replaced with a new guilt by association, this time with a former Weatherman.

PALLING AROUND WITH TERRORISTS

In trying to hype the book *O: A Presidential Novel,* its "anonymous" 2011 novel about President Obama, Simon & Schuster would say only that its author "had been in the same room with Barack Obama." By that meager standard, of course, the author could have been anyone who had ever attended a campaign event. But technically, the publisher wasn't telling a lie. Yes, we learned later, author and former McCain campaign manager Mark Salter had indeed been in the same room, or auditorium, with Obama—when he and John McCain met in their first presidential debate.

In fact, there wasn't much more of a connection between Barack Obama and William Ayers. Yet, no matter how passing their relationship, right-wing critics still asserted the worst about Obama. As Sarah Palin put it, this "is someone who sees America as imperfect enough to pal around with terrorists who targeted their own country."

As we saw, briefly, in the introduction, there is no way to back up the claim that Obama and Ayers were ever close enough to "pal around" together.

Here, again, is the truth about their relationship.

Fact: Obama lived in the same Hyde Park neighborhood as William Ayers and his wife, Bernardine Dohrn. So did tens of thousands of other people.

Fact: Obama met Ayers in 1995, when state senator Alice Palmer took him to Ayers's home. Palmer had decided not to run for reelection and wanted to introduce Obama, her handpicked successor, to her friends. Ayers was Palmer's friend, not Obama's, and she organized the gathering.

Fact: Obama and Ayers later served at the same time as trustees of the Woods Fund, a Chicago foundation board. Ayers, an education professor at the University of Illinois, was former top aide to Major Richard J. Daley.

Fact: Obama and Ayers were also both involved with the Chicago Annenberg Challenge, a major project to improve Chicago's public schools, founded and funded by former Republican ambassador Walter Annenberg. Obama served briefly as the first chairman of CAC's board of directors. Ayers was named cochair of a CAC advisory committee, the Chicago School Reform Collaborative.

And that's all there was to it. Period. End of story. *Finito. Nada mas.*

But that didn't stop the cascade of lies—gleefully and repeatedly spread on Fox News—linking Obama in some kind of bloodstained relationship with a man who was indeed the founder of the Weathermen but who had long ago moved on to become a respected member of the Chicago community. As author John K.

Wilson reported on the Huffington Post, the many lies about Obama and Ayers included the following.

Lie: Obama's job as community organizer was all part of a grand scheme orchestrated by Ayers to "test" Obama for future assignments (*Hannity's America*, October 5, 2008). Ayers, in fact, had nothing to do with Obama's work as community organizer.

Lie: "Obama's oldest friend in politics is a murderer and unrepentant terrorist" (ExposeObama.com, September 2008). Whoever Ayers is or was, he was a mere acquaintance, not Obama's oldest friend.

Lie: "The major media simply have not reported on Obama's two years at New York's Columbia University, where, among other things, he lived a mere quarter-mile from former terrorist Bill Ayers" (Tony Blankley, September 24, 2008). Really, Tony? How many other people in *Manhattan* lived within a quarter mile of Obama? And what evidence do you have that Obama even knew Ayers at the time?

Lie: "Who provided Obama with the only executive experience he has ever had in his young life? Bill Ayers, unrepentant domestic terrorist, communist revolutionary" (Joseph Farah, WorldNetDaily, October 2, 2008). Simply not true. Farah, by the way, was referencing Obama's brief volunteer position as chair of CAC's board of directors, for which he was recruited by Deborah Leff, president of the Joyce Foundation (on whose board Obama also served), not by Bill Ayers.

Lie: "I can't understand why somebody who wants to be president of the United States . . . would want to associate with or not condemn the actions of people in the past" (Paul Ragonese, *Hannity's America*, April 27, 2008). The truth is, Obama had often condemned the past actions of Bill Ayers, calling him somebody "who engaged in despicable acts 40 years ago."

Lie: "The most important smoking gun is that Barack Obama was funding Bill Ayers' radical educational projects" (Stanley Kurtz, *Fox & Friends*, September 29, 2008). As noted, the CAC was actually funded by Reagan friend and top Republican Walter Annenberg, and led by a broad-based board, of which Obama served briefly as chair.

Lie: "There is a secret group in the Obama-Biden campaign tasked with shutting off any leaks from the record that links Barack Obama to his longtime adviser and mentor Bill Ayers. . . . The source confirms that the unit is headed by Bill Ayers himself and likely includes [former Students for a Democratic Society head] Tom Hayden" (John Batchelor, *Human Events,* September 12, 2008). After all of the controversy surrounding him, the idea that the Obama campaign would let Bill Ayers get anywhere near campaign headquarters—with Tom Hayden in tow!—is laugh-out-loud funny.

Because his association with Bill Ayers and the Chicago Annenberg Challenge was so fleeting and so part-time, Obama easily survived the outrageous charge that he palled around with terrorists, or was a closet terrorist himself. But the fact that they were able to stir up so much controversy with such little material only served to embolden his critics. And they soon found another organization with which Obama had even weaker ties, but which they were able to whip up into an even bigger stink.

AGENT OF ACORN

The media controversy surrounding ACORN proved that you really can make something out of nothing—especially if you have unlimited funds, an entire cable network, and a powerful combination of both management and on-air personalities willing to engage in a relentless, reckless, partisan propaganda campaign. In 2008, that was certainly the case with Fox News and ACORN.

Again, I first debunked this scandal in *Toxic Talk.* But it's important in the context of this discussion to review the highlights.

ACORN, or the Association of Community Organizations for Reform Now, was created in the 1970s to band together neighborhood and community groups fighting for the urban poor and working-class families. By 2000, it had twelve hundred chapters in over one hundred cities nationwide. ACORN had some problems, too. For years, as part of its organizing efforts and in concert with other groups, ACORN had conducted voter-registration drives. But in 2008, evidence of irregularities—phony names, duplication, illegal immigrants—showed up in several state registration drives for which ACORN was responsible.

Because of their volunteer nature, voter-registration drives are notoriously inaccurate. And these problems would normally have been resolved by local election officials.

Except that in the case of ACORN, somebody discovered a link to Democratic presidential candidate Barack Obama. And, from that molehill, Fox made a mountain.

If you believed Fox (first mistake!), it was Obama who led and directed ACORN's every move. He was, according to Fox, using ACORN and its voter-registration volunteers to steal the election in state after state. Not only that; under his orders, ACORN representatives, with their "strong-arm tactics," had placed so much pressure on banks to make low-interest loans that they ultimately collapsed. ACORN itself, not high-flying hedge-fund managers, was directly responsible for the Wall Street implosion of September 2008.

Leading the charge, Sean Hannity branded Obama "the Senator from ACORN." Which was about as far from reality as Fox could possibly go.

Yes, as a community organizer, Obama had, naturally, run into Chicago leaders of ACORN. He must have impressed them, because they invited him to conduct a training session for their staff. Years later, when he was working for a public-interest law firm, they hired him to represent them in their efforts to force the state of Illinois to implement the federal Motor Voter Law.

And ACORN endorsed candidate Barack Obama when he ran for state senator, U.S. senator, and president.

But that's the extent of their relationship. Obama never worked for ACORN. He never belonged to ACORN. He never led any ACORN program. And he was definitely not "the Senator from ACORN."

As with his connection to Bill Ayers, the link between Barack Obama and ACORN was so thin that nobody other than Fox News, the propaganda arm of the Republican National Committee, took it seriously. The Fox-manufactured controversy didn't slow down Obama's drive to the White House, but it did significantly tarnish ACORN's reputation and make it a prime target for Republican politicians.

The final body blow came in July 2009 when right-wing blogger Andrew Breitbart sent two operatives disguised as a pimp and prostitute into ACORN offices in Baltimore, Washington, and Brooklyn, seeking—and receiving—advice on how to set up business in the neighborhood. It turns out the players were phony and the video was misleadingly edited. But the damage was done. As a result of the ensuing controversy, public and private funding dried up, and ACORN was forced to close its doors in November 2010.

FRIENDLY FIRE

Unfortunately, it was not just Republicans who played with the strategy of painting Barack Obama as "different" or "other," a not so veiled reminder of the color of his skin. In the heat of battle—the 2008 primary, to be exact—some Democrats were tempted to play with fire also.

In March 2008, Mark Penn, Hillary Clinton's campaign manager, sent her a memo, urging her to adopt a strategy of painting Barack Obama as "fundamentally foreign." Penn cited Obama's "diverse, multicultural" upbringing as an opportunity to emphasize his limited American "roots" and "values." In his memo, Penn anticipated almost word for word those charges that would soon be aimed against Obama by conservatives.

He wrote:

All of these articles about his boyhood in Indonesia and his life in Hawaii are geared towards showing his background is diverse, multicultural and putting that in a new light. Save it for 2050. It also exposes a very strong weakness for him—his roots to basic American values and culture are at best limited. *I cannot imagine America electing a president during a time of war who is not at his center fundamentally American in his thinking and in his values* [italics added].

He told the people of NH yesterday he has a Kansas accent because his mother was from there. His mother lived in many states as far as we can tell—but this is an example of the nonsense he uses to cover this up. How we could give some life to this contrast without turning negative: Every speech should contain the line you were born in the middle of America to the middle class in the middle of the last century. And talk about the basic bargain as about the deeply American values you grew up with, learned as a child and that drive you today. Values of fairness, compassion, responsibility, giving back. Let's explicitly own "American" in our programs, the speeches and the values. He doesn't. Make this a new American Century, the American Strategic Energy Fund. Let's use our logo to make some flags we can give out. Let's add flag symbols to the backgrounds.

In other words, Penn was telling his candidate to use any possible imagery to show that she was a real American and that Barack Obama was not.

To her credit, Hillary Clinton ignored Mark Penn's strategic advice. John McCain and Sarah Palin adopted it instead.

THE "OTHERING" OF OBAMA

If there's any image of the McCain/Palin campaign that defines the thrust of their strategy, it's Sarah Palin asking her frenzied supporters, "Who is the real Barack Obama?" and hearing a man in the audience cry out "Terrorist!"

Reporters noted she did not try to correct or caution him. Of course not. She might as well have planted him there. Because that's exactly the response that she and John McCain wanted. As has been noted earlier, their entire campaign was based on a series of charges aimed at portraying Barack Obama as exotic, different, foreign, untrustworthy—even un-American and dangerous.

In 2007 and 2008, the Obama Hate Machine spent millions of dollars, and Fox News and right-wing radio spent hundreds of hours, trying to paint Obama as "the other." As a result, *The Onion* deadpanned in September 2010, 20 percent of Americans believed Obama is a cactus!

To counter these attacks, the Obama campaign did its best to show Obama as just like the guy next door: He had a wife and two young kids, enjoyed a beer with his friends, worked out in the morning, played basketball on the weekends, loved bodysurfing and walking on the beach. Sometimes this strategy backfired, as when Obama went bowling during the Democratic primary . . . and scored a 37.

Still, in the end, Obama prevailed, thanks to four factors: a brilliant campaign, the yearning of the American people for change, an aimless, lackluster campaign by John McCain, and McCain's choice of perhaps the most inept and unqualified candidate for vice president in history.

But nobody around Obama really thought the vilification of him would cease once he was elected president of the United States. And it didn't. It just got worse.

3

THE "OTHERING" OF PRESIDENT OBAMA

When historians look back at the presidency of Barack Obama, many will begin by analyzing the remarkable contrast between the election of a new president in 2008 and the selection of a new president in 2000.

Not to beat a dead horse, but . . .

In 2000, Al Gore won the popular vote over George W. Bush by 543,895 votes. But, given the dispute over Florida's vote count, there was no clear winner in the electoral vote—that is, until the Supreme Court stepped in, stopped the recount, and, in a still-contentious 5–4 decision, declared George Bush our next president. At which point, Al Gore graciously conceded the election and the American people immediately—albeit, millions, reluctantly—accepted George W. Bush as our next president. Many questioned his policies, but hardly anyone questioned the fact that he was indeed president of the United States, no matter how he had gotten there.

Eight years later, the situation was just the opposite. Barack Obama won the popular vote by over 8.5 million votes. And he easily defeated John McCain in the Electoral College, 365 to 173. No recount. No court challenge. No doubt that Obama was the duly and constitutionally elected forty-fourth president of the

United States. Yet his political enemies refused to accept the legitimacy of his presidency from day one. And many of them still refuse to do so today.

Indeed, Obama has, unwittingly, opened a new chapter in American politics. Before Obama, members of one party would challenge the policies of the opposition, but seldom did they question their loyalty or Americanness. You know the drill: We all love our country, we all want what's best for our country, we all share the same goals, but we just have different ideas on how to get there.

But that "We're all in the same boat, just using a different set of oars" philosophy went out the window with the election of Barack Obama. To his political enemies, he doesn't just have the wrong ideas about where to lead America. To them, he's anti-America. He wants America to fail. To many of them, he's not even an American citizen.

With Obama's election, millions of Americans may have been looking for hope and change. But Republicans stuck to the same script they'd been using since 2007. The attacks they'd leveled during the campaign continued right into the Obama White House—with even more ugly ones piled on top.

OPEN SEASON ON NAME-CALLING

From the beginning, there's been no limit to the name-calling and the demagoguery against President Barack Obama. Trying to list them all here would be a fool's errand, but here are some of the more outrageous since Obama was elected to the nation's highest office.

RACIST

"This guy, I believe, is a racist," Glenn Beck told the hosts of *Fox & Friends* in July 2009. "This president, I think, has exposed himself as a guy, over and over and over again, who has a deep-seated hatred for white people, or the white culture, I don't know what it is." Which is, you must admit, an unusually un-Christian level of hatred coming from a man who professes to be a recent convert to Mormonism and a follower of Jesus. But Beck wasn't finished. In his view, Obama's not only a racist but a . . .

MARXIST

"This guy's a Marxist," Beck repeatedly warned his Fox TV audience—back when he still had a show. "He believes in the redistribution of wealth." And, as an avowed Marxist, Obama, Beck contended, was surrounding himself in the White House with "czars" whose secret mission was to turn America into a Communist dictatorship.

"Most of America doesn't have a clue as to what's going on," Beck warned. "There is a coup going on. There is a stealing of America, and the way it is done, it has been done through the—the guise of an election." Beck's warning was echoed by conservative talk-show hosts and others of the right-wing stripe. Janet Porter, an adviser to former presidential candidate Mike Huckabee, recycled in a 2009 WorldNetDaily column the outrageous claim that Barack Obama was actually a Soviet spy, groomed since birth to destroy the United States from within.

NEO-MARXIST FASCIST DICTATOR

In the game of smear the new president, however, Glenn Beck ran into a lot of competition from the savage Michael Savage, née Michael Weiner. The greater Obama's success, the uglier Savage's attacks became.

During the 2008 campaign, as we just saw, Savage had denounced Obama as an "Afro-Leninist," "America's first affirmative action candidate," and, of course, a "Muslim." By the time

Obama'd been in office for two months, Savage had already de-nounced him as "a neo-Marxist fascist dictator in the making," and, for good measure, "the biggest liar in the history of the presi-dency."

MAGIC NEGRO

No matter how mean-spirited they are, even Glenn Beck and Michael Savage must take a backseat to Rush Limbaugh in the Spewing Obama hate department. Limbaugh, with his penchant for, shall we say, racially charged remarks, was the first to call Obama the "affirmative action candidate." His radio show fea-tured a parody of an Obama campaign song, entitled "Barack, the Magic Negro."

As we saw in the previous chapter, Rush claimed that Obama had won for one reason only: because he's black, and guilty white liberals wouldn't dare vote against a black man. "If Barack Obama were Caucasian," Limbaugh stated as fact, "they would have taken this guy out on the basis of pure ignorance long ago." And Obama today, insisted Rush, would be nothing but "a tour guide in Honolulu."

It's not just the color of his skin; Limbaugh doesn't even like Obama's looks, and he doesn't hesitate to say so. "An American president has never had facial expressions like this," the right-wing blowhard told his listeners on October 19, 2010. "At least, we've never seen photos of an American president with facial expressions like this. These pictures, they look demonic." Well, if he looks like the devil, he must also be a . . .

MUSLIM

As already noted and as President Obama has affirmed on many occasions, he is a Christian by choice. He grew up with a mother and grandparents who didn't practice any religion. But he was attracted to the message and person of Jesus Christ and, later in life, embraced the Christian faith. For twenty years, he attended a Christian church in Chicago, where he was married and where his daughters were baptized. He still goes to church occasionally, reads the Bible, prays daily, and counts a small cadre of Christian preachers as his spiritual advisers.

In June 2009, the president even went to Cairo, the heart of the Arab world, and told his Muslim audience, "I'm a Christian." But that hasn't stopped his enemies from repeatedly suggesting he's actually a Muslim—thereby implying, of course, that he's also a terrorist.

Rush Limbaugh continues to feed the myth of Obama as a Muslim by regularly referring to him as "Imam Obama," or even "Imam Hussein Obama." Nothing wrong with that, he insists, even though he knows it's not true. "Since Bill Clinton was called the first black president," he asks, "why can't we call Imam Obama America's first Muslim president?"

Maybe because he's not? There are those pesky facts again.

Sarah Palin also got into the act, accusing Obama of issuing orders that the words *In God We Trust* be moved to the edge of coins. "Who calls a shot like that?" she demanded. "Who makes a decision like that? It's a disturbing trend."

No, what's really disturbing is that, once again, she hadn't bothered to do her homework. The change in the design of coins was ordered by the Bush administration in 2007 and was so unpopular, it was reversed by Congress a year later—both actions taken before Obama was even elected president.

With such nonstop questions about his faith, it came as no surprise when an August 2010 Pew Poll showed that one out of five Americans believed President Obama was a practicing Muslim. This was two years after Gen. Colin Powell gave the correct answer to those who insist on painting Obama as a Muslim: "What if he is? Is there something wrong with being a Muslim in this country?" And Powell pointed to the many graves in Arlington

National Cemetery of young Muslims who gave their lives fighting for this country in Iraq and Afghanistan. But, unfortunately for the country, Powell's words were ignored by most conservatives.

TERRORIST

As noted above, the not so subtle purpose in trying to brand Obama as a Muslim is to imply that he's also a terrorist. But some, like Michael Savage, disposed with the niceties. Savage just cut right to the quick, calling the president "even more of a terrorist than [Hugo] Chávez."

Attempts to label Obama a terrorist started during his presidential campaign. There was Sarah Palin, claiming that Obama "pals around with terrorists." While Rush Limbaugh asserted there would not be another terrorist attack before the 2008 election because terrorists wanted Obama to win and wouldn't do anything to derail his campaign. As it later turned out, notes found in Osama bin Laden's compound in May 2011 showed that the terrorist mastermind was in fact busy looking for ways to attack the American president and undermine his chances for reelection.

Limbaugh even went so far as to accuse Obama of being on the same page with Osama bin Laden, because both wanted to invade Pakistan. Bin Laden had, in fact, urged his followers in Pakistan to rise up and overthrow the government of then president Musharraf. Obama, on the other hand, merely and correctly promised that *if* the United States had "actionable intelligence" that terrorists from inside Pakistan were killing American troops—and *if* the Pakistani government failed to act—then, but only then, would American troops intervene. Which they, in fact, did on May 1, 2011, tracking down and killing the man whom Bush never could find.

Again, facts don't matter with Limbaugh. Nor do they with

Minnesota's zany congresswoman, Michele Bachmann, who suggested Obama was guilty of terrorism by causing an epidemic of swine flu in 2009—just like Jimmy Carter had done in 1976, she charged. Oops! In 1976, the president of the United States was actually Gerald Ford, a Republican.

With equal disregard for the facts, Liz Cheney—who held a minor State Department post while her daddy was in the White House, and went on to become a frequent guest on Fox—accused Obama of adopting an agenda of "apologize for America, abandon our allies, and appease our enemies."

But, in the "Can you top this?" terrorist department, zany Tom Tancredo won the prize. In his improbable 2010 campaign for governor of Colorado, the former congressman and presidential candidate declared that President Obama was actually a greater threat to the United States of America than al-Qaeda. Maybe because in his heart he was really a . . .

NAZI

In the worlds of politics and the Internet, it is known as Godwin's law: The longer any given conversation goes on, the more likely it is that someone will bring up Hitler or the Nazis. And the first person to stoop to that Hitler or Nazi analogy has lost the debate.

If true, Glenn Beck is the world's biggest loser. No matter the issue or context, the word *Nazi* is always on his lips. Indeed, it's remarkable how often Beck insists he is not calling Obama a Nazi or comparing him to Hitler—and then turns around and does just that.

When Obama moved to extend George W. Bush's loans to GM and Chrysler, for example, Beck told his radio audience, "I am not saying the Barack Obama is a fascist. But if I'm not mistaken, in the early days of Adolf Hitler, they [German auto companies] were very happy to line up for help there as well."

Earlier, when Obama had also followed Bush's lead in continuing the Troubled Asset Relief Program (TARP) to provide loans to financially strapped Wall Street firms, Beck saw the same evil connection. Again, notice first the denial, then the charge. "This is not comparing these people to the people in Germany, but this is exactly what happened to the lead-up with Hitler. Hitler opened up the door and said, 'Hey, companies, I can help you.' They all ran through the door. And then in the end, they all saw, 'Uh-oh. I'm in bed with the devil.'"

In August 2009, Beck invited former army staff sergeant David Bellavia on his program to discuss Obama's call for a "civilian national security force," which is how the president referred to his plans to expand two longtime successful volunteer programs, Americorps and the Peace Corps. But for Beck again, it brought back the specter of Hitler: "I'm finding this—this is the hardest part to connect to. Because this is—I mean, look, you know, David, what you just said is, you said, 'I'm not comparing'—but you are. I mean, this is what Hitler did with the SS. He had his own people. He had the brownshirts and then the SS."

And, of course, to Beck, Obama was never so Hitler-like as when he proposed national health-care reform. America's second-most popular talk-show host warned his audience that by not reading Obama's health-care plan, they would be making the same mistake Germans made by not reading *Mein Kampf.* First the denial: "I am not comparing him to this." Then the comparison: "But please, read *Mein Kampf* for this reason. If you read it now, you see that Hitler told you what he was going to do. He told the Germans. It outsold the Bible. Germans read *Mein Kampf,* but what did they do? They didn't listen. . . . They buried their hands in the sand, and then it became too late. Please, America, take this man for what he says."

Crazy? Totally. But Beck was not alone. His outrageous assertion that the drive for universal health care was nothing but a repeat of Hitler's Nazi Germany was also picked up by Rush

Limbaugh, who lives in fear every day that Beck will one day knock him off his throne as the nation's number-one radio talker. In October 2009, Limbaugh jumped on the Beck bandwagon: "Just as Obama's doing, Hitler—well, even prior to Hitler, German socialists attempted to remake and order their country using health care as the springboard and the foundation. Same thing that's happening here." Obama or Hitler, what's the difference? According to Limbaugh, "Adolph Hitler, like Barack Obama, also ruled by dictate."

Of course, Obama did not simply dictate a new health-care plan for America. He had to fight an uphill battle for it in the U.S. Congress. But facts have never prevented Limbaugh from taking a cheap shot at any Democrat.

Nor did it Michael Savage, who joined the Nazi right-wing chorus with this assertion: "It seems that the Obama appointees actually have almost the same exact policies as the Nazi Party did." And it wouldn't be long, Savage warned, before America's neo-Nazis showed their real stripes: "I'd say the likelihood is very high that the gang that has taken over this country will declare something—a pretext—they'll create it—the equivalent of the Reichstag fire. They will use it as a pretext to put in a form of martial law."

That was in August 2009. We're still waiting. Honestly, you'd think the secret Obama neo-Nazis would have scheduled something spectacular before the 2012 election.

FOREIGNER

The allegations that Barack Obama was either a Muslim or terrorist or Nazi only served to breathe new life into a far more insidious charge: that he wasn't even an American citizen.

As we saw in the previous chapter, doubts about Obama's birthplace in Hawaii began during the campaign and refused to go away—even after the campaign posted his birth certificate on

its Web site and reprinted birth announcements from two Honolulu newspapers that had appeared in print just a few days after
his birth.

Not even Obama's inauguration as forty-fourth president of
the United States could stop the crazies—led by the "queen of the
Birthers," California dentist and attorney Orly Taitz—from fan-
ning the flames of noncitizenship. And along the way, Taitz picked
up support from several members of Congress. Senators Richard
Shelby, David Vitter, and Roy Blunt and over a dozen Republican members of the House joined the chorus clamoring for
Obama to prove his American citizenship. On *Meet the Press*,
both Speaker John Boehner and majority leader Eric Cantor,
while insisting they themselves believed Obama was an American citizen, refused to criticize or condemn the Birthers in their
ranks.

To be fair, there were a few conservative voices who did stand
up to the Birthers. Mitt Romney dismissed the whole issue as a
waste of time. Conservative talk-show host Michael Medved
slammed the Birthers as "crazy, nutburger, demagogue, money-
hungry, exploitative, irresponsible, filthy conservative impos-
ters" who are "the worst enemy of the conservative movement"
and "make us look sick, troubled and not suitable for civilized
company." Even Ann Coulter dismissed them as "just a few
cranks."

But others eagerly kept the issue alive. Under founder Joseph
Farah, the Web site WorldNetDaily became "Birther Central."
Talk-show hosts Rush Limbaugh, Sean Hannity, Lou Dobbs, Michael Savage, and G. Gordon Liddy beat the citizenship drum
almost daily. Savage went so far as to warn, "We're getting ready
for the Communist takeover of America with a noncitizen at the
helm." And—evidence, once again, of the validity of the "Big Lie"
theory—the nonstop questioning of Obama's place of birth had a
definite impact on the American electorate.

By April 2011—over two years after President Obama took

office—one out of four Americans, according to a CBS News poll, did not believe the president was born in the United States.

And, of course, once again with zero evidence, Sarah Palin was only too happy to jump in, assuring radio talk-show host Rusty Humphries that she would not hesitate to make Obama's citizenship an issue if she decided to run for president in 2012. "I think it's a fair question," she told Humphries, "just like I think past associations and past voting records—all of that is fair game. The McCain-Palin campaign didn't do a good enough job in that area." (Or in most areas, frankly.)

But Sarah Palin never got a chance to make Obama's birth certificate an issue in the 2012 campaign. Donald Trump beat her to it. When "the Donald," who had already publicly toyed with the idea of running for president in 2000, 2004, and 2008, once again started making noises about 2012, most people laughed it off as a political bad joke. Then he jumped on the Birther issue and popped up on every network, charging that Obama's parents had paid for fake newspaper ads about baby Barack's birth so they could qualify for welfare. He vowed to hire private investigators to track down the truth about Obama's lineage. And he demanded that President Obama produce the "long form" of his birth certificate. Otherwise, the man with the worst comb-over in the world asserted, Obama might be guilty of perpetrating the worst "hoax" in history.

And suddenly, Donald Trump wasn't such a joke, anymore. Overnight, he soared in popularity among potential Republican nominees for 2012—either tied with or ahead of Mitt Romney.

Neil Abercrombie, Hawaii's new governor, tried to help bury the issue. As Obama's father's former teaching assistant at the University of Hawaii, he told his own story about getting to know Obama's parents and meeting the infant Barack shortly after he was born. In January 2011, Abercrombie also supported legislation that would allow any citizen to examine Obama's (or anyone else's) actual birth certificate—for a fee of one hundred dollars.

Still, the doubts persisted. Most ominously, the Southern Poverty Law Center reported that the Birther movement had taken root among some of the most "noxious elements" of the radical right, including white-supremacist and neo-Nazi groups, always looking for one more reason to hate our first black president. As one wonk put it on Twitter, Birtherism is to racism as intelligent design is to creationism.

At this point, those in the White House became increasingly concerned and decided to act—after watching an issue they thought they had buried long ago resurface and once again dominate the daily news cycle.

The climax came with a remarkable appearance by President Obama in the White House Briefing Room on the morning of April 27, 2011. It wasn't until 7:51 A.M. that we reporters were notified the president would make a statement to the press at 9:45. Most of us assumed he was showing up to confirm word leaked earlier that morning that he planned to nominate Leon Panetta as his new secretary of defense and Gen. David Petraeus to succeed Panetta as director of the CIA.

Imagine our surprise, then, when press secretary Jay Carney arrived for his 8:45 off-camera gaggle accompanied by communications director Dan Pfeiffer—and the two of them proceeded to hand out copies of President Obama's long-form birth certificate. Obama had finally had enough, they explained. Irritated by the media's paying so much attention to the Birther issue, he had directed his attorney to petition the state of Hawaii for access to his original "certificate of live birth," stored in state archives. Permission was granted. His attorney flew to Hawaii, picked up the original birth certificate, and delivered it to the White House—copies of which were then duly distributed to the press corps, together with copies of the correspondence between the White House and the Hawaii Department of Health.

For his part, President Obama used the occasion to scold the media for paying so much attention to a nonissue. This was the only issue on which he could get networks to break into regular programming, he pointed out. And that was nonsense. We have real things to worry about, he said. We have much more important things to talk about. "We can't just make stuff up," he said, chiding reporters. And, in a not so veiled swipe at Donald Trump, he warned the media about chasing "sideshows and carnival barkers."

The president also acknowledged that, for some crazies, even release of his long-form birth certificate, which they had long demanded, would not be enough. "I know that there's going to be a segment of people for which, no matter what we put out, this issue will not be put to rest," he told us in the Briefing Room. "But I'm speaking to the vast majority of the American people, as well as to the press. We do not have time for this kind of silliness. We've got better stuff to do. I've got better stuff to do."

And indeed, as the president predicted, Donald Trump and others refused to admit they were wrong. For a brief period, in fact, Trump not only questioned the authenticity of the long-form birth certificate released by Obama; he raised the stakes by demanding release of yet another document: Obama's college grades. Barack Obama was rumored to have been a "bad student," Trump charged. So how could he possibly have made it to Harvard?

But, with this latest attack, Trump clearly overplayed his hand. Obama, after all, had graduated from Harvard Law School magna cum laude, and had been elected president of the *Harvard Law Review*. He was clearly no academic slouch. There was only one possible explanation for why anyone would demand publication of his college grades, when no one had ever demanded release of George Bush's college grades. Everyone knew what was really behind that tactic, but it took CBS News anchor Bob Schieffer to express it publicly.

In an interview with then CBS News anchor Katie Couric, Schieffer didn't mince words: "I want to go on to what he said after he said this is out, and everything. He said we need to look at his grades and see if he was a good enough student to get into Harvard Law School. That's just code for saying he got into law school because he's black. This is an ugly strain of racism that's running through this whole thing. We can only hope that that kind of thing comes to an end too, but we'll have to see."

Good for Bob Schieffer. He was the first to say openly what most journalists were saying privately: Donald Trump was playing the race card. Like so many Tea Party members, he was engaging in personal, not policy, attacks against President Obama for one reason only: because he's black. In response, Trump insisted he had a great relationship with "the blacks." But, as *Saturday Night Live* chief comedy writer Seth Meyers cracked at the 2011 White House Correspondents Dinner, "Unless the Blacks are a family of white people, I bet he's mistaken."

By making a fool of himself on both issues, Obama's birth certificate and college grades, Donald Trump lost any credibility as a serious presidential candidate. His poll numbers and his candidacy sank like a rock. Three weeks after the White House Correspondents Dinner, on May 16, Trump accepted reality: He dropped out of the race, which he had never officially entered. Meanwhile, some media outlets weren't satisfied with merely questioning the president's country of birth. In trying to assert Obama's "foreignness," *Forbes* magazine—at one time, a respected nonpartisan business magazine—went where no one else had yet dared to go: Obama was not only a foreigner, they asserted in their October 2010 cover story; he was governing as a foreigner, with a foreigner's agenda.

For reasons that puzzled even its conservative business readers, *Forbes* featured a lengthy article by right-wing commentator Dinesh D'Souza, who seriously argued that Obama's entire political agenda had been shaped for him by his politically radical Kenyan father: a man, remember, who left Barack Obama when he was two, and whom Obama saw only one other time in his

THE "OTHERING" OF PRESIDENT OBAMA   89

life, when he was ten. Nonetheless, D'Souza contends, "The U.S. is being ruled according to the dreams of a Luo tribesman of the 1950's. This philandering, inebriated African socialist, who raged against the world for denying him the realization of his anti-colonial ambitions, is now setting the nation's agenda through the reincarnation of his dreams in his son."

Who knew? In putting forth his stimulus package, auto bailout, health-care reform, and Wall Street reforms, Barack Obama was merely following a plan mapped out for him fifty years ago by a philandering Kenyan socialist. Surely nobody in his right mind would believe that. Well, nobody but Newt Gingrich and Mike Huckabee—two leading Republicans, allegedly sane, one of them running for president.

Desperately seeking attention as a possible challenger to Obama, the disgraced former House Speaker publicly praised D'Souza's analysis—and then went on to draw what was, to him, the obvious conclusion: "What if Obama is so outside our comprehension, that only if you understand Kenyan, anti-colonial behavior, can you begin to piece together [his actions as president]?" Without that background, Gingrich insisted, you can never understand Barack Obama, because "[t]hat is the most accurate, predictive model for his behavior."

At this point, it's worth pointing out that a prolific Newt Gingrich had actually published two books in 2010 praising George Washington for his "anti-colonial" behavior. Presumably, American anticolonialism is to be praised, while Kenyan anticolonialism is to be feared. But I digress.

A few months later, in February 2011, Huckabee elaborated on Gingrich's Kenya-roots theme in an interview with radio talk-show host Steve Malzberg. When Malzberg again raised the issue of Obama's birth certificate and suggested Americans deserved to know more about Obama, Huckabee didn't hesitate: "I would love to know more," he said. "What I know is troubling enough. And one thing that I do know is his having grown up in

Kenya, his view of the Brits, for example, very different than the average American."

Then, just in case nobody knew what he was referring to, Huckabee elaborated: "But then, if you think about it, his perspective as growing up in Kenya with a Kenyan father and grandfather, their view of the Mau Mau Revolution in Kenya is very different than ours because he probably grew up hearing that the British were a bunch of imperialists."

Unbelievable! Isn't it amazing how uninformed you can be and still be taken seriously by the Republican party? Surely even most people in Arkansas must know that young Barack Obama did not grow up in Kenya. He grew up in Hawaii and Indonesia, a personal story told at great length in his memoir, *Dreams from My Father*. Obama didn't visit Kenya until he was in his twenties, long after his father—whom he'd met only twice—and his grandfather—whom he'd never met—were dead.

Rushing to cover his tracks, Huckabee lamely explained that he had simply misspoken. He had meant to say "Indonesia." Which, again, makes no sense at all. The Mau Mau revolution happened in Kenya in the 1950s, not in Indonesia. And, besides, Indonesia was a Dutch colony, not a British colony. As any stamp collector knows, it was called the Dutch East Indies.

And does Huckabee really believe it's wrong to consider leaders of the British Empire "imperialists?" That's what they were at the time. So were the Dutch, and the French, and the Spanish. And, under William McKinley and Teddy Roosevelt, for a time, so were we!

But Mike Huckabee, like Newt Gingrich and others, couldn't resist making a big issue of the fact that Barack Obama had spent part of his childhood outside the continental United States— precisely to make the point that Obama was somehow different, foreign, and not to be trusted. But even that wasn't the nadir of the name-calling.

JACKASS

In the fall of 2010, faced with expiration of the ten-year Bush tax cuts, President Obama proposed extending the tax cuts for all whose income was under $250,000 a year, but letting taxes revert back to their previous rate for those whose income was over $250,000 a year. And, at first, he dismissed Republican arguments that, without a continued tax cut, America's wealthiest individuals would refuse to invest in a growing economy, and thereby cause the loss of millions of jobs.

Eventually—and unfortunately—Obama dropped his demand and settled for a compromise that extended tax cuts for two more years on all income enjoyed by both middle-class and wealthy Americans. But the mere possibility of having to pay higher taxes on his own gazillionaire income sent Rush Limbaugh into orbit.

Abandoning any pretense of rational debate or disagreement, Limbaugh told the president on his radio show: "Mr. Obama, our imam-child, they have already taken their trillion dollar ball home, and they're sitting on it, you jackass." Because the president dared subscribe to the theory, held by most economists, that Americans could not afford to give its wealthiest citizens another one-trillion-dollar tax break while facing a fourteen-trillion-dollar national debt, Rush said of Obama, "He's a jackass. He's an economic illiterate. He's an economic ignoramus. And that's being charitable." Limbaugh, remember, is the same radio talk-show host who called Democrats critical of George W. Bush "disloyal" to America. But no liberal talk-show host ever called Bush a "jackass."

You couldn't go any lower than that. Right? . . . Wrong!

ADULTERER

It's the new rule of politics: When all else fails, accuse your opponent of cheating on his wife. And, frankly, in Washington, at least half the time you'd be correct. But not with Barack Obama.

Of course, that didn't stop Rush Limbaugh. Reporters who cover the White House know that weekends often find Barack and Michelle Obama, like millions of other parents across the country, at their kids' soccer or basketball games. Indeed, whenever the president takes in a game, reporters on pool duty travel with him, even though they're kept at a distance from the event.

Yet when Obama attended one game in early 2010, Limbaugh irresponsibly, and without one shred of evidence, suggested he might have been enjoying a "quickie" with a nearby girlfriend instead. "Nobody knows where he really went. . . . What was he doing out there? What was he doing?" Rush demanded of his audience.

Then he accused reporters of being accomplices in Obama's cheating by not reporting on it. "And, of course, the media, this breaks with decades of tradition, but they are not offended by this as they would be. I don't know if Michelle knows where he went. Nobody knows. He went to a soccer game that wasn't played."

Nobody knows? Every other parent at the game knew where Obama was. So did every kid on the field. And so did the entire White House press pool. ABC's chief White House correspondent, Jake Tapper, tweeted: "Don't know genesis of latest insane conspiracy theory, but yes: many ppl saw POTUS at daughter's soccer game at ft reno park soccer field."

As first reported by John K. Wilson in his book *The Most Dangerous Man in America,* Limbaugh never corrected his story and never apologized for accusing Obama of adultery.

OBAMA GETS OSAMA

Muslim, foreigner, terrorist, Marxist, fascist, or socialist . . .

Behind whatever name the Obama Hate Machine called the

president, there was one common theme: He didn't really love this country. Therefore, we couldn't trust him to keep us safe.

Indeed, that was the narrative Republicans had already woven for the 2012 presidential race: Obama might be a nice guy—even a nice black guy—but he was in over his head as commander in chief. He didn't have the experience, the expertise, or the backbone to make the tough decisions in our ongoing war on terror. Al-Qaeda and other terrorists knew they had nothing to fear as long as Barack Obama was in the White House.

That, of course, was nonsense. Check the record. According to the think tank Third Way, there were almost three times as many terrorist suspects killed by U.S. forces in Obama's first year in office as in the final four years of the Bush administration. And an October 2009 study by the New America Foundation reported that Obama authorized as many drone-launched missile strikes in his first nine and a half months in office as Bush did in his final three years.

But the narrative of Obama's being soft on terrorism collapsed, once and for all, when he walked into the East Room of the White House late on the evening of May 1, 2011, and announced, "Tonight I can report to the American people and the world that the United States has conducted an operation that has killed Osama bin Laden."

Details of the operation were soon revealed. Obama had ordered Leon Panetta, his new CIA director, to make finding bin Laden a top priority. CIA intelligence teams had located him—not in a remote cave in the mountains of Afghanistan, but in a mansion in Abbottabad, Pakistan. And Navy SEALs had then put together a bold plan to go in and capture or kill him, which the president personally authorized.

Obama didn't brag about what he did. He didn't have to. He recognized the heroic work of the CIA and the Navy SEALs, and thanked them accordingly. There was no need to say more. Everybody knew that Obama had accomplished in less than three years—bringing Osama bin Laden to justice—what George W. Bush had failed to do in seven. Still, Obama's enemies gamely tried to deny him any credit for getting bin Laden, or to find something wrong with the mission.

The *Washington Times* blasted Obama for allowing bin Laden to be buried at sea, in accordance with Islamic burial rites. "Obama bungled the Osama killing with too much respect for Islam," the right-wing propaganda sheet complained. "The White House went out its way to make certain that Osama bin Laden received full traditional Muslim burial rites. Obama officials claimed they did so to honor the Islamic religion, but they were also honoring bin Laden. Such acts are unacceptable on behalf of America's mortal enemy."

Glenn Beck also complained about the dignified burial at sea, adding, "I really would have put bin Laden in a meat grinder with a pig, honestly."

Claudia Rosett, writing for National Review Online, welcomed the news of bin Laden's death but said Obama made a big mistake "in delivering it himself." Rush Limbaugh claimed it was all political, insisting that if Obama were safe for reelection, "Osama bin Laden would still be alive today." On Fox News, host Andrew Napolitano accused President Obama of illegally murdering bin Laden, and warned that he might go after political enemies like Glenn Beck next. And in response to Obama's suggestion that, with bin Laden's capture and killing, we might recapture some of the spirit of unity that prevailed after September 11 to solve other problems, talk-show host Laura Ingraham tweeted: "BHO calling for unity? Republicans and conservatives must be aware of this trap. Sometimes disunity is good for us."

Taking criticism to the point of absurdity, Fox News also picked up on and amplified a complaint by the *Daily Mail* that Obama had taken too long to make up his mind. After military leaders presented their plan on Thursday, April 28, Obama said he wanted to sleep on it. He gave them the go-ahead on Friday morning, sixteen hours later—which doesn't seem like that much time, especially given the fact that the CIA told Obama they could be only 60 to 80 percent sure bin Laden was actually in the compound. But making the military wait that long, editorialized the *Mail*, was "feckless and indecisive" and not the sign of a true leader.

But, in the most desperate act of all, several conservatives went beyond denying Obama credit for getting Osama bin Laden by giving all the credit to George W. Bush. First, they asserted, it was Bush's war on terror that had led to the dramatic capture and killing of the world's number-one terrorist. Sean Hannity, on Fox News: "There was no way this would have happened, but for the policies of George W. Bush."

Karl Rove, on Fox News: "Important policy decisions made under Bush made bin Laden's death possible."

Columnist Brett Decker, in the *Washington Times*: "Bin Laden's death is more Mr. Bush's victory than Mr. Obama's."

Do they really think our memories are that short? Yes, we know that, immediately after September 11, Bush boasted that he was going to bring Osama bin Laden back "dead or alive." But we also know that he pulled American troops off the hunt for bin Laden when they were closing in on him in Tora Bora, then sent them to Afghanistan instead. And we know that Bush himself admits he soon lost interest in bin Laden altogether. "I truly am not that concerned about him," he told reporters on March 14, 2002. In July 2006, at the president's direction, the CIA shut down Alec Station, a special unit that, for a decade, had the special mission of hunting Osama bin Laden and his top lieutenants. It was Obama who directed the CIA to resume the long-cold search.

Bush loyalists and Obama haters were equally unconvincing when they claimed information gained through waterboarding September 11 mastermind Khalid Sheikh Mohammed was responsible for finding bin Laden—hence, another victory and justification for Bush's illegal actions while in the White House. Again, some of the same desperate voices were heard. Sean Hannity, on Fox News: "It is very obvious now that enhanced interrogations . . . led to the intelligence."

Karl Rove, on Fox News: "We now know that enhanced interrogation techniques . . . led to the code word, code name."

The *Wall Street Journal* ran the headline DEATH OF BIN LADEN LOOKS TO BE A VINDICATION OF MR. BUSH'S INTERROGATION POLICIES.

And former Bush attorney general Michael Mukasey bragged that, under waterboarding, KSM "broke like a dam" and revealed a torrent of information "including eventually the nickname of a trusted courier of bin Laden."

In fact, they were all wrong. Dead wrong. Not even close. For one simple reason, above all others. Think about it. The most important piece of intelligence about Osama bin Laden was where he was hiding out. He'd been living in Abbottabad, Pakistan, for six years, since 2005, when the walled compound was built. But the waterboarding of KSM—183 times!—took place in 2002. At that point, bin Laden's compound didn't even exist. There's no way KSM could have pinpointed its location.

Obama administration officials and other intelligence experts weighed in, throwing cold water on the claims so eagerly spread by Fox News. But nobody debunked the praise of waterboarding more conclusively than Republican senator John McCain. In an emotional speech on the Senate floor and a powerful op-ed in the *Washington Post*, McCain, himself a survivor of terrible torture, denounced the Bush apologists.

"I asked CIA Director Leon Panetta for the facts, and he told me the following," McCain wrote in the May 11, 2011, *Washington Post*. "The trail to bin Laden did not begin with a disclosure from Khalid Sheik Mohammed, who was waterboarded 183 times. . . . The first mention of Abu Ahmed al-Kuwaiti—the nickname of the al-Qaeda courier who ultimately led us to bin Laden—as well as a description of him as an important member of Al Qaeda, came from a detainee held in another country, who we believe was not tortured. None of the three detainees who were waterboarded provided Abu Ahmed's real name, his whereabouts or an accurate description of his role in al-Qaeda."

McCain continued: "In fact, the use of 'enhanced interrogation techniques' on Khalid Sheik Mohammed produced false and misleading information. He specifically told his interrogators that Abu Ahmed had moved to Peshawar, got married and ceased his role as an al-Qaeda facilitator—none of which was true. According to the staff of the Senate Intelligence Committee, the best intelligence gained from a CIA detainee—information describing Abu Ahmed al-Kuwaiti's real role in al-Qaeda and his true relationship to bin Laden—was obtained through standard, noncoercive means."

McCain's statements, in effect, killed GOP attempts to credit George W. Bush and Dick Cheney with finally bringing Osama bin Laden to justice. But, true to form, critics still had one ludicrous last arrow left in their quiver. A crazy band of Obama haters, led by Fox News anchor Andrew Napolitano, refused to believe that bin Laden was even dead—even though his wife, sons, and leaders of al-Qaeda had all confirmed his killing, by Navy SEALs.

Napolitano actually raised the question on Fox News whether Obama was "telling us the truth or pulling a fast one to save his lousy presidency."

Poor President Obama. His enemies had now come full circle. He now had to deal with both the Birthers and the "deathers."

AMERICA'S FIRST SOCIALIST PRESIDENT

Of all the names Obama has been called, one deserves special attention—and refutation: Barack Obama, the *socialist*!

He's a socialist! That is, in fact, the way he is most often and least accurately described by his critics—in one form or another.

As nutty freshman congressman Allen West of Florida charged, what do you expect from someone who started out as a community organizer? He told Greta van Susteren on Fox News, "I think that when you look at what a community organizer is turning out to be, it does seem to be like a low-level socialist agitator."

Which is absurd. Even a casual review of his actions as president would reveal that President Obama is, in fact, anything but a socialist. But that has never deterred the socialist smear, heard nonstop on Fox News—starting from the top.

How can Bill O'Reilly, Sean Hannity, and other Fox hosts get away with continuing to call President Obama a socialist? Because they're only following the example of their leader, Fox founder and president, and former Nixon strategist, Roger Ailes.

In November 2010, Ailes asserted that Obama was, in fact, even more of a socialist than the French or Germans. "The president has not been very successful," he told the Daily Beast's Howard Kurtz. "He just got kicked from Mumbai to South Korea, and he came home and attacked Republicans for it. He had to be told by the French and the Germans that his socialism was too far left for them to deal with."

There was zero evidence behind Ailes's claim. So what? His interview showed his Fox News hosts they had the green light to launch their own assaults on Obama the socialist. How could Ailes ask them to pull back, when he himself had set the tone? The mighty Foxers heard Ailes and marched behind him in lockstep.

Bill O'Reilly contended, "Most Americans reject the quasi-socialistic agenda they [Obama and the House Democrats] put out, but people like Nancy Pelosi and Barney Frank will never admit that, so tension remains inside the Democratic Party."

Well, at least he said "quasi-socialistic." Sean Hannity left any qualifiers behind. "You know what, I don't want his policies to succeed," he told his Fox audience. "I want him out of—I want him to be a one-term president because he's doing so much damage with his failed socialist policies." Hannity also called the Democratic party the "The Socialist Party of America" and declared that "the socialist in the White House has now smothered the private sector."

Everywhere he looked, Mike Huckabee, onetime presidential candidate and born-again weekend Fox News host, saw a socialist conspiracy under way. "The Union of Soviet Socialist Republics may be dead, but the Union of American Socialist Republics is being born," he exclaimed. The Republican leader also condemned TARP, or the Wall Street bailout, as a Communist plot. "Lenin and Stalin would love this stuff," insisted the former Arkansas governor, apparently ignorant of the fact that TARP was actually the result of legislation initiated and signed into law on October 3, 2008, by President George W. Bush—whom nobody ever accused of being a socialist.

Fox Washington bureau chief Bill Sammon agreed, telling viewers that Obama had an "agenda towards socialism." Even Joe Scarborough, who—as conservative as he is—generally avoids going off the deep end on MSNBC's *Morning Joe,* fell for this one. While discussing right-wing claims that, under Obama, America was "moving closer toward European-style socialism," the former Florida congressman commented without challenge, "That's not a right-wing claim; it's the truth."

Naturally, the Fox Business Network also jumped on the bash-Obama bandwagon. In September 2010, Wall Street analyst Stuart Varney, who hosts his own daily Fox Business program, joined Hannity's show to warn, "We've had an 18-month experiment with American socialism and we do not like it, we want to reverse it." Varney also declared that Obama's economic policies were not only socialist but also "un-American."

But no Fox personality took more delight in labeling Obama a socialist than Glenn Beck. Perhaps because it was the scariest word he could think of.

During the 2008 election, Beck had already charged that there was "strong evidence" Obama was "a socialist." After this, in a much-discredited survey, the *National Journal* labeled Obama the most liberal member of the Senate—even more liberal than Senator Bernie Sanders of Vermont, an actual self-described socialist. Or, as Beck preferred to categorize it: "past the socialists, left of the socialists." "That's a pretty good hint," concluded Beck, "that this guy is a radical." And it was up to Obama to prove otherwise. "So what is it?" Beck asked Obama rhetorically. "Will you denounce socialism as a failure that it is, or not?"

Then Beck turned to some of the people Obama had brought into the White House, directing his wrath at two in particular: green-jobs director Van Jones and science adviser John Holdren. "The president has aligned himself with these radical socialists," Beck warned. "Fact. They're radical Marxists. They're militant communists. Fact. The fact is, you cannot be with radical socialists, communists, and be also, you know, mom and Chevrolet and apple pie and baseball, you—you can't. It's one or the other. That's the fact."

Wow! So the president of the United States is a socialist. That's a pretty strong accusation, even coming from Fox News. What are the facts to support that charge? For now, let us simply offer the "airtight" case that Glenn Beck put forward to prove Obama was a socialist.

1. Obama's father was a "Nairobi bureaucrat who advised government to redistribute income through higher taxes."
2. Obama's mother was influenced by Nietzsche and Freud.
3. Obama's grandparents introduced him to poet and Communist Frank Marshall Davis.
4. As senator, Obama had voted for TARP.
5. As president, Obama had seized control of insurance giant AIG, initiated a $787 billion economic-recovery plan, appointed himself president of GM and Chrysler, and was a proponent of single-payer health care.

Any intelligent person would look at that case and laugh out loud at the weakness and absurdity of it. But that would be to underestimate the power of the Fox News megaphone.

Proving the effectiveness of the big-lie theory all over again: As a result of the nonstop "socialist" commentary from Fox News hosts and right-wing talk-show hosts, a national survey by Democracy Corps in July 2010 showed that 55 percent of likely voters actually believed Obama was a socialist. At which point, Fox News led with the headline IT'S OFFICIAL! OBAMA'S A SOCIALIST! The cover of *Newsweek* had earlier contributed to the hysteria with the headline: WE ARE ALL SOCIALISTS NOW.

So what's the truth?

Forget the alleged family influence. Obama's mother, grandparents, and father (whom he met only twice) did not raise him a socialist or a Communist.

As for the idea that his mother read little Barack bedtime stories by Nietzsche and Freud rather than ones by Dr. Seuss: It's worth pointing out that neither Nietzsche or Freud was a socialist nor held socialism in high regard. In *The Anti-Christ,* Nietzsche wrote, "Whom do I hate most among the rabble of today? The socialist rabble." As for Freud, the May 2006 issue of the *Socialist Standard* called his *Civilization and Its Discontents* "one of the most anti-socialist books ever written." Once again, Beck proved he doesn't know what he's talking about. He just likes throwing around the names Nietzsche and Freud—either because they sound so foreign and subversive or because it makes him sound well-read. And he can be sure his great unwashed audience won't know any better.

But what about Obama's actions as senator and president? The truth is, he's proved to be far from a socialist, as senator from Vermont and actual socialist Bernie Sanders and many others will attest. On many issues, it would even be a stretch to call him a liberal.

Without getting too wonky, socialism is generally defined as

an economic theory advocating collective or governmental ownership and administration of the means of production and distribu-
tion of goods. When government owns and runs the oil companies,
for example, that's socialism. When government regulates or taxes
the oil companies, that's not.

As we've seen, Beck and others generally cite three examples
of how Barack Obama is leading this country to socialism:
health-care reform, the auto industry bailout, and TARP. Yet a
brief look at each shows that just the opposite is true.

HEALTH-CARE REFORM

There is, indeed, a socialist model for delivering health care. It's
called "single-payer." It exists, with slight variations, in Canada,
the UK, France, Switzerland, Germany, Italy, Spain, and the Scandinavian countries. And it works.

Indeed, it works so well that Barack Obama was once a big
supporter of government-run, or single-payer, health care. In 2003,
as a candidate for the U.S. Senate, he praised it as the only way
to go, even though it would take a long time to get there: "I see
no reason why the United States of America, the wealthiest
country in the history of the world, spending 14 percent of its
Gross National Product on health care cannot provide basic
health insurance to everybody. And that's what Jim is talking
about when he says everybody in, nobody out. A single payer
health care plan, a universal health care plan. And that's what
I'd like to see. But as all of you know, we may not get there immediately. Because first we have to take back the White House,
we have to take back the Senate, and we have to take back the
House."

By the time he ran for president, however, Obama's views
about health care had been tempered by political reality. So much
so that when he declared his goal of establishing universal health
care in his first year in office, he said up front he was interested

in exploring every possible option, except one—a single-payer health-care system. Why? Not because he didn't believe in it. But because he knew that, despite the support of Speaker Nancy Pelosi and most Democrats in the House, there would never be enough votes in Congress for a single-payer system. Instead, Obama proposed a more pragmatic approach. "People don't have time to wait," he said in August 2008. "They need relief now. So my attitude is let's build up the system we got, let's make it more efficient, we may over time—as we make the system more efficient and everybody's covered—decide that there are other ways for us to provide care more effectively." In the first version of his plan, Obama did please liberals by including a "public plan" as one of the options available to families. For a while, Obama sold it vigorously as a neces_____ of any final health-care-reform plan in ord_____ choice and to give private insurance con_____ petition.

This "pub_____ r short of a single-payer system, because_____ n give people the choice of signing up fo_____ am that would be administered by the_____ re medical services, as in Medicare, wou_____ by private doctors and hospitals. But critics insisted it was a "foot in the door," which would eventually and inevitably lead to a single-payer health-care system. Facing intense opposition from the insurance industry, Obama soon dropped the idea.

Nevertheless, his critics continued to portray Obama's plan as a big government takeover of all health care, which would inevitably lead to rationing, cuts in coverage, and even "death panels." Sean Hannity described Obama's Affordable Care Act as "the single biggest power grab and move towards socialism in the history of the country." And, as will be discussed in more detail in chapter 6, Sarah Palin didn't hesitate to exploit her own child's health problems in scaring the public about the proposed health-care-reform legislation. "The America I know and love is not one in which my parents or my baby with Down Syndrome will have to stand in front of Obama's 'death panel' so his bureaucrats can decide, based on a subjective judgment of their 'level of productivity in society,' whether they are worthy of health care. Such a system is downright evil."

She's right. Such a system would be downright evil. But that's not what Obama delivered. Either Palin was woefully ignorant or deliberately lying. In the end, Obama fought for and signed a classic, government-free, private-sector extension of health care that represents Capitalism with a capital *C*.

Under the provisions of what his enemies insist on calling "Obamacare" (as if that proves it's socialist), every American must buy health insurance. And they must buy it from a private insurance company. For insurers, that's a gift of 32 million new customers who *must* buy their product. If that's socialism, I'm sure other business sectors, like home builders, would like a little socialism thrown their way, too.

Government's only role in the new health-care program is threefold: to provide subsidies to help those who can't afford to buy private health insurance; to hold private insurers to higher standards, such as not denying coverage because of a preexisting condition; and to make sure individuals and private companies are living up to their obligations under the law.

But even that is not necessarily the case in all states. Under one provision of Obama's plan—which nobody talks about—states may opt out of the federal program and adopt their own plan, if they can come up with a better way of providing universal and affordable coverage. Under the bill as passed by Congress, states would have that right in 2017. In March 2011, Obama endorsed legislation by Senators Ron Wyden and Scott Brown that would allow states to opt out beginning in 2014.

Another rarely talked about plank of Obama's health-insurance plan is the health-insurance exchanges. These are best defined as marketplaces, or exchanges, where businesses and individuals can come together and choose from a range of providers and plans (one of these plans was meant to be the aforementioned public option.)

Before the exchanges—which don't go into effect until 2014—when people in most parts of the country bought health-insurance coverage, they had only a few choices. Health-insurance companies, which enjoy regional monopolies, were under no obligation to reveal all the details of their plans or what options might be available to families, so customers often could not figure out what, in fact, they were getting.

What the exchanges are designed to do is break up monopoly power and introduce real competition into the marketplace. They force insurers to reveal basic information about their plans—cost, coverage, claim-denial rates—in a standardized format so that consumers can fully understand the plans being offered.

That's one of the reasons insurers hate the Affordable Care Act, even though it requires everyone to buy private insurance. Because it will force big insurers, who have until now enjoyed monopoly power in various regions across the country, to actually compete for business. Put simply, the way the ACA works to bring health-care costs down is by introducing real competition and free-market principles to the health-insurance market.

Yes, that's the essence of Obama's health-care reform: free-market competition. See what I mean? When you get beyond the Tea Party rhetoric and understand what's really in the new national health-care plan and what's not, there's no longer any question: It's the exact opposite of socialism.

AUTO INDUSTRY BAILOUT

No matter how hard you look, you won't find any socialism in America's new system of health-care reform. You won't find any in the auto bailout, either.

Again, socialism would be where the government actually

owns and runs auto manufacturers—like Russia's Lada, Czecho-slovakia's Skoda, or Yugoslavia's Yugo. You know the old joke about the Yugo: What's included in every owner's manual? A bus schedule.

That's nothing like what happened with the 2009 bailout of America's auto industry. For starters, the government didn't buy General Motors and Chrysler. It loaned them money to keep them afloat: a total of $85 billion, $25 billion under President Bush, and $60 billion under President Obama. President Obama did not become president of GM and Chrysler. Nor did the federal government take over management of the companies. It insisted on some changes in direction, such as the manufacture of more fuel-efficient cars, but it left GM and Chrysler executives in charge—although not the same executives as before.

Right-wing pundits and commentators exploded when, as a condition of government assistance under Obama, GM chairman and chief executive officer Richard Wagoner, Jr., was forced to step down. Senator John McCain deemed the move "unprecedented in the history of this country." The *Washington Times* called the move "unheard of in American history." *The American Spectator* spoke darkly of "a whiff of fascism emanating from the Obama White House."

Not surprisingly, Fox News screamed the loudest over Wagoner's resignation. Stuart Varney wrongly proclaimed this action "the first time in modern history that the government has fired the chief executive of a private corporation." Andrew Napolitano called it "an absolute power grab and it's the road to fascism. . . . This is Mussolini on the Potomac." One of Fox's business contributors huffed, "It's like when you read *Russia Today,* or *The Moscow Times.*" And on *Fox & Friends,* Steve Doocy claimed that "the last president who fired a CEO was Putin!"

Not so fast. Actually, the last president who fired a CEO was . . . George W. Bush, six months earlier. As the *Washington Post* reported on September 17, 2008, under Bush the terms of the bailout package for the insurance giant AIG included replacing chief executive Robert Willumstad with Edward Liddy, the former CEO of Allstate. And this highly socialist move by President Bush came ten days after Secretary of the Treasury Hank Paulson announced that new CEOs were coming to Fannie Mae and Freddie Mac as part of their forced move into government conservatorship.

In fact, not even George Bush was the first president to demand that an auto executive lose his job as a condition of federal aid. In September of 1979, Chrysler CEO John Riccardo resigned after the Carter administration made clear he would have to go before any aid was forthcoming—leading soon thereafter to congressional approval of the Chrysler Corporation Loan Guarantee Act. Then again, we all know Jimmy Carter was a socialist, too.

At any rate, the truth is that, far from being a socialist failure, as some contend, the auto bailout is, in fact, a capitalist triumph. Because of the temporary assistance received from the government, America's auto industry has not only survived; it has bounced back stronger than ever. Plants are being reopened, union workers are coming back, new lines of cars are being produced, and Americans are buying them. In September 2010, sales of new automobiles soared 29 percent, the biggest gain of the year.

By March 2011, a survey by KPMG of industry players around the world found top auto executives believing that U.S. car brands would increase their market share over the next five years. Forty percent thought General Motors would gain strength in the market, compared to 15 percent of executives in 2009 and 13 percent in 2010. Twenty-four percent of executives thought the same of Chrysler, compared to only 7.5 percent the year before.

No doubt, by lending a hand to GM and Chrysler, taxpayers saved one of America's last manufacturing bases from collapse. That's good news. But here's more. Because both companies have paid back a significant portion of their loans, with interest, the Treasury Department projects the actual cost of the bailout will end up being $17 billion, not the original $85 billion. That's still a lot of money, but most economists say it was worth it to prevent the loss of our auto industry and to save one million jobs.

But that's still not the end of the story. GM recently offered a new, public IPO to raise funds for the company. Depending on the speed and success of that IPO, GM plans to buy back all the stock the government now owns in the company. In which case, taxpayers will not only get all their $85 billion back; they may actually end up making money on the deal!

That's not socialism, folks. That's beautiful capitalism at work.

TROUBLED ASSET RELIEF PROGRAM

Even more than the aid given to the auto industry, it was TARP that made *bailout* a dirty word in politics today. Go to any Tea Party rally today, and, no doubt, it will come up. In fact, millions of Americans were outraged over the government's $700 billion bailout of Wall Street banks and financial institutions, the very companies that brought the American economy to its knees and caused millions of Americans to see their life savings and retirement accounts suddenly disappear. Particularly in the eyes of Tea Partiers—and their big corporate backers, who don't tend to hail from Wall Street—it was a colossal waste of money, a massive addition to the federal deficit, a dangerous, socialist, government takeover of the financial industry—and it was all the fault of that socialist Barack Obama.

But that view obscures a few important points.

For starters, it wasn't Obama's program. The collapse of Wall Street occurred in September 2008, while President Bush was still in the White House. And it was the Bush administration, with the full support of Republicans in Congress, that put together a $700 billion bailout, half of which was out the door before

Obama even walked in. Obama merely finished the job that Bush had started.

And even though it was unpopular at the time, and remains unpopular, TARP, like the auto industry bailout, has proven to be a good business proposition. In fact, when it officially ended at the end of September 2010, it was hailed as perhaps the most maligned, yet effective, government program in modern times.

Wall Street bankers, remember, didn't express any opposition to the federal government's bailing them out. It only objected when the Obama administration also began bailing out state governments and the auto industry. What was good for the goose, in other words, was not considered good for the gander.

One thing is for certain. TARP was a case of necessary, if unwelcome, government intervention. As distasteful as it was to assist the very banks that caused our economic collapse, without it the recession would have been much deeper and much longer.

TARP, in fact, enabled Wall Street firms to get back on their feet and saved us from a second Great Depression. And it did so at a cost far, far lower than originally anticipated.

Several banks have already paid back their loans in full, with interest. Others have paid substantial down payments. As a result, in March 2011, the Treasury Department announced that American taxpayers had already made $6 billion in profits on the $245 billion originally handed out to banks—and estimated that, in the end, bank investments under TARP would net taxpayers some $20 billion in profits. At the same time, treasury also predicted that all the $700 billion TARP programs combined—for banks, financial institutions, insurance companies, and domestic auto companies—would result in "little to no cost to taxpayers."

We lend money to American firms to prevent their collapse. We get our money back, and make substantial profits on the deal. Again, that's far from socialism. That's a good investment. That's capitalism at work.

NOT EXACTLY EUGENE DEBS

In the end, for the final word on whether or not President Obama is a bona fide card-carrying socialist, we turn to—who else?—a real socialist. Billy Wharton, editor of *The Socialist* newspaper, tried to set the record straight in an op-ed in the *Washington Post* in March 2009.

For starters, Wharton argued, no self-respecting socialist could support two of Obama's initiatives: his health-care-reform plan or his continuation of TARP.

On health care, Wharton pointed out: "A national health insurance system as embodied in the single-payer health plan reintroduced in legislation this year by Representative John Conyers, Jr. (D-Mich.) makes perfect sense to us. That bill would provide comprehensive coverage, offer a full range of choice of doctors and services, and eliminate the primary cause of personal bankruptcy—health-care bills. Obama's plan would do the opposite."

And on the Wall Street bailout, or TARP, Wharton slammed Obama for not daring to do what a real socialist would do—nationalize the banks. "The first indication that Obama is not, in fact, a socialist, is the way his administration is avoiding structural changes to the financial system. Nationalization is simply not in the playbook of Treasury Secretary Timothy Geithner and his team." Nor in President Obama's playbook, one might add.

Bottom line, according to Wharton: "[We] socialists know that Barack Obama is not one of us. Not only is he not a socialist, he may in fact not even be a liberal. Socialists understand him more as a hedge-fund Democrat—one of a generation of neoliberal politicians firmly committed to free-market policies."

So there you have it, from a leading socialist himself: President Obama is not a socialist. Which doesn't mean Glenn Beck and other crazies will ever stop calling him a one. They like the sound of it. It scares people.

OBAMA DERANGEMENT SYNDROME

Believe it or not, as nasty as it was, all of the name-calling described so far isn't the worst abuse President Obama has had to face.

Much more insidious is the political theory behind the name-calling: that Obama is actually and deliberately trying to undermine our democratic system and standing in the world, perhaps in the service of a foreign—or extraterrestrial?—power.

This level of attack wanders so far from legitimate disagreement with Obama's policies that some conservatives are worried it makes it look like their entire movement has gone off the deep end and been taken over by the extreme fringe. Early in the Obama administration, leading conservative author David Horowitz—at any normal political time, a fringe dweller himself— noted "an interesting phenomenon on the Right, which is beginning to cause me concern." Horowitz identified his concern as "the over-the-top hysteria [among conservative critics] in response to the first months in office of our new president." Horowitz, no fan of Obama, memorably dubbed such extremism the "Obama Derangement Syndrome."

When David Horowitz is the voice of reason, you know you're swimming deep in the crazy zone. But Horowitz's caution was ignored by most of his fellow conservatives in the media. The doomsday warnings about Obama not only continued; they became more extreme in direct relationship to how successful Obama was in accomplishing his goals. Still today, his critics use a combination of anti-Obama rhetoric and antigovernment rhetoric to spread fear and paranoia about Obama's plans to disrupt life the way we know it.

NEW WORLD ORDER

The black helicopters are back!

If there's one conspiracy that will never die, it's the rumor about the Trilateral Commission: that group of evildoers that supposedly sits around with Henry Kissinger all day long, plotting the rise of a one-world government—under which the United States would surrender all sovereignty and become only a minor player. George H. W. Bush was a member, don't you know. And so was Bill Clinton. Not sure about George W. Bush. What was he up to anyway? But there's no doubt that the newest Trilateralist is Barack Obama.

Before he was kicked off of Fox for being too crazy—which is really crazy—Glenn Beck used to say flat out that "a new world order" and a "global government" are "being cobbled together today" by the Obama administration. Which, of course, would require a universal monetary system. But, no worry. Rush Limbaugh has already announced that President Obama is "all for a single world currency."

When the global economic crisis struck in the spring of 2009 and leaders of the G-20 nations met to coordinate economic-recovery strategies, Fox Business Network contributor Charles Payne smelled trouble: "One day, I think that we are heading toward a one-world sort of government," he predicted. And he added, "I think Obama probably likes that."

Citing the financial rescue of the auto industry and passage of health-care reform as evidence, Fox News contributor Dick Morris—who, like members of a similar profession, will service any client who knocks on his door, for a fee—accused President Obama of engineering a federal government takeover of vital elements of private industry as the first step to the "new world order." Against which, Morris suggested, the only recourse was violence: "Those crazies in Montana who say, 'We're going to kill ATF agents because the U.N.'s going to take over—well, they're beginning to have a case."

UNDERMINE AMERICA

The Obama Derangement Syndrome rolls on!

If you buy their logic, then it makes sense: Before he can make America part of a new-world, twenty-first-century global government, Barack Obama must first destabilize, if not destroy, our existing political and financial structures. Which, deranged conservatives fear, he's already begun.

Obama's ultimate goal, they insist, is to make the United States a second-rate power. Rush Limbaugh has repeatedly stated his concern that Obama wants to cut America "down to size." After which, he foresees "our greatness is going to be redefined in such a way that it won't be great, that we're just going to become average."

By providing temporary assistance to Wall Street and auto manufacturers, Obama was doing nothing more than continuing the policies of George W. Bush—policies that won nothing but praise from Limbaugh and others at the time. But, under Obama's hand, they were little short of treason. Leaders of the Obama administration were "focused on the destruction of the private sector," Limbaugh charged. "This is an all-out assault on capitalism." And he thanked Obama for "doing the job that everybody expects of you, taking every tradition and institution that defined this country's greatness and trying to rip it to shreds."

No matter that, in the end, both the auto bailout and TARP proved to be two of the smartest investments this country ever made.

Making a good investment and reaping the reward: Aren't TARP and the auto bailout perfect examples of what capitalism is all about? Not according to lead Obama critic Sean Hannity:

"The administration is on a mission to hijack capitalism in favor of collectivism," he warns. "The Bolsheviks have already arrived." Lou Dobbs agrees, although with a different historical model in mind. To the former host of CNN's *Moneyline*, America is "moving toward a combination of corporate power and political power," which he finds "disturbingly similar to what we witnessed in Italy in the 1930s."

Other commentators have looked for analogies closer to home. They have accused Obama of seeking a black man's revenge for the worst catastrophe to happen on American soil. Glenn Beck saw it coming: "I think we're headed for civil war." As did the ever-paranoid Michael Savage: "I almost feel as though Obama's trying to create a civil war in America for his own reasons."

Who would undertake such a mission to destroy the very nation he was elected to lead? Only someone who has allegiance to a foreign power. On that score, talk-show host Jay Severin—echoing the remarks of Huckabee aide Janet Porter—won a spot in the front ranks of Obama Derangement Syndrome wackos with this observation: "If it comes out that Barack Obama is a Russian spy, I will have been right." OMG!

MY GOD, IT'S FULL OF CZARS

Of course, if Obama were to succeed in undermining America, he could not do so by himself. Nor has he tried to. From the beginning, he surrounded himself with a subversive band of comrades in arms dedicated to the same destructive mission.

There is only one word to describe such all-powerful secret agents of evil: *czars*! At one time, according to Politico, Obama had twenty-nine of them. Others claim thirty-seven, even though some jobs were short-lived. Whatever the actual number, they included economic czar Paul Volker; energy and environment czar Carol Browner; green-jobs czar Van Jones; border czar Alan Bersin; Afghanistan/Pakistan czar Richard Holbrooke; pay czar

Kenneth Feinberg; Mideast peace czar George Mitchell; health czar Nancy-Ann DeParle; car czar Ron Bloom; and science czar John Holdren.

Now, most people would be impressed by such a collection of outstanding Americans, each highly qualified for and willing to take on a particular assignment to serve the country. But not those who believed in the vast Obama conspiracy. To them, these White House aides were the most dangerous public officials of all—because they were not elected, did not, in most cases, require Senate confirmation, and were therefore answerable to no one but Obama in the exercise of their duties.

True to form, Fox News led the attacks on these special-assignment Obama appointees. With ominous undertones, Sean Hannity warned of a "shadow government right here in the U.S." Neil Cavuto called them "evil despots accountable to no one." (Not even the president?) And a then Fox contributor, Angela McGlowan, helped lead the smear campaign that forced green-jobs coordinator Van Jones to resign his post. "People like this czar goes against the Constitution," she argued. "What are we, in Russia? Having czars?"

Lost in all the commotion over White House "czars," however, was the fact that Obama was hardly the first to name such special assistants. The practice started under Franklin Roosevelt and has been continued by every president since. Ronald Reagan, who signed a bill authorizing presidents to name special assistants without Senate confirmation, named the first drug czar.

According to most counts, the Bush 41 White House employed two czars; Bill Clinton, eight; and Bush 43, thirty-three of them—including "domestic policy czar" Karl Rove. Which is especially ironic, given that later, as a Fox News contributor, Rove became one of the most outspoken critics of Obama's nomination of czars, which he condemned as "a giant expansion of presidential power." At no time, however, did Rove mention that, as George W. Bush's senior policy adviser, he himself participated in the hiring of a food-safety czar, a cybersecurity czar, a regulatory czar, an AIDS czar, a manufacturing czar, an intelligence czar, a bird-flu czar, and a Katrina czar.

Although, to be fair and balanced, Rove wasn't the only hypocrite on Fox when it came to czardom. Like Sean Hannity, Bill O'Reilly railed against the impropriety, if not danger, of czars appointed by President Obama. Yet, just a couple of years earlier, he had publicly called on President George W. Bush to name an "immigration czar," as well as a "charity czar" and a "disaster relief victims family czar." And, in order to manage two wars at a time, in Afghanistan and Iraq, chief Obama critic and Fox contributor Newt Gingrich had earlier urged Bush to create a "war czar."

Czars, like beauty, it seems, are in the eyes of the beholder.

ANYTHING BUT CAPITALISM

It's obvious that, in their attempts to discredit President Obama, his political enemies were confused.

They knew they didn't like him; they just couldn't figure out why.

They knew he wasn't pro-democracy, but they didn't know what he wanted to replace it with.

The result was a lineup of critics who accused Obama of introducing to America communism, or socialism, or fascism, or corporatism—anything but capitalism. And it was obvious from their comments that none of them had any idea what communism, socialism, fascism, or corporatism really stood for. They just liked throwing the words out there, knowing that a certain percentage of the unlearned masses would believe them, no matter what they accused Obama of.

For Glenn Beck, Obama was—eventually—not a capitalist, or even a socialist. He was a fascist. "I was wrong," Beck told his vast radio audience. "Our government is not marching down the road towards communism or even socialism. They're marching us to a brand of non-violent fascism . . . toward 1984." Later, appearing on *The O'Reilly Factor* with fellow Foxer Bill O'Reilly, Beck elaborated on his claim: "We are really truly stepping beyond socialism and starting to look at fascism."

As if he hadn't already made his point, Beck felt compelled to add, "The government is a heroin pusher using smiley-faced fascism to grow the nanny state."

So who was Obama? Was he Mussolini on the Potomac, or Karl Marx on the Potomac? There's a big difference, but Fox personalities couldn't seem to make up their minds. Perhaps because he is neither.

RULING WITH AN IRON FIST

In June 2010, a resident of Hartlepool, England, summoned police after a neighbor called to say he'd seen a man climbing into a window of this man's house. After the police came and searched the house, without finding anybody, the relieved home owner retired for the night. But his head had no sooner hit the pillow than he heard a rustling noise and discovered the intruder climbing out from under his bed.

I cite this incident as evidence that, sometimes, there really is such a thing as a burglar hiding under the bed—but not nearly so often as Obama haters believe. Ever paranoid, they see a burglar—excessive government control—hiding under the bed of everything Obama does, no matter how harmless. Consider just two examples, among many, both of them Internet-related.

For years, the Federal Communications Commission wrestled with the question of "network neutrality." At issue was whether Internet service providers or government could place any restrictions on content, sites, platforms, or kinds of equipment chosen by Internet users.

Consumer groups and other advocates of net neutrality argue

that Internet access should be completely unfettered, as it has been up to now. They support new rules that would prevent broadband providers from using a pricing structure to block access to the Internet platforms and content of their competitors. Phone companies, cable television companies, and other providers insisted they had no intention of blocking access and that therefore any new regulations were unnecessary. Just trust us, they said. (Wink, wink!)

In December 2010, under Chairman Julius Genachowski, the Obama FCC—after much back-and-forth—adopted a heavily diluted form of net neutrality rules that leaned toward what the companies had asked for. The FCC plan exempted wireless communications, one of the growing areas of Internet usage, and it included no ban on "paid priority"—meaning that companies can still pay more to see their data move to the front of the line, which, by default, is the opposite of staying net-neutral. But even this industry-friendly version of net neutrality proved too much for the industry-friendlier Republicans in Congress, who vowed to overrule the FCC by legislation.

That is, if the courts don't first rule that the FCC has exceeded its rule-making authority. A U.S. appeals court had already come to that decision in April 2010, when they said the FCC did not currently have the power to prevent Comcast from blocking some of its users. This is because, under George W. Bush and his spirit of deregulation, the FCC had reclassified broadband Internet access from a "Title II," or "telecommunications service," to a "Title I," or "information service." The FCC has much less regulatory authority over Title I services than it does over Title II services.

So unless the FCC officially went back to the old system, and classified Internet access once again as a Title II "telecommunications service," the court argued it does not have the authority it once had to regulate the activity of broadband companies. Even this reclassification, which is strongly encouraged by net neutrality advocates, has been resisted by the Obama FCC.

So, as you can see, the issue of net neutrality is a big and complicated one. But it is hard to argue that the FCC is attempting a power grab here. If anything, it is going out of its way not to retake powers it already had.

It's a big issue, with legitimate differences of opinion. Nonetheless, in it the Obama haters saw something much more sinister in net neutrality: a government takeover of the Internet. As usual, Glenn Beck led the paranoia parade, arguing that by moving forward with plans for net neutrality, the FCC was putting a "boot on your throat." Raising the specter of a government-controlled Web, Beck warned, "This will control every aspect of the Internet. . . . We are losing our country."

Beck and others raised equally dire warnings about legislation introduced by Senators Joe Lieberman and Tom Carper that would give any president emergency power to respond to a future cyberattack.

In the event of a cyberemergency, the Lieberman bill would enable the president, acting through the Department of Homeland Security, to protect the Pentagon, NASA, air-traffic networks, banks, the power grid, or other prime targets by shutting down Internet communications for up to 120 days. The approval of Congress would be required to extend the Internet blackout any longer. Such emergency powers are needed, Lieberman argues, because "[t]he Department of Homeland Security has actually shown that vulnerabilities in key private sector networks like utilities and communications could bring our economy down for a period of time if attacked or commandeered by a foreign power or cyber terrorists."

Actually, cybersecurity has long been a major concern of President Obama. He talked about it during the 2008 campaign. In one of his first interviews as president, he said it was the one thing that kept him awake at night. Early on, he named a White House coordinator on cybersecurity. And in his May 29, 2009, speech about national security, he made it a top priority: "From now on, our digital infrastructure . . . will be treated as they should be: as a strategic security asset. Protecting this infrastructure will be a national security priority."

But again, especially after the governments of Egypt, Iran, and Libya shut down all Internet communications in an attempt to prevent pro-democracy advocates from organizing mass protests, Obama's political enemies suspected him of evil intent—and dubbed the administration-supported legislation "the Internet kill switch bill."

It's all a Communist plot, charged Glenn Beck, because the Chinese government already has a similar authority. His acolyte Andrew Napolitano accused Obama of conspiring with Democrats in Congress to gain the same "power over the Internet that the Chinese have." And, anticipating that the legislation would pass and Obama would immediately manufacture a phony emergency and shut down the Internet, Beck urged his listeners to rush out and "buy a short-wave radio."

Paranoia, thy name is Glenn Beck.

Or maybe it's Mark Levin. You can't get much more paranoid than this: "The government's bigger than it's ever been. It's massive. It's a massive conglomerate. It is into everything out there. I dare you to tell me what it's not into. It reaches all the way down. The iron fist is in your toilet, it's in your light socket. It's everywhere, you can't escape it."

You heard the man. Get big government out of his toilet!

TEARING APART OBAMA'S SPEECHES

On top of all the above, Barack Obama has faced one more direct line of attack: a line-by-line criticism of almost every speech he's given as president.

It's no surprise his enemies went there, of course. It's a classic jujitsu (and Lee Atwater) move to use an opponent's greatest strength against him. It's the same reason John Kerry the war hero was "swift-boated" in 2004. And if there's one great gift God gave Obama, it's his mastery of the spoken word. Before him, Ronald Reagan and Bill Clinton had both worn the crown of "the Great Communicator." But no longer. Reagan had his moments, and Clinton was great, no doubt about it. He's still good. But Obama, in his ability to inspire and move an audience, is second to none. He's the most effective public speaker the White House has seen in decades.

Which is why Obama haters have rushed to trash every speech President Obama has ever given—starting with the fact that he, like every president in the modern age, often gives speeches with the aid of a teleprompter.

Privately, White House aides admit they push for the teleprompter in order to keep Obama on-script and prevent him from wandering off into long-winded asides. But, as veteran White House CBS Radio correspondent Mark Knoller reports, there's a much more important reason: He's so good at it, delivering an impassioned speech while maintaining good eye contact with his audience. Ronald Reagan also was very much at ease using a teleprompter. George W. Bush was not.

Nonetheless, Obama's skill with the teleprompter soon came under attack. Rush Limbaugh even charged that Obama was incapable of delivering a speech without it: "Barack Obama's use of teleprompters is becoming legendary. He doesn't go anywhere without them and rarely, if ever, speaks without their assistance."

Take it from me, as a regular member of the White House press corps: That's simply not true. Yes, many times I have seen President Obama use a teleprompter: for speeches, for announcements in the Rose Garden, for presentations in the East Room. But, just as many times, I have seen him, without a teleprompter, speak from notes, or a printed text, or off the top of his head. In fact, Obama, I believe, is most persuasive and most impressive in his news conferences, where he fields reporters' questions on a wide range of issues—live and unscripted—with no chance of using a teleprompter.

It is ironic that even members of the media, who make a living reading from a teleprompter, would criticize Obama's use of one. But the truth is, he's a great communicator, with or without the teleprompter. Maybe they're just jealous.

STUDY HARD TO GET GOOD GRADES

Of course, Obama haters have also focused on the content of the president's speeches, searching for any word or sentence to buttress their contention that Obama is on a mission to destroy America. In so doing, they haven't hesitated to paint the most innocent of ideas as the most dangerous of messages—sometimes with ludicrous results.

It's just one of countless examples, but nothing demonstrates their paranoia or the depth of their hypocrisy more than the absolute hysteria they whipped up over President Obama's first address to the nation's schoolchildren, delivered on September 8, 2009.

Like other presidents before him, President Obama agreed to give a "back to school" speech to students, encouraging them to pay attention in class, obey their teachers, study hard, get good grades, and stay in school. Others can help, Obama told them, but, in the end, whether or not they got a good education was up to them: "But at the end of the day, we can have the most dedicated teachers, the most supportive parents, and the best schools in the world—and none of it will matter unless all of you fulfill your responsibilities. Unless you show up to those schools; pay attention to those teachers; listen to your parents, grandparents and other adults; and put in the hard work it takes to succeed."

Study hard. Behave in class. Do your homework. That's as American as apple pie, don't you think?

Not if you're a member of the Obama Hate Machine. To hear

their complaints, you'd think Obama had told kids the only way to succeed was to drop out of school, sell drugs, buy a gun, and rob a bank.

Seriously! Talk about being over the top. Despite his offering advice any parent, teacher, or principal would give, critics accused Obama of attempting to "brainwash" and "indoctrinate" America's children—just like Mao Tse-tung, Mussolini, and Adolf Hitler had done. You don't believe it? Here they are, crazier than ever.

No sooner was the speech announced than Glenn Beck sounded the alarm, warning parents that President Obama planned "the indoctrination of your children." How serious was it? "Gang, you have a system that is wildly, wildly out of control, and they are capturing your kids.

"As [green-jobs czar] Van Jones himself has said, the earlier we get the kids, the earlier we make this adjustment with the youth, the easier this transition is going to be. Stand guard, America. Your republic is under attack!"

On the conservative Web site NewsBusters.org, Mark Finkelstein compared Obama's planned speech to propaganda campaigns of the Chinese Communist party. Alongside a photo of the book *Quotations from Chairman Mao Tse-tung,* Finkelstein asked, "Will our MSM report on the interesting parallel between our president's plan for our children and the approach of another Great Leader from the past?"

On Fox News, conservative commentator Monica Crowley saw the same danger: "Just when you think that this administration can't get any more surreal and Orwellian, here he comes to indoctrinate our children. This is what Chairman Mao did. This is like Max Headroom. This is going into every single classroom. There is no escape from him."

Bob Unruh, editor of WorldNetDaily, accused Obama of using his back-to-school speech to recruit a Civilian National Security Force, prompting many readers to worry about the creation of another "Hitler youth brigade." Wrote one blogger, "Totalitarian regimes around the world have sought to spread their propaganda and entrench their power by brainwashing the children. I guess it's easier to indoctrinate a six-year-old instead of fighting a 26-year-old or being challenged by a 46-year-old in the voting booth."

Writing in *American Thinker* magazine, Lauri Regan vowed to keep her children home: "Obama has turned his team of brainwashers on the task of indoctrinating America's youth. . . . My children are off limits."

At Newsmax.com, Pamela Geller urged all parents to do the same: "The fascist-in-chief is taking his special brand of brainwashing to the classroom. Keep your kids home. I think this man is a threat to our basic inalienable rights. I don't want him indoctrinating my children."

And, of course, you could see this coming. Others traced Obama's school speech all the way back to "Communist and domestic terrorist" Bill Ayers. What was the connection? Only the fact that, at one time, both Obama and Ayers served on the board of a foundation that made grants to schools for innovative education reforms. But that was enough for the editors of the *Washington Times*.

After repeating allegations of a radical partnership between Obama and Ayers, they warned readers, "Radicals always have viewed children as wards of the state to be shaped into shock troops to advance their revolutionary agendas. It is an idea of ancient provenance. Plato said that 'children must attend school, whether their parents like it or not; for they belong to the state more than to their parents.' Every radical leader of the 20th century put indoctrinating children at the top of his agenda. So when someone with Mr. Obama's background reaches directly into every school in America, parents are rightly concerned."

Again linking Obama and Ayers, Fox News contributor Michelle Malkin went further: "We're coming full circle with regard to the second story of them abusing—abusing and exploiting children. It all goes back to Bill Ayers in Chicago. . . . We know that the left has always used kids in public schools as guinea pigs and as junior lobbyists for their social liberal agenda." Jim Greer, chairman of the Florida Republican party, saw it the same way: Obama was indoctrinating kids to support his entire "socialist agenda." "The idea that schoolchildren across our nation will be forced to watch the president justify his plans for government-run health care, banks, and automobile companies, increasing taxes on those who created jobs, and racking up more debt than any other president," fumed Greer, "is not only infuriating but goes against the beliefs of the majority of Americans, while bypassing American parents through an invasive abuse of power."

But, in the end, what do you know. Obama went to Arlington, Virginia, and gave his speech, which was broadcast nationwide. It was not mandatory. Teachers could choose to have their classes watch or not. Parents could keep their kids home, if they so chose. And President Obama gave the same "obey your teachers, study hard, and get good grades so you can graduate and get a good job" advice that both President George H. W. Bush and President George W. Bush had given in their own back-to-school speeches—which, naturally, raised not a peep of concern from right-wing fanatics.

Obama's speech was so noncontroversial and so inspiring, in fact, that one year later, when he scheduled his second back-to-school speech, the Florida Republican chairman did something highly unusual for a conservative: He actually admitted he was wrong. Said Jim Greer in September 2010, "In the year since I issued a prepared statement regarding President Obama speaking to the nation's schoolchildren, I have learned a great deal about the party I so deeply loved and served. Unfortunately, I found that many within the GOP have racist views and I apologize to the President for my opposition to his speech last year and my efforts to placate the extremists who dominate our party today. My children and I look forward to the President's speech."

Why the change of heart? Perhaps Greer wanted Obama in a pardoning mood. Three months earlier, the former Republican party chair in Florida was arrested on six felony counts, including fraud, money laundering, and grand theft—he had allegedly been funneling party funds into his own accounts. Now that's something you don't want to teach the schoolchildren.

EVEN TEATIME GETS UGLY

Take a major piece of legislation, brand it as "socialized medicine," then, as we'll see in chapter 5, toss in millions of the Koch brothers' dollars for recruiting volunteers, busing them to congressional town halls with printed instructions on how to disrupt the proceedings and get on television—and, presto—the Tea Party is born!

Make no mistake about it. Despite its innocent-sounding name, the Tea Party was never just a bunch of old ladies sitting around talking politics over afternoon tea—nor a bunch of fiscal conservatives genuinely concerned about government spending. From the beginning, it was a manufactured, corporate-funded campaign aimed at stirring up hatred of President Barack Obama.

If you don't believe it, walk through any so-called Tea Party rally. I've walked through several of them. The ostensible purpose may have been to oppose health-care reform. But the signs they carried gave away the real agenda.

The Huffington Post featured the ten most offensive signs at the first big Tea Party protests, on tax day, April 16, 2009. They included:

- OBAMA'S PLAN: WHITE SLAVERY
- THE AMERICAN TAXPAYERS ARE THE JEWS FOR OBAMA'S OVENS
- BARACK HUSSEIN OBAMA: THE NEW FACE OF HITLER

- OUR TAX $$ GIVEN TO HAMAS TO KILL WOMEN, CHILDREN, AMERICANS—THANKS, MR. O
- NO TAXES. OBAMA LOVES TAXES. BANKRUPT USA. LOVES BABY-KILLING.
- OBAMA—WHAT YOU TALKIN' ABOUT, WILLIS? SPEND MY MONEY?

Mad as a hatter, right? At every Tea Party protest, some of the signs went far beyond the issue of taxes, health-care reform, or global warming. They were blatantly, unapologetically racist. Most notably, the omnipresent representation of a "socialist" Obama wearing the white face of Batman's nemesis, the Joker, like a reverse minstrel figure. Other signs spotted at Tea Party events:

- CONGRESS = SLAVEOWNER; TAXPAYER = NIGGAR [sic]
- OBAMA BIN LYIN'—IMPEACH HIM NOW
- SOMEWHERE IN KENYA A VILLAGE IS MISSING ITS IDIOT

Tea Party leaders, to the extent that there is any such thing as "Tea Party leaders" beyond Koch operatives, insisted that racism played no part in their movement. But, having attended several Tea Party rallies, take it from me. The crowds who came to Tea Party events were overwhelmingly conservative, old—and white. Walking around Glenn Beck's August 2010 Tea Party rally at the Lincoln Memorial, for example, with so many older white citizens in wheelchairs or on walkers, I felt like I was attending the annual picnic of a Mississippi nursing home.

TOXIC TALK

Once corporate funders like the Koch Brothers wound up their crowds into an anti-Obama froth, they did not care much what happened when they were let loose. In far too many cases, anti-Obama rhetoric from Tea Partiers was not only ugly and racist; it also became dangerously violent and filled with gun-centered rhetoric—aimed directly at Obama or at members of Congress who dared to support his agenda.

Violent words, of course, do not always lead to violent actions. But there is always the risk that they can and will. Because, as former president Bill Clinton observed in April 2010, on the fifteenth anniversary of the Oklahoma City bombing, "words matter."

"What we learned from Oklahoma City is not that we should gag each other or reduce our passion from the positions we hold," Clinton reminded the crowd in Oklahoma City," but that the words we use really do matter, because there's this vast echo chamber and they go across space and they fall on the serious and the delirious alike. They fall on the connected and the unhinged alike. And I am not trying to muzzle anybody. But . . . no law can replace personal responsibility. And the more power you have and the more influence you have, the more responsibility you have."

Clinton was referring particularly to right-wing talk-show hosts—I covered them at length in my last book, *Toxic Talk*—but his warning applies equally to those active in the political arena, who should know better. People like Wayne LaPierre, head of the National Rifle Association, who told the 2009 Conservative Political Action Committee conference, "Our Founding Fathers understood that the guys with the guns make the rules." Even more dangerous was the desire expressed by Minnesota congresswoman and Tea Party darling Michele Bachmann that, on the issue of cap and trade, she wanted her constituents to be "armed and dangerous on this issue of the energy tax because we need to fight back."

Part of the reason for all the gun rhetoric against Barack Obama was the fact that, in the 2008 campaign, the NRA painted him as an extreme antigun radical. In fact, Obama—both as state senator and U.S. senator—had always been very supportive of gun owners. Nevertheless, to bolster their own political standing with the Republican party, the NRA launched a GunBaN-Obama Web site, declaring that Obama, if elected, "would be the most anti-gun president in American history." Which, of course, has not happened. To the dismay of his liberal base, President Obama has, as of this writing, done nothing about gun control except write an op-ed about it in the *Arizona Daily Star*. In 2010, the Brady Campaign to Prevent Gun Violence gave Obama an F on gun control because of his "extraordinary silence and passivity" on the issue.

Nevertheless, his political enemies continued to aim gun-filled threats at Obama and his administration. In almost identical language—talking points from the NRA?—conservative candidates from coast to coast warned that Obama's expansion of federal government and assault on individual liberties were the very reason our Founding Fathers gave us the Second Amendment. They didn't give us the right to bear arms in order to hunt, in other words. They gave us the right to bear arms to shoot agents of the federal government—starting, Obama haters clearly implied, with the president of the United States. When a Georgia yokel asked Republican congressman Paul Broun, "Who is going to shoot Obama?" in February 2011, Broun didn't even respond.

As a result of that message, or call to arms, the Southern Poverty Law Center reported that the number of known antigovernment "Patriot" forces in the United States leaped 244 percent in the year following Obama's election: from 149 (including 42 militias) to 512 (including 127 militias). And they all marched to the same drumbeat: Take up arms against the federal government, represented by Barack Obama.

In April 2010, for example, Republican state senator Randy Brogdon met with Tea Partiers in Oklahoma to discuss formation of a new "volunteer militia." It was important they take up arms, Brogdon warned, to defend against unlawful infringement of the federal government on state sovereignty. In writing the Second Amendment, he argued, our Founding Fathers "were not referring to a turkey shoot or a quail hunt. They really weren't even talking about us having the ability to protect ourselves against each other. The Second Amendment deals directly with the right of an individual to keep and bear arms to protect themselves from an overreaching federal government."

Actually, most constitutional scholars agree that the Founding Fathers' original intent behind the Second Amendment was to equip state militias with the firearms needed to protect and defend the nation's newly formed government, not to take up arms against it. Nevertheless, there were even more strident, violent voices from the Hate Obama Echo Chamber, making the same point, almost word for word.

In Virginia, Republican House of Delegates candidate Catherine Crabill urged Tea Party followers to keep their guns handy as the next line of political action: "We have a chance to fight this battle at the ballot box before we have to resort to the bullet box. But that's the beauty of our Second Amendment right. I am glad for all of us who enjoy the use of firearms for hunting. But make no mistake. That was not the intent of the Founding Fathers. Our Second Amendment right was to guard against tyranny."

Sharron Angle, Republican U.S. Senate candidate in Nevada, told the *Reno Gazette-Journal,* "You know, our Founding Fathers, they put that Second Amendment in there for a good reason and that was for the people to protect themselves against a tyrannical government. And in fact Thomas Jefferson said it's good for a country to have a revolution every 20 years. I hope that's not where we're going, but, you know, if this Congress keeps going the way it is, people are really looking toward those Second Amendment remedies and saying my goodness what can we do to turn this country around?"

Former House Speaker Newt Gingrich to the 2010 annual convention of the NRA: "The Second Amendment is not in defense of hunting. It is not in defense of target shooting. It is not in defense of collecting. The Second Amendment is in defense of freedom from the state." Radio talk-show host Joyce Kaufman, on Florida's WFTL: "I am convinced that the most important thing the Founding Fathers did to ensure me my First Amendment rights was they gave me a Second Amendment. And if ballots don't work, bullets will. . . . This is the stand-off. When I say I'll put my microphone down on November 2nd if we haven't achieved substantial victory, I mean it. Because if at that point I'm going up into the hills of Kentucky, I'm going to go out into the Midwest, I'm going to go up in the Vermont and New Hampshire outreaches, and I'm going to gather together men and women who understand that some things are worth fighting for and some things are worth dying for." (After the 2010 midterm elections, newly elected Florida congressman Allen West named Kaufman his chief of staff, but he withdrew his job offer after the above remarks received national attention.)

CNN commentator Erick Erickson even went so far as to identify census workers as the real federal threat and, on his radio show on WMAC-AM in Macon, Georgia, warned what would happen if one of them happened to walk up to his front door: "We have become, or are becoming, enslaved by the government. . . . I dare 'em to try to come throw me in jail. I dare 'em to. I'll pull out my wife's shotgun and see how that little ACS twerp likes being scared at the door. They're not going on my property."

And after Congress approved Obama's health-care-reform legislation, one conservative blogger, identified as Solomon "Solly" Forell, twice used his Twitter account to make the threat against Obama real and personal. First tweet: "Assassination! America, we survived the #Assassinations of #Lincoln & #Kennedy. We'll surely get over a bullet 2 #BarackObama's head!" Followed by: "The next #American with a #Clear #Shot should drop #Obama like a bad habit."

After several examples of that kind of hate talk, it's no surprise that the Secret Service reported an unprecedented number of death threats against President Obama in his first year in office: a 400 percent increase in serious threats over those directed at George W. Bush.

TOXIC ACTION

President Obama wasn't the only one to experience right-wing rage. Democrats in Congress who supported his agenda were also targeted—and, in too many cases, not just with hate talk, but with hateful acts.

Among many examples we remember:

- On March 20, 2010, several Democratic members of Congress were verbally abused by Tea Partiers as they walked into the Capitol. Civil rights leader John Lewis was called a "nigger." Massachusetts congressman Barney Frank was called a "faggot." Emanuel Cleaver of Missouri was spat upon.
- The brother of freshman congressman Tom Perriello discovered a propane line cut at his Virginia home after Tea Partiers posted his home address and suggested opponents of health-care reform "drop by."
- Arkansas congressman Vic Snyder received a letter that warned, "It is apparent that it will take a few assassinations to stop Obamacare. Militia central has selected you for assassination. If we cannot stalk and find you in Washington, D.C., we will get you in Little Rock.
- Arizona congressman Raul Grijalva shut down his Yuma district headquarters after someone shot a bullet through the office window.
- In Niagara Falls, a brick was thrown through the window of the office of Congresswoman Louise Slaughter.
- Senator Patty Murray (D-Washington) received a phone call from a citizen who was outraged over her vote for health care, telling her she had "a target on her back." He went on:

"Since you are going to put my life at risk, and some bureaucrat is going to determine my health care, your life is at risk,
dear. . . . I hope somebody puts a bullet between your eyes."

- In Denver, a man was arrested for threatening to set fire to the
  offices of Senator Michael Bennet. He originally called to tell
  staffers, "I'm just going to come down there and shoot you all."

- And in Seattle, another man was arrested after leaving the
  following voice mail for Congressman Jim McDermott's staff:
  "You let that fucking scumbag know, that if he ever fucks with
  my money, ever the fuck again, I'll fucking kill him, okay. I'll
  round them up. I'll kill them. I'll kill his friends. I'll kill his
  family. I will kill everybody he fucking knows."

MURDER AND HOPE IN TUCSON

Eventually, of course, this series of verbal and physical attacks
against members of Congress escalated even further. They led to
the tragic events of Saturday, January 8, 2011, in Tucson, Arizona.

Congresswoman Gabrielle Giffords stood outside a local Safe-
way market, greeting her constituents, when a lone gunman,
twenty-two-year-old Jared Lee Loughner, walked up and opened
fire, first shooting Giffords in the head and then randomly turning his gun on the crowd. Giffords miraculously survived a shot
through the brain, and, as of this writing, is still recovering slowly.
Eighteen other innocent bystanders were shot, six of whom were
killed instantly—including federal judge John Roll, top Giffords
staffer Gabe Zimmerman, and nine-year old Christina-Taylor
Green, who began her short life on September 11, 2001.

As a nation in shock tried to comprehend how such a horrific
and mindless act of mass murder could occur, the blunt-speaking
sheriff of Pima County, Clarence Dupnik, laid the finger of blame
squarely on the atmosphere of hate over immigration and health
care that had turned Arizona into a "mecca for racism and big-
otry."

"Let me say one thing, because people tend to pooh-pooh this business about all the vitriol that we hear inflaming the American public by people who make a living off of doing that," Dupnik told reporters the morning after the shooting. "That may be free speech, but it's not without consequences." Earlier, the sheriff had told MSNBC, "It's time that this country take a little introspective look at the crap that comes out on radio and TV."

There was no evidence that Loughner ever listened to conservative talk radio, or, indeed, that he was active or interested in politics at all. But he committed a political act of murder: carefully planning to assassinate a member of Congress, hunting and gunning her down at a political event as she met with members of the community, and then turning his gun on voters who had come out on a Saturday morning to greet and entreat their elected representative. And he did so in the hothouse political environment of Arizona, home to the ugliest and most vitriolic political rhetoric in the country.

President Obama, reflecting Sheriff Dupnik's comments, addressed the need for self-examination about the quality of our political discourse when he spoke a few days later in Tucson, in what was, undoubtedly, the most moving and powerful speech of his presidency so far. Perhaps we'll never know what motivated anyone to commit such a heinous crime, Obama acknowledged. "But at a time when our discourse has become so sharply polarized, at a time when we are far too eager to lay the blame for all that ails the world at the feet of those who happen to think differently than we do, it's important for us to pause for a moment and make sure that we're talking with each other in a way that—that heals, not in a way that wounds." Of course, we have to examine all the facts behind the tragic shooting in Tucson and see what changes have to be made and what we can learn from it, Obama acknowledged. But, he cautioned, "what we cannot do is use this tragedy as one more occasion to turn on each other. That we cannot do. That we cannot do."

In fact, Obama suggested, reflection on the Tucson shooting could serve as an opportunity to better our political discourse: "Rather than pointing fingers or assigning blame, let's use this occasion to expand our moral imaginations, to listen to each other more carefully, to sharpen our instincts for empathy, and remind ourselves of all the ways that our hopes and dreams are bound together."

And we should do so, Obama noted, in memory of those good citizens of Tucson who were killed for doing no more than exercising their civic duty. We owe them that effort, to be better than we have been, he said. "If this tragedy prompts reflection and debate, as it should, let's make sure it's worthy of those we have lost. Let's make sure it's not on the usual plane of politics and point-scoring and pettiness that drifts away in the next news cycle. The loss of these wonderful people should make every one of us strive to be better, to be better in our private lives, to be better friends and neighbours and co-workers and parents."

President Obama also pointed out the good that could come out of this tragedy, and why that was important for the whole nation. "And if, as has been discussed in recent days, their death helps usher in more civility in our public discourse, let us remember it is not because a simple lack of civility caused this tragedy—it did not—but rather because only a more civil and honest public discourse can help us face up to the challenges of our nation in a way that would make them proud."

So what, finally, should be the nature of our political debate? President Obama concluded by saying, "We should be civil because we want to live up to the example of public servants like John Roll and Gabby Giffords, who knew first and foremost that we are all Americans, and that we can question each other's ideas without questioning each other's love of country, and that our task, working together, is to constantly widen the circle of our concern so that we bequeath the American dream to future generations."

Imagine that: "we are all Americans . . . we can question each other's ideas without questioning each other's love of country."

Or maybe even what country someone else was born in?

What a novel idea. What an old-fashioned, all-American idea.

If only President Obama's enemies were listening. Instead, they probably had their noses stuck in one of a mountain of anti-Obama books.

4

THE I HATE OBAMA BOOK CLUB

The American landscape, unfortunately, is peppered with presidential libraries, most of which are not worth the time or money for a visit. But they exist because every president since FDR, no matter how insignificant his accomplishments, has had one built in his memory.

The presidential library, usually located in the president's hometown, is today considered an expected and necessary footnote to any presidency. Yet somehow George Washington, John Adams, Thomas Jefferson, James Monroe, and James Madison were able to live without one.

But with Barack Obama, it's going to be different. He will become the first former president to require two presidential libraries: one to house the personal papers and historical record of America's first African-American president; the second to house the mountain of Obama hate books that have been published during his time in office.

Hate Obama tomes have been a boon to the publishing industry, much as hate Obama rhetoric has become the lifeline of right-wing talk radio. Who says President Obama hasn't helped grow the economy? Just ask Regnery Publishing or Encounter Books, especially.

Columnist John Avlon, writing for the Daily Beast, was the first to track down the anti-Obama literature in detail. By his count, there were five books attacking Obama published even before he reached the White House. By year three of his presidency, a staggering sixty-seven books, at least, had been published that demonized Barack Obama—far more than either Bill Clinton or George W. Bush had to contend with—and the number keeps growing.

Even though throwing mud at Bill Clinton was a favorite pastime of the far right, keeping Regnery and other publishers busy, only eleven anti-Clinton books had been published by his two-year anniversary.

George Bush got off even easier. According to Avlon, only five anti-Dubya books had hit the shelves by the same time in his presidency. Only in 2004, after his contentious reelection campaign, did the number of anti-Bush books reach forty-six. That collection, of course, included my own *Bush Must Go!* Alas, if only a few more people in Ohio had read it, he might not have been reelected.

The library of hate Obama books is noteworthy, not just because of its numbers but because of its titles. True, you can't tell a book by its cover. But you can figure out a lot about the anti-Obama books simply by their titles, each meaner and more breathless than the last. Among the more colorful:

- *The Manchurian President: Barack Obama's Ties to Communists, Socialists and Other Anti-American Extremists*
- *To Save America: Stopping Obama's Secular Socialist Machine*
- *Barack Obama's Plan to Socialize America and Destroy Capitalism*
- *The Post-American Presidency: The Obama Administration's War on America*
- *Barack Obama and Larry Sinclair: Cocaine, Sex, Lies and Murder?*

And then there's everybody's favorite: *Whiny Little Bitch: The Excuse-Filled Presidency of Barack Obama.*

Granted, some of these books can be dismissed as nutty screeds written by crazies nobody ever heard of and self-published through services like CreateSpace; but not all of them, by any means. Most were released by mainstream publishing houses. And the list of authors includes a former attorney general of the United States, a former ambassador to the United Nations, a former Speaker of the House, a former Ohio secretary of state, prominent conservative commentators, and at least four top national radio and TV talk-show hosts: Sean Hannity, Bill O'Reilly, Michael Savage, and Laura Ingraham.

Together, they command a broad audience. And together, in print as on the airwaves, they have decided that the only way to bring down President Obama is not to challenge his policies but to undermine his personal credibility. In their warped world, Obama is not just wrong on the economy; he is a Marxist-socialist Manchurian candidate channeling the radical, antiimperial politics of his father and grandfather.

With such a flood of hate literature—its lies duly repeated and promoted on radio, cable television, and online—it's no surprise, as noted earlier, that so many Americans are willing to believe the worst about Barack Obama. As this book goes to print, 25 percent of all Americans, and 41 percent of all Republicans, believe Obama was not born in the United States. One of every five Americans still believes he is a Muslim, and a whopping 55 percent are convinced he's a socialist. "I read it in a book, I saw it on television, so it must be true."

As we saw in chapter 1, publication of opposing opinion has been part of America's political tradition since the beginning. Vice President Thomas Jefferson, you remember, even hired his own publisher to undermine President John Adams. And each president since has seen a handful of critical books about him. It goes with the territory. And it should.

But, as with all the other arms of the Obama Hate Machine, the hate Obama literature differs both in quantity and intensity. It's not a handful; it's an avalanche. It's not thoughtful political dissent; it's a wave of ugly personal attacks—as evidenced by even a quick glance through each of the anti-Obama titles.

Don't worry. You don't have to read them all. I've skimmed them for you. Here's a survey of the hate Obama library, listed alphabetically by author, with a brief summary of each—which I label "Between the Covers," shamelessly stealing the name my friend Tom Connaughton adopted for his outstanding rare-book dealership.

Note: Most, but not all, books critical of Obama have been written by right-wingers. So, just so I can brag about being "fair and balanced," I also include those negative volumes on Obama authored by commentators on the Left.

BLASTING OBAMA FROM THE RIGHT

1. Babbin, Jed. *How Obama Is Transforming America's Military from Superpower to Paper Tiger.*
   Publisher: Encounter Books, July 2010.

Between the Covers: According to former air force officer Jed Babbin, President Obama wants America to be a second-rate military power and, in league with Defense Secretary Robert Gates—in the real world, a Bush appointee—is moving fast in that direction by cutting military spending, abandoning our allies, and not investing in new technology. Apparently, Babbin was AWOL when Obama drove his liberal base crazy by continuing the war in Iraq, expanding the war in Afghanistan, providing military assistance to the rebels in Libya, and increasing the Pentagon's budget while cutting heating-oil funding for the poor. Another right-wing charge without any supporting evidence.

2. Blackwell, Ken and Ken Klukowski. *The Blueprint: Obama's Plan to Subvert the Constitution and Build an Imperial Presidency.*
Publisher: Lyons Press, April 2010.

Between the Covers: Blackwell, Ohio's former Republican secretary of state, teams with conservative constitutional attorney Ken Klukowski to argue that Obama intends to pack the Supreme Court with liberal justices who will support his "power grab" and his plans to subvert the Constitution and turn America into "a militant, secular welfare state dominated by an overbearing central government." This is fearmongering at its worst, with not a shred of evidence. When Ed Meese praises it as "an important and timely book," you know it's pure right-wing propaganda.

3. Bolton, John R. *How Barack Obama Is Endangering Our National Sovereignty.*
Publisher: Encounter Books, May 2010.

Between the Covers: It's like a dog whistle. One of the tried-and-true ways to drive right-wingers crazy is to raise the specter of Democrats who are destroying America's leadership in the world by surrendering our national sovereignty to foreign powers and international institutions—you know, the black helicopters of the United Nations and all that. It's a serious charge, which deserves at least one example, one bit of evidence, of where President Obama is doing just that. John Bolton, George Bush's former appointment to the UN, who thinks most every problem can be solved by bombing Iran, provides none.

4. Brown, Floyd. *Obama Unmasked: Did Slick Hollywood Handlers Create the Perfect Candidate?*
Publisher: Merril Press, August 2008.

Between the Covers: The very name Floyd Brown is enough to put fear in the hearts of many Democrats. For years, he was the Republican party's number-one behind-the-scenes attack dog, best known for creating the Willie Horton ad that sank Michael Dukakis in 1988. But in this campaign book, he seems to have lost his teeth, accusing Obama of being nothing but a creature of spin doctors and focus groups and just coasting his way through the general election until George Soros would pull off an "October Surprise" and propel him into the White House. Nobody, not even Fox News, pretended this book was fair, evenhanded, or even factual during the election. And in the end, of course, McCain was such an inept candidate, and his pick of Sarah Palin so disastrous, that Obama didn't need Soros's "October Surprise."

5. Cashill, Jack. *Deconstructing Obama: The Life, Loves, and Letters of America's First Postmodern President.*
   Publisher: Threshold Editions, February 2011.

Between the Covers: By most accounts, before being elected president, Barack Obama had written two books: *Dreams from My Father* and *The Audacity of Hope*. Not true, says business writer Jack Cashill. Obama was intellectually incapable of writing either book, he asserts. Not only that; after exploring similarities in their two memoirs, he concludes that *Dreams* was, in fact, written by—guess who? Wait for it, wait for it!—Obama's friend (not really) the former Weatherman Bill Ayers. Consequently, Cashill concludes, Obama is nothing but a "calculating phony." He may have been born in Hawaii, according to Cashill, but his father was actually author and alleged Communist Frank Marshall Davis, not Barack Obama. As an added bonus, Cashill also says he "discovered" that Obama is bisexual. Amazing what trash you can get published, as long as it's anti-Obama.

6. Cook, Terry L. *America's Communist Revolution!: Terrifying Change Without Hope!*
   Publisher: CreateSpace, February 2010.

Between the Covers: You know you're in for a wild ride when his publicity package says Terry Cook, like the Blues Brothers, is "a man called by God for this particular mission" (and when there are so many exclamation points in the title—it reads like a line from Allen Ginsburg's "Howl"). Cook's mission in this book is to expose Barack Obama as the true Manchurian candidate—carefully programmed by his father, as well as Frank Marshall Davis and Chicago pals Tony Rezko, Bill Ayers, and Jeremiah Wright, to sneak into the White House under cover as a Democrat and then rip off his mask as a Communist. "God help us!" Cook concludes. Yes, God help us from paranoid Christian nut jobs like Terry L. Cook.

7. Cook, Terry L. *The Making of an American Dictator!: Barack Hussein Obama.*
   Publisher: CreateSpace, June 2010.

Between the Covers: The "man called by God" is back again, with more titular exclamation points. This time, he's warning Americans about the catastrophic changes that can be expected in 2011. Under Obama's direction, Cook warns, America will be transformed from a Constitutional republic to a full-fledged socialist police state and, later, to a Communist dictatorship. All in one year's time! Also, it will all be triggered by another broad economic collapse deliberately induced by Rothschild-controlled international bankers—paging George Soros!— just like they conspired with George W. Bush to bring about the crash of September 2008.

8. Corsi, Jerome. *The Obama Nation: Leftist Politics and the Cult of Personality.*
   Publisher: Threshold Editions, Simon & Schuster, August 2008.

Between the Covers: In 2004, Corsi almost single-handedly torpedoed the candidacy of John Kerry with publication of *Unfit for Command,* challenging the accuracy of Kerry's record of heroism in Vietnam. In

2008, he was back with *The Obama Nation*, which he admitted was written solely to defeat Obama in the 2008 presidential primary. Very sloppily written and with very little evidence, this book accuses Obama of being an extreme leftist with close ties to Tony Rezko, Bill Ayers, Ayers's wife, Weather Underground member Bernadine Dohrn, and Jeremiah Wright. He also asserts that Obama was secretly a Muslim, who wanted "to will all the white blood out of himself so he can become pure black." Fortunately for Obama, unfortunately for Corsi, the book was so filled with factual mistakes that it was dismissed as pure right-wing nonsense—by everybody except Sean Hannity, Bill O'Reilly, and all the other usual suspects on Fox News.

9. Corsi, Jerome. *Where's the Birth Certificate? The Case That Barack Obama Is Not Eligible to Be President.*
   Publisher: WND Books, May 2011.

Between the Covers: If at first you don't succeed, try, try again. The Web site WorldNetDaily continues to fan the flames of the absurd theory that Barack Obama was not born in the United States and is therefore an illegitimate president, long after most rational people, including the Roberts Supreme Court, have rejected it. Not surprising, then, that they should publish Corsi's latest attempt at making a buck. According to Corsi, the very fact that Obama has spent millions of dollars in attorney's fees to oppose having to produce a "long-form birth certificate"—whatever that is—proves he's lying about where he was born. Three years into Obama's administration, Corsi is still arguing that Obama is "constitutionally ineligible for the office of the presidency." And there are still too many idiots—I'm talking about you, Donald Trump—who believe him. Even before it was published, Corsi's book zoomed to the number-one position on Amazon.

10. Cullen, Mike. *Whiny Little Bitch: The Excuse-Filled Presidency of Barack Obama.*
    Publisher: Quite Right Books, June 2010.

Between the Covers: The title says it all. Don't expect much from this book, and you won't be disappointed. Even one sympathetic reviewer had to acknowledge that it's no "in-depth" account of the Obama administration. It's a thin book, full of thin and stale criticisms of Obama's messianic complex, his slighting of allies, his being too hard on Wall Street, his surrounding himself with cronies, his race-baiting, etc., etc. Cullen proves there's an audience for any anti-Obama drivel, no matter how shallow.

11. DeBrecht, Katharine. *Help, Mom, Radicals Are Ruining My Country!*
    Publisher: Kids Ahead.

Between the Covers: Are you ready for this? The first anti-Obama children's book. God spare us. Or, better yet, God spare our kids. Described by the publisher as "a hilarious and entertaining way for parents to sit down with their children and teach them the origins of the new Tea Party movement and the importance of standing up for liberty and the American Dream." In this gripping drama, sure to keep any three-year-old sitting on the edge of his seat, Tommy and Lou are trying to set up their swing-set business, but first they have to fight off the "onerous regulations and sky-high taxes" thrown in their path by Nancy Pelosi, Harry Reid, Barney Frank, Chris Dodd, and Charles Schumer. In the end—are you paying attention, children?—the big test is whether they will "join the other kids on the corner in standing up for freedom or will they continue to fear being vilified by the press and demeaned" by the big, bad, and black "Marxus Obundus." Any parent who reads this book to their child should be charged with child abuse.

12. D'Souza, Dinesh. *The Roots of Obama's Rage.*
    Publisher: Regnery Publishing, September 2010.

Between the Covers: Obama's critics have called him many things: a socialist, a Marxist, a Chicago-machine politician, and worse. But actually, Barack Obama is none of the above, says conservative writer

Dinesh D'Souza. He is best understood as an angry anticolonialist, still upset at the injustices his father and grandfather suffered at the hands of the British in Kenya—and determined to get revenge. Never mind that Obama never met his grandfather, and only met his father twice. At least D'Souza accomplished one thing with this book: He convinced both Newt Gingrich and Mike Huckabee to make total fools of themselves by swallowing his ridiculous theory whole—and repeating it verbatim. After which, neither of them was ever again taken seriously as a presidential candidate.

13. Ferrara, Peter—*President Obama's Tax Piracy*.
    Publisher: Encounter Books, October 2010.

Between the Covers: There's nothing new in this little book, so don't look for it. Ferrara wastes forty-eight pages making the argument that Ronald Reagan's tax policies saved the nation, while Barack Obama's tax policies will destroy it. He conveniently omits the fact that 95 percent of Americans actually received a tax cut in Obama's 2009 stimulus package. And his book was published before Obama made a deal with Republicans in Congress to extend the Bush tax cuts to all taxpayers, middle-class and wealthy. Ferrara, who served in the Reagan White House, also seems to have forgotten that Reagan raised taxes in seven out of his eight years in office.

14. Freddoso, David. *The Case Against Barack Obama: The Unlikely Rise and Unexamined Agenda of the Media's Favorite Candidate*.
    Publisher: Regnery Publishing, August 2008.

Between the Covers: Another campaign book aimed at stopping Obama's surge toward the White House. But Freddoso, a writer for the *National Review*, takes a different approach. He thinks Corsi and others are making a mistake by focusing on Obama's life history or instant celebrity. (Remember McCain's Paris Hilton ad?) He suggests a stronger case against Obama could be made by examining his record in the Illinois state senate and, briefly, in the U.S. Senate—where, Freddoso argues, Obama accomplished nothing. He conveniently omits Obama's work in the Illinois state senate to fashion bipartisan reforms of campaign financing and the death penalty, and, to take one example, his work on arms control in the U.S. Senate with Richard Lugar. Obama's not "a bad person," Freddoso admits. "It's just that he's like all the rest of them. Not a reformer. Not a Messiah. Just like all the rest of them in Washington." And, of course, Freddoso adds, he doesn't walk on water, either.

15. Fredrick, Don. *The Obama Timeline: From His Birth in 1961 Through His First 100 Days in Office.*
    Publisher: iUniverse, July 2009.

Between the Covers: The media didn't tell us everything about Barack Obama—and had they done so, he would never have been elected president. That, in a nutshell, is the thesis of this sore-loser book. In rushing to Obama, Fredrick insists, voters had no idea of his "overwhelmingly radical history." He traces Obama's life from cradle to the White House and lists, by his definition, all the unsavory characters Obama met and hung out with along the way: the Marxists, Communists, and socialists who shaped his character and politics—you know their names by now. Fredrick puts special emphasis on Rahm Emanuel, the new "communist" mayor of Chicago.

16. Furchtgott-Roth, Diana. *How Obama's Gender Policies Undermine America.*
    Publisher: Encounter Books, September 2010.

Between the Covers: The first bill President Obama signed into law was the Lilly Ledbetter Fair Pay Act, making it easier for women to sue for discrimination in pay—for which he was applauded by all women, except Furchtgott-Roth, researcher at the conservative Hudson Institute. Here, she makes the bizarre argument that Obama is actually hurting women by helping them. Women are doing fine on their own without government help, she insists. Giving them any special protection only reinforces the notion that they are a weaker sex, and also hurts men in the process. By her logic, of course, women would still be denied the right to vote.

17. Gasparino, Charles. *Bought and Paid For: The Unholy Alliance Between Barack Obama and Wall Street.*
    Publisher: Sentinel HC, October 2010.

Between the Covers: To Barack Obama, it must often feel like he can't win for losing. On the one hand, conservatives accuse him of being antibusiness, an avowed enemy of big business. On the other hand, others, like Charles Gasparino of the Fox Business Network, accuse him of being in bed with big business. For Gasparino, defying conventional conservative commentary, the Obama administration is nothing but "business as usual" when it comes to Wall Street. Obama talks a tough game, he says, but in the end his economic policies benefit the big banks and financial institutions, while small business and individual taxpayers suffer. Fox Business . . . always looking out for the little guy.

18. Geller, Pamela and Robert Spencer. *The Post-American Presidency: The Obama Administration's War on America.*
    Publisher: Threshold Editions, July 2010.

Between the Covers: If you truly believe that Barack Obama is "the most radical individual ever to occupy the White House," this is the book for you. Geller and Spencer sound yet another call to arms to Americans concerned about Obama's plot to destroy our free-market system and nationalize major segments of our economy. As proof, they accuse Obama of seizing control of three key economic engines: health care, energy, and education. (The ridiculousness of this argument was covered in the previous chapter.) Billed as "the true patriot's handbook," Geller's book urges conservatives to rise up and stop Obama in his tracks, while there is still any America left to defend.

19. Gingrich, Newt. *To Save America: Stopping Obama's Secular-Socialist Machine.*
    Publisher: Regnery Publishing, January 2011.

Between the Covers: In one of the most dramatic personality changes since George Jorgensen underwent a sex-change operation to become Christine Jorgensen, Newt Gingrich has transformed himself from notorious wife cheater and sinner to Christian preacher and reformer. In his new role, he accuses Barack Obama of leading the fight to banish religion from the public square and attempting to remake America from "a land of free enterprise, faith, and personal freedom" into a morass of "endless bureaucracy, secularism, and state control." That's not what Americans voted for, says Gingrich, but we are being steamrolled by the secular-socialist Obama machine—a machine he plans to stop himself in the 2012 election. Um, good luck with that, Newt.

20. Goldberg, Bernard. *A Slobbering Love Affair: The True (and Pathetic) Story of the Torrid Romance Between Barack Obama and the Mainstream Media.*
    Publisher: Regnery Publishing, January 2009.

Between the Covers: Having made a good living in print and on Fox News bashing the "liberal news media," Goldberg expands his attack by accusing the mainstream media of falling so head over heels for Barack Obama during the 2008 campaign that they failed to report the true story and therefore handed Obama a victory over John McCain. Without the "slobbering" help of the media, as Goldberg sees it, Obama would have won neither the Democratic primary nor the general election. The truth is quite different, as we will see in chapter 6. Goldberg complains that reporters presented Obama as young and energetic, while portraying McCain as old and tired. Hey, but wasn't that the truth?

21. Graham, John. *Obama's Change: Communism in America.*
    Publisher: Dorrance Publishing, September 2010.

Between the Covers: Bad news! If you wanted to prevent a Communist takeover of America, you're too late. We already have one. In fact, we've had one for over sixty-five years, insists John Graham, under three Communist dictators. (I guess that explains why we all speak Russian): first, FDR, who gave Stalin all of Eastern Europe in return for helping us during World War II; then, Bill and Hillary Clinton, who gave China the secrets to our long-range-missile system in return for a campaign loan; and now, Barack Obama, who is setting up "a communist dictatorship right before our very eyes." In some parts of the world, news does travel slowly. But you'd think Graham would have heard by now that the Cold War is over.

22. Graham, Michael. *That's No Angry Mob, That's My Mom: Team Obama's Assault on Tea-Party, Talk-Radio Americans.*
    Publisher: Regnery Publishing, March 2010.

Between the Covers: Nobody ever tried to shut talk-show host Michael Graham up. They couldn't if they tried. Yet he insists the Obama administration is trying to muzzle Tea Partiers and listeners to right-wing talk radio. As if. Tea Partiers aren't racists or crazies, he argues. They're like his mom, nothing but honest Americans, frustrated with the growth of government and eager "to restore the home-spun values of hard work, fair play, and individual responsibility." That statement alone proves that Graham doesn't attend many Tea Party rallies. Nor does he realize, as we will see in the next chapter, that the whole Tea Party was invented and funded by Charles and David Koch as the "grassroots" front lines of the Obama Hate Machine. Does his mom know she was part of the "Kochtopus?"

23. Gratzer, David. *Why Obama's Government Takeover of Health Care Will Be a Disaster.*
Publisher: Encounter Books, November 2009.

Between the Covers: Notice when this book was published: five months before President Obama signed America's Affordable Care Act. Had he only waited, Dr. Gratzer could have saved himself a lot of time. But then again, he would not have been able to attack the president's bill as "socialized medicine," which would create a massive new government bureaucracy, introduce rationing, and stifle innovation that has made America a world leader in developing new miracle drugs. I'm surprised he didn't predict "death panels" also. Maybe because Sarah Palin beat him to the punch. None of Gratzer's dire predictions came to pass, of course. Obama did little more than sign legislation forcing everybody to buy health insurance from private insurance companies. But why wait for the facts?

24. Hannity, Sean. *Conservative Victory: Defeating Obama's Agenda.*
Publisher: Harper Paperbacks, March 2010.

Between the Covers: If you watched any Fox News coverage of the last presidential campaign, you don't have to read Hannity's book, because you've heard it all before. For his most loyal, unthinking, and extremist followers, Hannity merely repeats all the arguments he made against candidate Obama in 2008. You know the litany: Bill Ayers, ACORN, the Reverend Jeremiah Wright, community organizer, Communist sympathizer, and all the rest. And because not enough believed him, Hannity warns, Obama has now surrounded himself with a bunch of "self-professed socialists, fringe activists, and others" who have kicked off "an alarming assault on our capitalist system." It's the end of the world as we know it, says Hannity.

25. Hanson, Victor Davis. *How the Obama Administration Threatens Our National Security.*
Publisher: Encounter Books, December 2009.

Between the Covers: In yet one more of Encounter's forty-eight-page publishing wonders, Hoover Institution fellow Victor Davis Hanson sets out to show how President Obama has "imprinted his domestic ideology of victimhood onto a therapeutic, Carter-inspired foreign policy." You try to explain what that means. I can't. And neither can Hanson, a classicist who once called Donald Rumsfeld "a rare sort of secretary of the caliber of George Marshall." He projects that Obama may be successful in forging better relationships with Iran, Russia, and China—but that all three will eventually turn on the United States because they perceive us as weak. Only a confirmed Obama hater to begin with would take this book seriously.

26. Hedrick, David. *The Liberal Claus: Socialism on a Sleigh.*
     Publisher: FreedomsAnswer, October 2010.

Between the Covers: In the sick world of Tea Partiers, it's never too early to start brainwashing your kids. So here we go with another anti-Obama children's book. And a Christmas book, no less. This one is written by a failed congressional candidate from Washington State (who once suggested Nancy Pelosi wore Nazi insignia on her sleeve)—and is dedicated to his kids. And it tells the story of how underhanded liberals stole an election in the Great Elf Council, kicked out Santa Claus, and replaced him with a skinny imposter who wasn't even born at the North Pole and can't even give a speech without a teleprompter. Oh, and did I mention he's black? Liberal Claus forces all elves to join a union and decrees that from now on they make only little "red" train cars. You can figure out the rest. Pity the poor kids who have to fall asleep listening to this propaganda while waiting to hear the sounds of reindeer prancing on the roof.

27. Horner, Christopher C. *Power Grab: How Obama's Green Policies Will Steal Your Freedom and Bankrupt America.*
     Publisher: Regnery Publishing, April 2010.

Between the Covers: If you didn't figure it out from the title, you know what to expect here when Christopher Horner is hailed as a "watchdog" by Glenn Beck and praised by Rush Limbaugh as the "longtime go-to guy on global warming extremism." You expect a grossly exaggerated account of Obama's role in seeking climate-change legislation and the economic disaster that would result. And, in that sense, Horner does not disappoint. No matter that Obama failed completely to enact any legislation on global warming in his first three years in office and, with Republicans in control of the House, is even less likely to do so in 2012. Horner still prophesies economic, not environmental, doomsday. Even without legislation, the very fact that Obama favors renewable sources of energy, according to Horner, means that he has declared war on oil, coal, and natural gas. Unless Obama is stopped in his tracks, Horner fears, it's only a matter of time before we flip a switch and the lights don't come on. Don't say he didn't warn you.

28. Ingraham, Laura. *The Obama Diaries.*
    Publisher: Threshold Editions, July 2010.

Between the Covers: There are people who are born to be stand-up comics. And there are those who should not even try. I belong in the latter category. So does Laura Ingraham. She just doesn't know it. Instead, she's published a supposedly yuck-yuck fake Obama diary: a joke setup that might have been worth five minutes on her radio show but not a whole book. Instead, Ingraham stretches it out to four hundred painful pages, forcing readers to suffer such rib-splitting lines as Obama on Sarah Palin: "Hell, doesn't Palin have anything better to do than criticize me? Shouldn't she be back home shooting some endangered wolf species from a helicopter?" Or Obama, weighing the next step in his career while visiting the Vatican: "If I can ingratiate myself with a few more of these red-hats, the pope thing might not be a bad follow-up to the presidency." There are good joke writers out there. Ingraham should think of hiring one for her next book.

29. Johnson, Donald. *Black but Not My Brother: Why I Cannot Vote for Barack Hussein Obama.*
   Publisher: AuthorHouse, November 2008.

Between the Covers: This is a sick book, written by a sick man, in a feeble last-minute attempt to help block Barack Obama from the White House. Pastor Donald William Johnson believes that the very survival of the African-American community is threatened by abortion and homosexuality, both of which, he says, Obama supports. Therefore, unlike many leading black conservatives, he says he could not even consider voting for his black brother. "If we choose Mr. Obama because of his color," Johnson warns, "we choose a champion for abortion and the homosexual agenda; we choose our own destruction." Obama, says Johnson, is in league with Planned Parenthood's campaign of genocide to wipe out America's black population. The question facing black voters in November 2008 was, "Can we afford a leader who champions racial suicide—even if he is black?" Fortunately, few blacks believed or had heard of Johnson. Obama got 96 percent of the black vote.

30. Joscelyn, Thomas. *What President Obama Doesn't Know About Guantanamo.*
   Publisher: Encounter Books, May 2010.

Between the Covers: President Obama's first executive order, signed on January 22, 2009, was to close the naval prison at Guantánamo Bay in one year. He did so, Obama said, in order for America to reclaim the "moral high ground" in the war on terror and to deny al-Qaeda one of its chief recruiting tools. But Joscelyn condemned the order as "pure folly," undertaken by people who knew nothing about the detainees in Gitmo, what intelligence we were getting out of them, how complex their cases were, and where we might house them once Gitmo was closed. True or not, his case was undercut anyway by the fact that, despite his best intentions, Obama was unable to persuade Congress to approve shutting down Gitmo. In March 2011, he signed another executive order, keeping the prison open and resuming military trials.

31. Kirby, Stephen M. *Islam and Barack Hussein Obama: A Handbook on Islam.*
    Publisher: CreateSpace, July 2010.

Between the Covers: How violent a religion is Islam and how much a supporter of Islam is Barack Obama? Former LAPD officer Stephen Kirby takes a roundabout way of answering those questions by contrasting the positive things Obama said about Islam in his June 4, 2009, speech at Cairo University with the ugly reality of what Kirby believes Islam is really all about. The author also accuses Obama of failing to express sufficient public regret for the shooting of two army officers by a Muslim convert at a Little Rock recruiting station three days earlier. Indirectly, Kirby's message is, Don't believe anything he says. Obama's really a Muslim; make no mistake about it.

32. Klein, Aaron and Brenda J. Elliott. *The Manchurian President: Barack Obama's Ties to Communists, Socialists, and Other Anti-American Extremists.*
    Publisher: WND Books, May 2010.

Between the Covers: Gather all the paranoia about Barack Obama between the covers of one book—and this is what you get. The man portrayed by Aaron Klein and Brenda Elliott is not just a Democrat, not just a liberal, not just a socialist. Oh, no. He is—as so many other books on this list concur—"the most radical—and therefore the most dangerous—president this country has ever seen." And, of course, Obama didn't just get there on his own. Like any self-respecting Manchurian candidate, he was programmed on his way to power by a long-standing, "far-leftist, anti-American nexus" that, now that Obama is in the White House, is busy writing and directing his policies in order to turn America into a Communist dictatorship. Wait till you hear about "Obama's mysterious college years unearthed!" And bet you didn't know that Obama's "hope" and "change" slogans actually stem from Communist activism. So little time, so much to fear. Here's the place to start.

33. Krikorian, Mark. *How Obama Is Transforming America Through Immigration.*
Publisher: Encounter Books, May 2010.

Between the Covers: You would think that the executive director of the Center for Immigration Studies would know something about immigration. Apparently not. Krikorian slams President Obama for his policy of "open borders," leading to easy amnesty, loose enforcement, and ever-higher levels of legal immigration. The truth is just the opposite. President Reagan granted wholesale amnesty to immigrants living here illegally; President Obama never has. Instead, Obama put forth the same plan for comprehensive immigration reform proposed by President George W. Bush. Meanwhile, under Obama, there are more guards at the border than ever, fewer immigrants are crossing the border illegally, and the illegal-immigrant population in the United States dropped by one million in 2010, a year that saw a record number of deportations. Mark Krikorian, call home!

34. Kurtz, Stanley. *Radical-in-Chief: Barack Obama and the Untold Story of American Socialism.*
Publisher: Threshold Editions, October 2010.

Between the Covers: President Obama has a secret: a secret he's managed to hide through the first two years of his presidency from everyone but right-wing authors and talk-show hosts. His secret? According to *National Review* writer Stanley Kurtz, it's his "socialist convictions and tactical ruthlessness." But Kurtz lets the cat out of the bag: "Our Commander-in-Chief is really a Radical-in-Chief." OMG. Here we go again. This book has been written by several others under different titles. It's but another rehash of the "Manchurian candidate" theory:

that Obama is a closet socialist, shaped by his experience as a community organizer and his connections with Bill Ayers, ACORN, and Jeremiah Wright. Like others, Kurtz speculates that Obama fully embraced socialism during the mysterious "lost chapter" of his life, when he was a student at Columbia—even though Obama writes extensively about his days at Columbia in *Dreams from My Father*. If Obama has his way, Kurtz warns, capitalist America will soon resemble a "socialist-inspired Scandinavian welfare state." But, of course, there's no sign of that yet.

35. Ledeen, Michael A. *Obama's Betrayal of Israel.*
    Publisher: Encounter Books, November 2009.

Between the Covers: One of the biggest canards among right-wingers today is that President Obama is an enemy of Israel—which is nothing but an indirect way of keeping alive the theory that he's a closet Muslim. There is certainly no evidence of Obama's enmity toward Israel, as Ledeen, unwittingly perhaps, proves in this essay. He accuses Obama of pursuing a two-state solution for Israel and the Palestinian territories for the same reason the North Vietnamese once agreed to a two-state division of Vietnam: only as a temporary diversion until they could take over the entire country. In fact, the two-state solution was first officially proposed by President George W. Bush and accepted as their mutual goal by leaders of both Israel and the Palestinian territories. In the Middle East, as in so many other areas, and to the dismay of his liberal base, Obama has continued the policies of his predecessor.

36. Limbaugh, David. *Crimes Against Liberty: An Indictment of President Obama.*
    Publisher: Regnery Publishing, August 2010.

Between the Covers: Okay, what do you expect from Rush's little brother? Exactly what you get: Obama accused of criminal behavior in "encroaching upon and stripping us of our individual and sovereign rights" as Americans. Obama sees individual liberty as a threat to government power, according to Limbaugh, something to be squashed by any means possible. So, he's out to do so through health-care reform, the stimulus package, environmental policies, "bail out upon bail out," and Wall Street reforms. Sometimes you really have to wonder if junior Limbaugh is just making this stuff up. Or maybe he's just repeating stuff he heard his big brother talk about while popping pills. Where, for example, is Obama's "blatant pursuit of race-based justice" that Limbaugh complains about? Or "the administration's gagging of the honest discussion of the threat of radical Islam?" And, frankly, I haven't seen any sign of Obama's "Chicago-style bully boy tactics," but I wish he'd use a little more of it in dealing with John Boehner.

37. Malkin, Michelle. *Culture of Corruption: Obama and His Team of Tax Cheats, Crooks, and Cronies.*
    Publisher: Regnery Publishing, August 2009.

Between the Covers: As part of the Fox News army of conservative commentators, blogger Michelle Malkin did her best to prevent Barack Obama from becoming president. Six months later, she pronounced him a complete failure. Her complaints are familiar fodder to any Fox viewer: Obama surrounded himself with power-hungry "czars"; he named ethically challenged people like Hillary Clinton and Timothy Geithner to his cabinet; he funneled millions of dollars to ACORN and labor unions. A year later, August 2010, she published a paperback edition of her book, in which she also accuses Michelle Obama of taking on the cause of child obesity only in order to create 400,000 new food-service jobs for her friends at the SEIU. This is brass-knuckle Chicago politics at its worst, she charges. Again, this is a pack of lies that would never be considered for publication by any mainstream media outlet. But Malkin doesn't care. She knows it's enough to guarantee her a continued job at Fox.

38. Martin, Andy. *Obama: The Man Behind the Mask.*
    Publisher: Orange State Press, July 2008.

Between the Covers: As you can see from this list so far, there have been many attempts in print to "rip the mask off Barack Obama" and expose the real monster hiding beneath. Andy Martin goes about this tilting at windmills through the prism of Chicago. With forty years of experience in Chicago politics under his belt, Martin paints Obama as just another lackluster, ineffective, corrupt Chicago politician, remarkably unqualified to be president. Don't expect anything new. All we get is the same old litany of community organizers: Saul Alinsky, Bill Ayers, Tony Rezko, Richie Daley, and Jeremiah Wright. Martin honestly thought his exposé would stop Obama dead in his tracks. Imagine his chagrin today, knowing not only that Obama is in the White House—with a Daley as his chief of staff—but that his former chief of staff, Rahm Emanuel, is Chicago's new mayor.

39. Mattera, Jason. *Obama Zombies: How the Liberal Machine Brainwashed My Generation.*
    Publisher: Threshold Editions, February 2011.

Between the Covers: You may not know Jason Mattera's name, but you've seen him at work online, a precursor to Andrew Breitbart and James O'Keefe, and a pioneer in ambush "journalism," capturing young political activists at their worst. Here, he paints a scary picture of "the Obama generation" as a brainwashed cadre of clueless college students hoodwinked by the charismatic community organizer from Chicago. It's no secret how Obama won in 2008, claims Mattera. He simply "lobotomized" an entire generation who went on to elect the "most radical and untested president in U.S. history." (Are you sensing a theme to this list yet?) The only way conservatives can win back the White House, Mattera concludes, is to infiltrate the Web and lure the youth vote away from Obama. But, of course, in order to do that, they're going to need somebody a little more compelling than Mitt Romney, Tim Pawlenty, Michele Bachmann, or Rick Perry.

40. McCarthy, Andrew C. *How Obama Embraces Islam's Sharia Agenda.*
    Publisher: Encounter Books, December 2010.
       See comments below.

41. McCarthy, Andrew C. *How the Obama Administration Has Politicized Justice.*
    Publisher: Encounter Books, January 2010.

Between the Covers: Andrew McCarthy, former assistant U.S. attorney for the Southern District of New York, worked in the Bush Justice Department under Attorney General John Ashcroft, where he was actually a supporter of waterboarding. In these two Encounter broadsides, he basically argues that everything Bush and Ashcroft did in the so-called "war on terror" was right—and that everything President Obama's doing is wrong. He objects especially to Obama's initial plans to bring September 11 mastermind Khalid Sheikh Mohammed to trial in Manhattan's federal courthouse. Which is ironic given that, as assistant U.S. attorney, McCarthy helped prosecute World Trade Center bomber Sheih Omar Abdel-Rahman—in the same federal courthouse! Earlier, McCarthy had accused Obama of being a proponent of introducing Sharia law to the United States by supporting the activities of the international Muslim Brotherhood and the Organization of the Islamic Conference. This is so preposterous and so totally without foundation, it almost defies a response. But seasoned Obama haters will believe every word of it.

42. McCaughey, Betsy. *Obama Health Law: What It Says and How to Overturn It.*
    Publisher: Encounter Books, June 2010.

Between the Covers: In 1994, before becoming New York's lieutenant governor, Betsy McCaughey gained fame as one of the chief critics of President Clinton's 1,362-page health-care-reform legislation. Some reporters, in fact, gave her credit for killing the whole plan with the cover story "No Exit," which she wrote for *The New Republic*. Sixteen years later, she tried to do the same for President Obama's health-care-reform package, and failed. In this long essay, published three months after the Obama plan was signed into law, she merely repeats the lies heard from Republicans in Congress. This new law will "destroy your constitutional rights." As if that's not bad enough: "For the first time in history, the federal government will dictate how doctors treat their privately-insured patients." The problem for her, and other critics, is that none of the horrors she warns about have come true.

43. McMahon, Edmund J. *Obama and America's Public Sector Plague.*
    Publisher: Encounter Books, September 2010.

Between the Covers: This is an interesting book—not for any truth it contains, but because it shows that right-wingers had been planning for and encouraging an attack on public-sector workers long before Republican governors like New Jersey's Chris Christie, Ohio's John Kasich, and Wisconsin's Scott Walker tried to destroy public-employee unions in their states. McMahon, in effect, wrote the patently false talking points that Kasich and company would stick to about public employees enjoying higher salaries and better benefits than all other workers. But he blames President Obama, especially, because it was only with the assistance of his stimulus funds that local governments were able to keep so many teachers, nurses, firefighters, and cops on the job. McMahon would have been happier if they'd all been fired. And, of course, he'd like to see them all lose their right of collective bargaining.

44. Moore, Stephen. *How Barack Obama Is Bankrupting the U.S. Economy.*
    Publisher: Encounter Books, December 2009.

Between the Covers: Stephen Moore, former head of the Club for Growth, now sits on the editorial board of the *Wall Street Journal*, where his job is to appear on cable television or write occasional broadsides like this one, always with the same theme: Liberals can't do anything right. And besides, they are destroying the economy. Here, Moore reports this shocking news: "In his first nine months in office, Barack Obama has pursued the most aggressive government expansionist agenda since Franklin Roosevelt's New Deal was launched in 1933." Duh! What Moore doesn't point out is that Obama also inherited the worst economic crisis since FDR inherited the Great Depression. Moore also fails to point out that it was George W. Bush, not Obama, who began the necessary bailouts of Wall Street and the American auto industry— and that both programs, continued by Obama, have proven phenomenally successful and have actually earned taxpayers money. But that may be asking too much from a Rupert Murdoch acolyte.

45. Morris, Dick and Eileen McGann. *Fleeced: How Barack Obama, Media Mockery of Terrorist Threats, Liberals Who Want to Kill Talk Radio, the Do-Nothing Congress, Companies That Help Iran, and Washington Lobbyists for Foreign Governments Are Scamming Us . . . and What to Do About It.*
Publisher: HarperCollins, June 2008.
    See comments below.

46. Morris, Dick and Eileen McGann. *Catastrophe: How Obama, Congress, and the Special Interests Are Transforming . . . a Slump into a Crash, Freedom into Socialism, and a Disaster into a Catastrophe . . . and How to Fight Back.*
Publisher: HarperCollins, June 2009.
    See comments below.

47. Morris, Dick and Eileen McGann. *Revolt! How to Defeat Obama and Repeal His Socialist Programs.*
Publisher: Broadside Books, March 2011.

Between the Covers: One thing for sure. Barack Obama has certainly been good to the Dick Morris household. He and his wife have turned their animosity toward Obama into three best-selling and long-titled books, each less original than the last. In *Fleeced,* Morris joins with Mrs. Morris to show how Americans are being ripped off today by just about everybody—bankers, bureaucrats, and politicians. There is very little about Barack Obama. It seems Morris added his name to the title only in order to sell more books. The second, *Catastrophe,* published halfway through Obama's first year in office, merely repeats the standard right-wing scare stories about Obama's plans to destroy the economy, nationalize banks and auto companies, let terrorists go free, enfranchise illegal immigrants, force everyone into a government-run health plan, and shut down talk radio. The happy couple strikes again with *Revolt!*—a fervent plea to conservatives to use their newfound power after the 2010 midterm elections to stop the Obama agenda in its tracks. You can pretty much judge the Morris family's powers of prognostication by looking at the title of their 2005 book: *Condi vs. Hillary: The Next Great Presidential Race.* My question is, Why would anybody, including his wife, believe anything from a guy who let his highly paid prostitute listen in on his conversations with the president of the United States? And why does Fox still keep him on the payroll?

48. Mukasey, Michael B. *How Obama Has Mishandled the War on Terror.*
    Publisher: Encounter Books, March 2010.

Between the Covers: I must say, this book surprised me. Because, being somewhat old-fashioned, I expected more from a highly respected New York judge and former attorney general of the United States than a purely partisan screed based on a pack of lies. Mukasey accuses Obama of being "soft on terror" for wanting to try terrorist suspects in federal criminal courts, for example, when it was Mukasey himself who presided over the successful trial of World Trade Center bomber Sheikh Omar Abdel-Rahman in lower Manhattan. He also attacks Obama for wanting to "provide better conditions for terrorists than common criminals," when, in fact, Obama retained terrorist suspects in the same prison George Bush established at Guantánamo Bay. Mukasey obviously drank too much of the Bush Kool-Aid while in Washington, where he spent his days making excuses for Bush-era waterboarding.

49. Muravchik, Joshua. *Obama's Radical Transformation of America: Year One.*
Publisher: Encounter Books, February 2010.

Between the Covers: If, from the title, you get the impression that Joshua Muravchik, senior fellow at the conservative Foreign Policy Institute, wasn't a big fan of President Obama's first year in office, you're right. This from the book's promotion materials: "In only one year, Obama has saddled Americans with a skyrocketing deficit that will leave future generations deeply in debt; a health-care plan that prescribes a cure worse than the illness; catastrophically expensive environmental schemes; and a foreign policy that appeases enemies and punishes friends." One can only guess what he thought of years two and three.

50. Newberry, Tommy. *The War on Success: How the Obama Agenda Is Shattering the American Dream.*
Publisher: Regnery Publishing, January 2010.

Between the Covers: Tommy Newberry has made a good living and sold a lot of books as an expert on small business. Unfortunately, he also decided to jump into politics, where he quickly found himself over his head and forced to repeat the same old canard about how Republicans are good for business—and Democrats are bad—when just the opposite is true. Newberry brings nothing to the table we haven't already heard from even less informed conservatives and offers no new insights. Ignoring the reality of a slow but consistent economic recovery from the Bush recession under Obama, Newberry accuses the president of staging a "fundamental assault on the very concept of success" by delivering "higher taxes, nationalized industries, and suffocating regulations." Only those totally ignorant of today's economy might believe him.

51. O'Leary, Brad. *The Audacity of Deceit: Barack Obama's War on American Values*.
    Publisher: WND Books, September 2008.

Between the Covers: Lucky for Barack Obama I didn't read this book before the 2008 election, or I would never have voted for him. How could anyone other than an outright Communist vote for him after Brad O'Leary told you what his real agenda was. No kidding. Few people realized that Barack Obama had these seven top goals: to raise the top tax rate to 60 percent; to grant citizenship to twelve million illegal immigrants; to appoint Supreme Court justices who would overturn the Second Amendment; to take 25 percent of farmland out of production; to transfer care of children under five from parents to government; to set up a new government agency to decide which medical procedures seniors qualify for; and to make it easier for more Democrats to get elected by allowing felons to vote. Of course, that may have been a good way to scare people. But it didn't work. And, needless to say, not one of O'Leary's predictions has come true.

52. O'Reilly, Bill. *Pinheads and Patriots: Where You Stand in the Age of Obama*.
    Publisher: William Morrow, September 2010.

Between the Covers: The insufferable Bill O'Reilly has written—well, at least published—another insufferable book. He divides all Americans into two camps. "Patriots" are those who agree with him politically. All the rest of us are "Pinheads." Personally, I've never been so proud to be a pinhead. One-third of this book is a transcript of O'Reilly's interview with Obama during the 2008 presidential campaign, at the end of which O'Reilly does a fairly sloppy job of comparing what Obama said then with what he's actually done as president. Surprisingly, for Fox's number-one anchor, O'Reilly is relatively easy on Obama. After all, he once praised him as the perfect role model for America's schoolchildren today. He still attends Obama's annual White House Christmas party with his daughter. And he scored an interview with Obama during the 2010 Super Bowl. O'Reilly's careful not to cut off that kind of access.

53. Ott, Scott. *Laughing at Obama: Volume I.*
    Publisher: MacMenamin Press, July 2010.

Between the Covers: Among the dozens of books critical of President Obama, this one is a refreshing change. Because it's funny. And it's meant to be funny. In fact, it's political satire at its best, which even Obama supporters can laugh at. And it's exactly what you'd expect from the editor of Scrappleface.com, whose slogan is "News fairly unbalanced. We report. You decipher." Ott pokes fun at the highlights of the Obama campaign and the Obama presidency, which is also a recurring theme of his Web site. Did you realize, for example, that President Obama, following the example of John F. Kennedy, has announced his goal of putting a "Muslim on the Moon"—and "returning him safely to earth using only Muslim technology?" Meanwhile, the White House refuses to comment on reports that Obama plans to order a fatwa against the 24 percent of Americans who still believe, incorrectly, that he's a Muslim. Obama told reporters, "Whether I've asked for a fatwa or not is between me and my mufti." Through his satirical Web site and book, Ott provides what is too often lacking in politics: a good belly laugh.

54. Patterson, Robert. *Conduct Unbecoming: How Barack Obama Is Destroying the Military and Endangering Our Security.*
    Publisher: Regnery Publishing, September 2010.

Between the Covers: As a military aide assigned to the Clinton White House, Buzz Patterson's job was to carry the briefcase holding the "nuclear football"—a job any well-trained ape could do. Yet, somehow, Regnery believes that experience qualifies him to pontificate on American foreign policy and declare President Obama a danger to the military and the nation. The book is full of contradictions. Obama's slashed funding for the military, complains Patterson. In fact, he's increased it substantially. Obama's ignored the war in Afghanistan, according to Patterson. In fact, he's more than doubled the number of American troops. Obama's only the second president since World War II with no military experience. In fact, he's the third—because nobody counts George W. Bush's work on a U.S. Senate campaign while serving in the Texas National Guard as true "military" experience. And, just for good measure, Patterson also attacks Obama for "bowing to the King of Saudi Arabia." It's so much more manly to do what George Bush did and just hold the king's hand. There's nothing in this book, in other words, except just what you'd expect from a bona fide Obama hater.

55. Pipes, Sally C. *The Truth About Obamacare.*
   Publisher: Regnery Publishing, August 2010.

Between the Covers: As we've seen in so many other books, criticism of President Obama's health-care-reform plan, both while it was being debated in Congress and since it's become the law of the land, has been way, way over the top. Sally Pipes, with the long-established conservative Pacific Research Institute, does a typical hatchet job: tells a bunch of lies about the plan and then refutes them. In conservative circles today, this is known as "research." For starters, she condemns Obama's plan as "the largest expansion of government in the history of the United States." In truth, there is a vast expansion of private insurance, and no government expansion. The greatest expansion of government since Medicare was actually George W. Bush's creation of Medicare Part D, which conservatives widely applauded, even though there was never any pay-for passed along with it. As part of the right-wing echo chamber, Pipes declares that "Obamacare" will destroy the American economy and "fundamentally alter the way we live, work, and see our doctors." And, she might have added, brush our teeth. Unfortunately, for Pipes and others, "Obamacare" is already in place, and none of her dire predictions have come true. So much for all that "research."

56. Prescott, R. Lee. *Barack Obama's Plan to Socialize America and Destroy Capitalism.*
    Publisher: Madrona Books, March 2009.

Between the Covers: Obama sure works fast. He'd been in office only two months before Lee Prescott accused him of successfully destroying capitalism and turning the United States into the world's new socialist empire. Good work, comrade! Sounds like Prescott's been listening to too much Glenn Beck. Like Beck, he believes that behind Obama's attractive, articulate, charismatic personality lurks his "dangerous agenda" for America: socialized medicine, education, finance, manufacturing, and energy production. Of course, there never was any truth to that charge. Obama a socialist? Nonsense. By this time in his presidency, many of us progressives are wondering whether we can still call him a liberal.

57. Savage, Michael. *Trickle Up Poverty: Stopping Obama's Attack on Our Borders, Economy, and Security.*
    Publisher: William Morrow, October 2010.

Between the Covers: If you've ever been unlucky enough to catch his radio program, you know that Michael Savage is the worst of the worst: the nuttiest and ugliest conservative talk-show host on the air—and that's saying something. And he has a particular loathing of Barack Obama. You know what you're getting when Savage begins by warning, "No longer can we be Barack Obama's sheeple and let the American Dream be trampled, beaten, and burned to the ground." Followed by: "The Naked Marxist must be stopped. Obama's trickle up poverty is infecting everything we hold to be true and self-evident." Like every other Obama hater, Savage never bothers with reality. He accuses Obama of favoring illegal immigration, for example, when, in fact, Obama has doubled the number of agents on the border and presided over a record number of deportations. But why let the facts get in the way of a good, frothing tirade?

58. Sinclair, Lawrence W. *Barack Obama and Larry Sinclair: Cocaine, Sex, Lies, and Murder?*
Publisher: Sinclair Publishing, Inc., June 2009.

Between the Covers: How low can you go in politics? Meet Larry Sinclair, who stooped so low that he could not get anyone to publish his explosive charges—not even Regnery Publishing!—so he set up his own company and published them himself. His story is hardly worth repeating, but just to show you how far some people will go to bring down Barack Obama, Sinclair claims that on November 6 and 7, 1999, he engaged in consensual homosexual acts with then Illinois state senator Barack Obama in a Chicago hotel room. During those trysts, Sinclair says, Obama procured cocaine for him and smoked crack cocaine while being fellated. It wasn't until Obama gave his famous speech at the 2004 Democratic National Convention that Sinclair realized whom he'd had sex with. As if that's not bad enough, Sinclair also claims that on December 23, 2007, after rumors of Obama's homosexual activities had begun to surface, Obama ordered the murder of his former lover and Trinity United Church's choir director Donald Young, just days before the 2008 Iowa Democratic caucuses. Now here's what's really disgusting: Sinclair was not only able to publish his grotesque charges; he was granted permission to repeat them publicly in a news conference at the National Press Club during the 2008 campaign. Shame on the Press Club!

59. Spencer, Roy W. *The Bad Science and Bad Policy of Obama's Global Warming Agenda.*
Publisher: Encounter Books, January 2010.

Between the Covers: Welcome to the Flat Earth Society. Roy Spencer is a former NASA scientist, now at the University of Alabama. He admits that global warming may be real, but he denies that it's man-made. The melting of the ice caps and glaciers has nothing to do with all the greenhouse gases we're pumping into the air, he claims. It's just Mother

Nature trying out a few new temperature levels, like a new set of clothes. Government should stay out of global warming, Spencer argues. Let Mother Nature do her thing. And let the free market work. Because we know that corporate interests will always do what's in the public's best interest and never act purely for bigger profits, the environment be damned. It's no surprise that Spencer's at the University of Alabama (sorry, Crimson Tide fans!), but how'd he ever get a job with NASA?

60. Tarpley, Webster Griffin, Bruce Marshall, and Jonathan Mowat. *Obama: The Postmodern Coup: Making of a Manchurian Candidate.* Publisher: Progressive Press, June 2008.

Between the Covers: Here's the first hint of what lies between the covers of this book: the dust jacket features side-by-side photos of Barack Obama and Benito Mussolini waving to campaign crowds. Building to their conclusion that Obama is the architect of "postmodern fascism," whatever that is, the three authors produce what must be the most outrageous and incredible of all the hate Obama literature. They seriously want us to believe that while he was still a student at Columbia, Obama was recruited by Zbigniew Brzezinski, on behalf of the Trilateral Commission, to become president of the United States and lead a global confrontation against China and Russia. Obama himself, of course, did not win the 2008 election. A "deeply troubled personality," he merely allowed himself to be used as "the megalomaniac front man for a postmodern coup by the intelligence agencies, using fake polls, mobs of swarming adolescents, super-rich contributors, and orchestrated media hysteria." It's hard to imagine anybody believes this stuff. But there are still many Americans who believe September 11 was an inside job, planned by George Bush and Dick Cheney.

61. Thiessen, Marc A. *Courting Disaster: How the CIA Kept America Safe and How Barack Obama Is Inviting the Next Attack.* Publisher: Regnery Publishing, January 2010.

Between the Covers: Caveat emptor! This book has been endorsed by both Dick Cheney and Donald Rumsfeld. Don't say I didn't warn you. But, if you're looking for a defense of torture—why it's morally justifiable, why it's necessary, how much information was gained, how many lives were saved, and how many new terrorist attacks were prevented because of it—this is your baby. And, as the title shouts, by banning torture—which is, after all, illegal, both under international and U.S. law—President Obama is naïvely inviting another terrorist attack. It is no surprise that Marc Thiessen would argue this point of view. He is, after all, the former White House aide who wrote George W. Bush's speech defending the use of torture. Now that torture's illegal again, he's lucky he, Bush, Cheney, and Rumsfeld are not all in jail.

Whew!

So the Right *have* been busy at their typewriters—but they are not the only ones to go after Obama in print. With that in mind, a look now at those books about Obama by disgruntled liberals. Their complaint is just the opposite, of course: not that Obama has gone too far in many areas, but that he has not gone far enough—or been willing to use the powers of the presidency to fight for the things liberals believe in.

This proved to be a big problem for Democrats nationwide in 2010, when many Democratic voters, disenchanted with Obama's perceived failure to deliver, simply stayed home—and when many dissatisfied independents, having given Democrats a chance in 2008, moved back to the Republican column.

Indeed, given the frustration with Obama expressed by so many liberals, I'm surprised there haven't been more books critical of Obama published on the Left. Those that have been written, however, make their case very strongly—but also more gently and kindly than books coming from the other side. Naturally! They're written by liberals!

BLASTING OBAMA FROM THE LEFT

1. Ali, Tariq. *The Obama Syndrome: Surrender at Home, War Abroad.*
   Publisher: Verso, October 2010.

Between the Covers: Here is one of the first criticisms of President Obama from the Left. British Pakistani military historian Tariq Ali, regular contributor to the *New Left Review* and *The Guardian,* accuses Obama of reneging on his campaign promises—at home by bailing out Wall Street and falling short on health care; abroad by continuing the occupation of Iraq, sending more troops to Afghanistan, and launching more drone attacks on Pakistan. Ali argues that very little changed between Obama and Bush, which will inevitably lead Republicans to victory in 2012.

2. Carney, Timothy P. *Obamanomics: How Barack Obama Is Bankrupting You and Enriching His Wall Street Friends, Corporate Lobbyists, and Union Bosses.*
   Publisher: Regnery Publishing, November 2009.

Between the Covers: This is a searing indictment from the Left of Obama's economic policies, reflecting the disappointment felt by many liberals. Investigative reporter Tim Carney credits candidate Barack Obama for wanting to help protect average Americans from corporate interests. But, Carney argues, the economic policies of President Barack Obama have done just the opposite. Under Obama, the only people getting bigger and richer are the Wall Street banks, pharmaceutical companies, oil companies, auto companies, and big polluters. For Carney, "Obamanomics" is just another term for corporatism, which Obama has done little to change.

3. Hodge, Roger D. *The Mendacity of Hope: Barack Obama and the Betrayal of American Liberalism.*
   Publisher: HarperCollins, October 2010.

Between the Covers: Roger Hodge is a respected veteran journalist, a former editor of *Harper's,* and a deeply disappointed Obama supporter. Indeed, he had great expectations for "Archangel" Obama and the "Audacity of Hope," only to see his hopes crushed by the reality of what he cleverly calls the "Mendacity of Hope." Like many liberals, Hodge feels betrayed by the president, who promised to fight for the middle class and—on health care, tax cuts, the economy, and other issues—ended up, instead, favoring the very corporate interests he had campaigned against. What we got with Obama, he argues, is not change, but continuity. On Iraq, Afghanistan, and the war on terror, there's not much difference between Barack Obama and George W. Bush. This is the strongest indictment of Obama I've seen from the Left, and one the administration should take seriously.

4. Jocelyn, John Michael and Dirk Brewer. *President Obama's Broken Promises: Race, Religion, and Gay Rights.*
   Publisher: Iuniverse, January 2010.

Between the Covers: Where does President Obama stand on gay rights, and what influenced his thinking on this important civil rights issue? Jocelyn and Brewer relate their conclusions, based on interviews with many Obama associates over the years. His support of gay rights in general, but opposition to same-sex marriage in particular, they believe, is based on the overwhelming influence of the Reverend Jeremiah Wright, Obama's pastor for twenty years in Chicago. Even on the Left, Wright is a bogeyman of sorts. His experience at Trinity United Church, the authors contend, left Obama both "unashamedly black" and "unapologetically Christian." And, as such, he has ended up disappointing his gay and lesbian constituents by not being more supportive of their issues in the White House.

5. Street, Paul. *Barack Obama and the Future of American Politics.*
   Publisher: Paradigm Publishers, September 2008.

Between the Covers: Paul Street's critique is unique in two ways: It is thoughtful and analytical, and it comes from the Left, not the Right. As one who has followed Obama as an Illinois state senator and in his early days as a U.S. senator, Street warns liberals to be careful. What you see is not necessarily what you get. Obama's not as liberal as he pretends to be on the campaign trail. Street notes, for example, that Obama opposed legislation creating universal health care for Illinois until it was watered down to authorize only the creation of a commission to study the issue. As U.S. senator, he also parted with liberals in supporting George W. Bush's plan for tort reform. Street is especially critical of Obama for, he says, ignoring the deep-seated problem of racism in this country, other than giving an occasional mild "Bill Cosby-like lecture." Everybody's expecting something radically new and different about an Obama administration. Lower your expectations, Street advises. Instead of breaking the mold, Obama, he predicts, will easily fit into the mold of narrow-thinking, cautiously acting, corporate-controlled Republican and Democratic presidents of the past.

6. Street, Paul. *The Empire's New Clothes: Barack Obama in the Real World of Power.*
   Publisher: Paradigm Publishers, September 2010.

Between the Covers: Two years later, Paul Street can't wait to shout out, "I told you so!" Again, coming from the Left, Street compares Obama's original progressive agenda for change to what he actually delivered in his first two years on the job. Needless to say, like many liberals, he is frustrated with what we got, compared to what we expected. He accuses Obama of letting his base down by settling on a weak health-care-reform plan, expanding the war in Afghanistan, not fighting harder for the poor and unemployed, increasing the Pentagon's budget, and not cracking down harder on Wall Street bankers. If you're a progressive Democrat frustrated with the Obama administration, take heart. Paul Street is your voice. This is the book for you.

Buried under a pile of books a mile high? By this time, you almost have to feel sorry for Barack Obama. As we've seen, he's faced an unprecedented wave of personal attacks: in speeches, on radio and television, online, and in print.

But, the discontent of the Left not withstanding, you'd be naïve to think this just happened spontaneously. Just the opposite. From the beginning, the right-wing Obama attack machine was created, fueled, and funded by a pair of extremely wealthy conservative brothers from the heartland.

As we have seen throughout this book, others have voiced the same criticism. But only the Koch Brothers had the money to build an entire anti-Obama movement—and were more than willing to spend it.

5

THE BROTHERS

As documented in the preceding chapters, we've seen years of ugly attacks leveled against Barack Obama as candidate, senator, and president.

Yet, as offensive as that hate talk is—and as important as it is to counter the anti-Obama lies with the truth—the intensity and ubiquity of attacks is not surprising once you understand their source. At its heart, the Obama Hate Machine is directed and paid for by two billionaires who share the same father, the same mother, the same antigovernment political philosophy—and the same hatred of our forty-fourth president. Franklin Roosevelt had the du Ponts, Bill Clinton had Richard Mellon Scaife, and Barack Obama has the Brothers Koch.

MEET THE KOCH BROTHERS

"If not us, who? If not now, when?"

With that Thomas Paine–like call to arms, Charles Koch and his brother David summoned their fellow conservative fat cats to meet in Palm Springs in January 2011.

If nothing else, notice of the meeting answered two questions once and for all: Yes, the vast right-wing conspiracy really does exist—and, yes, it actually holds meetings.

Charles Koch had hoped this would be another secret gathering, like all the previous ones he had assembled. But this time, he failed to reckon with the relentless digging of ThinkProgress, the investigative journalism arm of the Center for American Progress. They not only revealed plans for Koch's Palm Springs meet; they published the list of politicians, financiers, and conservative journalists who had attended the previous year's meeting in Aspen.

When word got out, the progressive organizations Common Cause and Code Pink also joined the battle, inviting their volunteers to rally outside the gathering under the banner UNCLOAK THE KOCHS, THE BILLIONAIRES CAUCUS, and sponsoring an opposition panel discussion in a nearby hotel. The panel featured former labor secretary Robert Reich, former Obama green-jobs czar Van Jones, and ThinkProgress researcher Lee Fang, who had done so much of the legwork in breaking this story.

As a result, when Charles and David Koch arrived at the Rancho Las Palmas Resort in Rancho Mirage, just outside Palm Springs, they were met by hundreds of protestors and a swarm of TV news cameras. Their cover was blown. And for the first time, the whole world met the Koch Brothers. Their powerful right-wing political machine was a secret no longer.

FROM WICHITA TO MANHATTAN

Although Palm Springs became an unwelcome coming-out party for the Koch Brothers, their long history of political machinations had earlier been exposed in the pages of *The New Yorker* magazine. In its issue of August 30, 2010, *The New Yorker* published an in-depth article by investigative reporter Jane Mayer, entitled "Covert Operations: The Billionaire Brothers Who Are Waging a War Against Obama."

Mayer clearly touched a nerve. The Kochs subsequently hired investigators to dig up dirt on Mayer and accuse her of plagiarism. Though they were unsuccessful in this attempt, they nevertheless protested to the American Society of Magazine Editors when Mayer's story was nominated for a National Magazine Award. "Her article is ideologically slanted and a prime example of a disturbing trend in journalism," the chief counsel for Koch Industries charged in a letter to ASME, "where agenda-driven advocacy masquerades as objective reporting."

Even though Mayer did not win the ASME 2011 award, her article, along with the outstanding work done by ThinkProgress, remains the definitive source of much of today's Kochology.

So, who are the Brothers?

As Mayer carefully documents, the influence of Charles and David Koch, like that of most obscenely wealthy people, operates on several fronts: business, philanthropy, family, and politics.

As businessmen, they are the heads of Koch Industries, an energy and manufacturing conglomerate based in Wichita, Kansas, which they inherited from their father and have expanded many fold. Today, Koch Industries has seventy thousand employees in sixty different countries. Its corporate activity stretches over ten major business groups, from its original mission of refining oil and natural gas to ranching, fertilizer, finance, asphalt, pipelines, and paper, among other endeavors. They operate oil refineries in Alaska, Texas, and Minnesota. They control four thousand miles of pipelines. In 2004, they bought Invista from DuPont (who were, remember, the Kochs of FDR's day), which means they own Lycra, Stainmaster, Anton, and other polymer brands. The following year, they bought Georgia-Pacific, which gave them ownership of Dixie cups, Brawny paper towels, and Angel Soft and Soft 'n Gentle toilet paper.

In his attempt to defend the Koch Brothers from their liberal critics, *The Weekly Standard*'s Matthew Continetti only slightly exaggerated their awesome reach:

You wake up in the morning and turn on a light using electricity generated by oil and natural gas that Koch Industries discovered, sold, refined, and delivered to the power plant. You get out of bed and your feet touch a carpet made from Koch polymers. You drink from a paper cup manufactured by Koch. You use a Koch paper towel to clean up water spilled from the cup. You get dressed in Lycra products made by Koch. You leave the house, built from materials that in all likelihood have at some point intersected with a Koch company, and get into a car powered by gasoline made by Koch Industries. You drive to the airport where you get on an airplane using fuel refined at a Koch facility. If the airplane is Air Force One, when you get thirsty you have some coffee from the Koch-produced official presidential coffee cup. You hijack the plane and demand that the pilot take you to a country where there is no Koch presence, no Koch employee, no Koch brand. But he can't. He just stares into space. Because there is no escape.

It is no exaggeration to say that we live in the kingdom of Koch. With over $100 billion in annual revenues, Koch Industries ranks as either the largest or the second-largest privately held company in America, alternating the top spot with agricultural giant Cargill.

It's no surprise, then, that Charles and David, as principal owners of Koch Industries, are two of the richest men in the country. Their combined wealth, now estimated at $50 billion, puts them in third place in American family fortunes, after Bill Gates and Warren Buffett. And, like Gates and Buffett, the Koch Brothers give a lot of their money away, through various family foundations, to many good causes. In 2010, *The Chronicle of Philanthropy* listed David Koch number forty-five among donors who gave the most to charity.

David Koch lives on Manhattan's Upper East Side, where he recently surpassed Mayor Michael Bloomberg as the city's richest resident, and is frequently spotted in photographs on the society pages of the *New York Times*. In NYC, David is known not for his extreme right-wing political views, but for his extreme generosity to some of the city's most revered institutions: Lincoln Center, the American Museum of Natural History, the Metropolitan Museum of Art, and the American Ballet Theatre. A survivor of prostate cancer himself, he has also given over $200 million for cancer research at Johns Hopkins University, the Memorial Sloan-Kettering Cancer Center, the new David H. Koch Institute for Integrative Cancer Research at MIT, and other medical centers around the country.

On at least one occasion, David Koch's philanthropy ended up on a collision course with company business. While serving on the National Cancer Institute's Advisory Board, his company, Koch Industries, one of the country's top producers of formaldehyde, was lobbying hard to stop the federal government from formally classifying the chemical as a carcinogen. Pressure from Greenpeace and others in the scientific community, and the resulting bad publicity, coincided with Koch's departure from the board in October 2010, several months after his term had expired in any event. Eight months later, the Department of Health and Human Services finally added formaldehyde to the list of known cancer-causing agents. Although he does not deny that Koch subsidiary, Georgia-Pacific, was lobbying against the classification, Koch has denied any conflict of interest, claiming that his service on the Cancer Advisory Board had nothing to do with that decision.

Charles Koch, who stayed behind in Wichita, has focused more on academia, founding and funding economic research centers on many college campuses, all dedicated to furthering the free-market and unfettered capitalism theories put forth by Austrian economist Friedrich von Hayek in his 1944 book, *The Road to Serfdom*—as well as the Koch's own business philosophy, which he calls "Market-Based Management."

Their good works and right-wing think tanks aside, it is their blatantly political activity that has gained the Koch Brothers the most notoriety. David Koch liked to joke that Koch Industries was "the biggest company you've never heard of." But no longer. Now the Kochs are two of the nation's biggest political donors. They have built a vast propaganda machine. They are worshiped as heroes by the Right, while being vilified as villains by the Left—and rightly so. And in political giving today, there is nobody—not George Soros, not Bill Gates, not Steve Bing, not David Geffen—in their league. Charles Lewis, founder of the Center for Public Integrity, has been tracking political contributions longer than anybody in Washington. He told Jane Mayer, "The Kochs are on a whole different level. There's no one else who has spent this much money. The sheer dimension of it is what sets them apart. They have a pattern of lawbreaking, political manipulation, and obfuscation. I've been in Washington since Watergate, and I've never seen anything like it. They are the Standard Oil of our times."

THE "KOCHTOPUS"

When it comes to politics in the Koch family, Charles and David are living proof that "the apple does not fall far from the tree." In fact, for all the Kochs now complain about the creeping tendrils of socialism, Fred Koch, their father, made his fortune thanks to communism. He built fifteen oil refineries for the Stalin government, but returned to the United States a fierce anti-Communist conservative warrior.

As Mayer revealed in her *New Yorker* article, Fred Koch was one of the original members of the John Birch Society, known for its belief that Communists had infiltrated the American government all the way up to the White House, where President Eisenhower himself, they suspected, was a Communist spy. Koch was also a big fan of Benito Mussolini because of his suppression of communism in Italy. He encouraged Barry Goldwater to run for president in 1964 in order to counter the moderate, Nelson Rockefeller drift of the Republican party. And he distrusted the civil rights movement because he believed its leaders were either Communist sympathizers or members of the Party. He once warned, "The colored man looms large in the Communist plan to take over America."

In many ways, Koch was a Tea Partier long before there was a Tea Party. He transferred his hatred of Stalin's Soviet Union into a profound distrust of our own government: a passion, Mayer recounts, that Fred Koch pounded into his four children. "He was constantly speaking to us children about what was wrong with government," David Koch told Brian Doherty, editor of the libertarian magazine *Reason*. "It's something I grew up with—a fundamental point of view that big government was bad, and imposition of government controls on our lives and economic fortunes was not good."

In a 1963 speech, the senior Koch predicted that Communists would "infiltrate the highest offices of government in the U.S. until the President is a Communist, unknown to the rest of us." Substitute *socialist* for "Communist," and he could give the same speech today—this time about Barack Obama.

But, of course, Fred can't. He died in 1967. Nor does he have to. Charles and David do it for him. Charles told Continetti that Obama inherited an antibusiness, anti–free market, anti–free enterprise philosophy from his Kenyan father (whom Obama had almost no contact with, as pointed out parlier). "I'm not saying he's a Marxist," Charles insisted, "but he's internalized some Marxist models—that is, that business tends to be successful by exploiting its customers and workers." Brother David added that he believes Obama to be "the most radical president we've ever had as a nation. He's done more damage to the free enterprise system and long-term prosperity than any president we've ever had." Their father would be proud of them.

Of course, as with so many accusations from the Obama-hating camp, their charge that President Obama has been bad for business has no basis in the real world. As Glenn Greenwald pointed out on Salon.com, big business has never had it better. Consider the statistics today.

U.S. corporate profits hit an all-time high at the end of 2010, with corporations reporting $1.68 trillion in profit in the fourth quarter—surpassing the previous record of $1.65 trillion in the third quarter of 2006. GE alone posted $14.2 billion in world-wide profits, and paid zero federal corporate taxes. And financial firms, which benefited most from the Bush/Obama Wall Street bailout, showed some of the biggest gains. JPMorgan Chase, for example, reported profits up 47 percent.

Since Obama was inaugurated, in fact, the Dow Jones has increased over 50 percent—from eight thousand to over twelve thousand—at the time of this writing. The wealthiest Americans received a continued tax break. And, according to the Huffington Post, the share of U.S. taxes paid by corporations has fallen from 30 percent of federal revenue in the 1950s to 6.6 percent in 2009.

Meanwhile, under Obama, the unemployment rate soared from 7.7 to over 10 percent at its peak, before starting to fall gradually. Millions of Americans have lost their homes to foreclosure. And the number of Americans living below the poverty line has increased dramatically.

Exactly where in that record is Obama's "Marxist model" shining through? Given the surge in corporate profits since Obama's been in the White House, the Koch Brothers might argue we need more of what the president is doing, not less. Certainly Marx would have a hard time seeing our forty-fourth president as a fellow traveler.

At any rate, by the time Charles and David became interested in politics, the John Birch Society no longer existed, so they had to chart their own course. Which they did, starting out as libertarians advocating the principles of smaller government, less regulation, lower taxes, and greater reliance on the free market. Too much government, whether led by Democrats or Republicans, they believed, was bad for business.

When parachuting into politics, the Koch boys, like other wealthy conservatives before them, followed the path laid out in 1971 by Lewis Powell, two months before Richard Nixon named him to the Supreme Court. As I documented in my last book, *Toxic Talk*, in a memo prepared for the U.S. Chamber of Commerce, at Nixon's suggestion, on how to build a lasting conservative movement, Powell proposed raising millions of dollars to build a network of related organizations that would control everything from the development of policies to the dissemination of those policies in the media. Conservatives followed Powell's plan to a tee. Which is why the Right has such a powerful message machine today—and the Left has practically none.

The Koch Brothers were very much influenced by what became known in conservative circles as the "Powell Doctrine." Charles Koch understood it better than anybody. The only way to bring about major social change, he explained, was to develop a "vertically and horizontally integrated" strategy that spanned "from idea creation to policy development to education to grassroots organizations to lobbying to litigation to political action." On the Right, the Kochs are major players in every one of those areas today.

Following the Powell script, in 1977 the Charles G. Koch Foundation donated funds for the creation of Washington's Cato Institute, the nation's leading libertarian think tank, which has emerged today as one of the main centers of opposition to climate-change legislation. They joined others in helping found the Heritage Foundation, a stone's throw from the U.S. Capitol and the premier source of its conservative position papers.

A few years later, Charles endowed the Center for the Study of Market Processes at George Mason University, located just outside Washington, in suburban Virginia. Later renamed the Mercatus Center, it occupies a very powerful role today as the chief architect of Republican legislation to gut EPA's regulatory authority. Its influence was confirmed by a 2004 *Wall Street Journal* article noting that out of twenty-three environmental regulations targeted for elimination by the Bush administration, fourteen had been suggested by Mercatus. Richard Fink, first president of Mercatus, is now the chief lobbyist for Koch Industries in Washington. The Institute for Humane Studies, another Koch-funded project, has also been established at George Mason. And in 2008, the Charles G. Koch Charitable Foundation entered into an agreement with Florida State University to create two new programs in their economics department: The Study of Political Economy and Free Enterprise (SPEFE) and Excellence in Economics Education (EEE). As with other Koch-funded campus think tanks, however, his millions to FSU came with one big string attached: Charles had to directly approve those appointed to leadership positions.

But an interest in academics was never enough for the Brothers. In 1980, David Koch made a quixotic run for vice president on the Libertarian party ticket, with Ed Clark as the presidential candidate. Their platform included not only the elimination of Social Security, welfare, federal regulations, minimum-wage laws, and all personal and corporate income taxes; they also proposed shutting down the FBI, the CIA, and all public schools— and legalizing prostitution, recreational drugs, and suicide. What was left for government to do?

Despite David's dumping two million dollars of his personal funds into the campaign, Clark and Koch managed to win only 1.1 percent of the national vote. That still represented more votes than any other Libertarian party ticket in history, yet the Koch Brothers realized they needed to build a bigger and broader organization if they were ever going to achieve the broad political influence they desired. They knew they needed a mechanism to move the ideas generated by the think tanks they funded into political reality.

In 1984, therefore, they established Citizens for a Sound Economy (CSE), which was intended to built "grassroots" support for the libertarian agenda developed at Cato and Mercatus. For Koch acolyte Richard Fink, who left his job at Mercatus to become the first CEO of CSE, what they were doing was taking Friedrich von Hayek's ideas about manufacturing and marketing products— and applying them to the realm of ideas. To influence policy, Fink argued, you must first develop the "intellectual raw materials" (think tanks); then develop these into policy "products" (legislation); and finally "market" (via the media) and "distribute" them to "consumers" (citizen organizations). Matt Kibbe, who joined CSE as lead economist and now serves the Koch empire as president of FreedomWorks (see page 189), further explained that the organization's mission was "to take these heavy ideas and translate them for mass America. . . . We learned we needed boots on the ground to sell ideas. Not candidates."

From the beginning, however, there was one other factor unique to the Koch Brothers' foundation grants. They weren't just sponsoring research for the sake of research. They were also seeking opportunities to marry their philanthropic side with their business side: establishing or assisting think tanks that would develop arguments for getting rid of environmental regulations, for example, so that their oil refineries and utilities could continue to pollute the air and water without government interference.

The Koch Brothers are not disinterested donors, in other words. They very deliberately, and diabolically, use their money in order to make more money.

Citizens for a Sound Economy was the first of what *The New Yorker*'s Jane Mayer described as "slippery organizations with generic-sounding names" created by the Koch Brothers. Its purpose was to further their political goals, while helping their corporate bottom line. In fact, CSE was fashioned to provide exactly what the Tea Party, another creature of Koch family largesse, would provide a quarter of a century later. As brother David explained at the time, "What we needed was a sales force that participated in political campaigns or town hall meetings, in rallies, to communicate to the public at large much of the information that these think tanks were creating."

Corporate money and grassroots support are an inherent contradiction, of course. There was nothing "grassroots" about CSE from the beginning. According to the Center for Public Integrity, the organization gobbled up $7.9 million in Koch funds from 1986 to 1993. Yet, even with lavish corporate funding, it still took time to build the appearances of a national citizens' organization. Within a few years, CSE could boast fifty paid organizers in twenty-six states. It had also created a sister organization, Concerned Citizens for the Environment, which the *Pittsburgh Post-Gazette* reported had "no citizen membership of its own," but which did publish papers calling acid rain a myth—just as Koch-funded groups would later call global warming a myth. Finally, in 1993, Citizens for a Sound Economy found the enemy it was made for: President Bill Clinton's proposal to levy a BTU energy tax, or carbon tax, which had been hugely successful in reducing air pollution in the EU, but which the Koch Brothers saw as a stake to the heart of their business empire if applied in this country. "Our belief is that the tax, over time, may have destroyed our business," Richard Fink told the *Wichita Eagle*. CSE ran newspaper and television ads against the plan, staged media events, commissioned public opinion polls, and whipped up opposition to members of Congress who supported it, including Wichita's then congressman, Democrat Dan Glickman. Anticipating the same tactics Koch organizers would later use under the guise of the Tea Party, CSE organizers also staged mass faux-grassroots rallies outside House office buildings in Washington, designed, said one NPR report, "to strike fear into the hearts of wavering Democrats."

It worked. Nervous House and Senate Democrats ran for the hills, and President Clinton dropped the plan. But around the same time, troubles of a different nature struck the Brothers Koch—on several fronts.

Before the Clinton era, the Senate Select Committee on Indian Affairs accused Koch Industries in 1989 of "a widespread and sophisticated scheme to steal crude oil from Indians and others through fraudulent mis-measuring." An investigation was conducted and a grand jury was empaneled, but no charges were eventually filed.

In 1997, during its investigation of campaign irregularities, the Senate Committee on Governmental Affairs uncovered a phony corporation called Triad Management, Inc., which had pumped three million dollars into attack ads against twenty-six House Democrats and three Democratic senators running for reelection. More than half of Triad's ad budget—$1.79 million— had come from a nonprofit organization, the Economic Education Trust, which, of course, turned out to be just another front group for Charles and David Koch, as confirmed by the *Wall Street Journal*. Two years later, a Texas jury found Koch Industries guilty of negligence and malice in the deaths of two teens killed in the explosion of an underground butane pipeline.

Meanwhile, the Clinton Justice Department accused Koch Industries of causing more than three hundred oil spills, which dumped an estimated three million gallons of oil into America's waterways. Koch agreed to pay a $35 million fine and spend $5 million on cleanup. In still another matter, the Justice Department sued Koch Industries for covering up the release of ninety-one tons of cancer-causing benzene from its refinery in Corpus Christi. Again, the company pleaded guilty and paid a twenty-million-dollar fine.

At which point, the Kochs set out to get their political revenge. In 2000, they spent $900,000 supporting George W. Bush and other Republican candidates—and hundreds of thousands more getting Bush reelected in 2004. But they ran into trouble when Oregon Democrats accused Citizens for a Sound Economy of attempting to get Ralph Nader on the presidential ballot in order to siphon votes from John Kerry and deny Kerry a big West Coast win. (An FEC complaint against CFSE was later dismissed.)

But the beleaguered brothers didn't give up on politics. They just regrouped. They deep-sixed Citizens for a Sound Economy and replaced it with two successor organizations: FreedomWorks and Americans for Prosperity, both bankrolled by the Koch family, and both of which would play important roles in the formation of the Obama Hate Machine.

FREEDOMWORKS

For CEO of FreedomWorks, the Koch Brothers turned to former House Republican majority leader Dick Armey, with whom they had long enjoyed a close working relationship, both in his role as Texas congressman and in their role as principal funders of the Cato and Heritage institutes, which provided much of the conservative agenda for the Tom DeLay/Dick Armey–controlled Congress.

Like its parent organization, Citizens for a Sound Economy, FreedomWorks floundered for a few years without any real purpose (other than booking Armey on TV talk shows)—until it found its real enemy: Barack Obama. Bingo! Armey has admitted that he immediately saw an opportunity to rally disaffected conservatives against Obama, just like MoveOn.org had successfully mobilized liberals against the policies of George W. Bush.

And what do you know? Suddenly, like weeds, six hundred different tax day rallies popped up on April 15, 2009, which led to countless protests at town hall meetings held by members of

Congress across the country the following summer. The raucous disruptions of town hall gatherings were celebrated by the media as a genuine, spontaneous, homespun display of voter outrage— the birth of a new movement, called the "Tea Party." In reality, they were anything but.

Most of the protestors, in fact, probably didn't realize what was going on. Their so-called grassroots events were, in fact, organized and funded by corporate lobbyists back in Washington, D.C., under the direction of Dick Armey. The FreedomWorks Web site helped them find a congressional meeting near their home and told them where to show up for free bus transportation to and from the event. Once at the meeting, Tea Partiers were given written instructions on how to disrupt the meeting, how to prevent the member of Congress from maintaining order, and what to say in front of the TV cameras.

Armey even scheduled himself as keynote speaker at a big tax day rally in Atlanta. He never denied his role in directing the Tea Party phenomenon. He just tried to minimize it instead, telling Fox News, "We'd like to say we are one of the main driving forces, but we are not THE driving force behind the protests. We're mainly helping activists get in touch with each other."

At the same time, true top-dog corporate lobbyist that he is, Armey wasn't just helping create a citizens movement for no reason. As reported by ThinkProgress, in many cases there was a direct connection between the issues Tea Party members were protesting and the clients Armey represented in Washington.

Among his biggest clients, for example, were giant pharmaceutical companies like Bristol-Myers Squibb, which opposed money-saving comparative-effectiveness research in Obama's health-care-reform legislation because it might allow cheaper generic drugs to cut into their historically high profits. Drug companies were only too happy to see senior citizens in Armey's army. After all, everybody expected them to welcome universal health care, since they already enjoyed it. Instead, Armey was able to convince a good number of them to denounce Obama's plan as "socialized medicine."

"We believe that hard work beats daddy's money," Armey gushed at the time. Yet it was only with big money from corporate daddies like Charles and David Koch—with the help of Richard Mellon Scaife, the Olin and Bradley foundations, ExxonMobil, Bristol-Myers Squibb, and other predictable funders of right-wing propaganda—that FreedomWorks was born.

AMERICANS FOR PROSPERITY

Americans for Prosperity, the second spin-off of Citizens for a Sound Economy, remains under the direct control of Charles and David Koch. Day-to-day operations are led by its president, Tim Phillips, a veteran Republican campaign strategist and former business partner of Ralph Reed, whose reputation has been tarnished by his association with disgraced Republican überlobbyist Jack Abramoff.

As partners in Century Strategies, building on Reed's reputation as former executive director of the Christian Coalition, Phillips and Reed had assembled an unusual collection of clients, starting with Enron. They charged Enron $380,000 for recruiting "religious leaders and pro-family groups" to support energy deregulation in Congress—as if that had anything to do with the Bible. Although, as Christians, they were theoretically opposed to all forms of gambling, they signed a contract with Jack Abramoff to generate Christian opposition to Indian gambling—because it might compete with traditional casinos he represented.

Perhaps their most infamous lobbying campaign was urging conservative Christians to pressure members of Congress to oppose applying federal wage and worker-safety laws in the U.S. commonwealth of the Northern Mariana Islands. Even though a federal report found that female Chinese workers in the Marianas "were subject to forced prostitution in the local sex-tourism industry," Phillips and Reed sent out mailers claiming that Chinese workers in the Marianas "are exposed to the teachings of Jesus Christ" and that many "are converted to the Christian faith and return to China with Bibles in hand." It was a disgustingly dishonest campaign—and good preparation for the lies Tim Phillips would perpetuate as one of the Koch Brothers' top lieutenants and head of their "grassroots" political operation.

The Koch boys gave their pet project an innocuous-sounding name: Americans for Prosperity. After all, who's *not* for prosperity? But it might better be called "Obama Hate Headquarters," because no organization is more responsible for the intense level of white-hot hate directed against President Obama, his person and his policies. It is their sole mission. They are the twenty-first-century edition of the du Ponts' Liberty League.

No sooner had Obama stepped into the Oval Office, for example, than Americans for Prosperity organized "Porkulus" rallies across the country against Obama's $787 billion stimulus, or economic-recovery, package. In true Tim Phillips fashion, they formed a spin-off group called No Stimulus to try to block passage of the Economic Recovery Act. Later, the Mercatus Center even released a report accusing Obama of giving priority for stimulus funds to Democratic congressional districts, a report they later had to admit was erroneous.

THE ARMS OF THE KOCHTOPUS

FreedomWorks and Americans for Prosperity are just the tip of the Koch iceberg. Because they operate through various family foundations, and because not all organizations receiving Koch contributions are required to reveal the names of donors, no one but the Koch Brothers themselves knows how much money they have poured into their anti-Obama crusade. But it certainly adds up to hundreds of millions of dollars.

The Kochs pour their money out of three family foundations,

with combined assets of over sixty million dollars: the Charles
G. Koch Charitable Foundation, the David H. Koch Charitable
Foundation, and the Claude R. Lambe Foundation (named after
a close family friend who died). Again, we don't know them all,
but among those organizations fully or partly funded by the Koch
family foundations are the following:

- The Cato Institute
- Citizens for a Sound Economy
- Mercatus Center, George Mason University
- Institute for Humane Studies, George Mason University
- Heritage Foundation
- Institute for Justice
- Foundation for Research on Economics and the Environment
- Reason Foundation
- Federalist Society for Law and Public Policy Studies
- Pacific Research Institute for Public Policy
- Washington Legal Foundation
- Capital Research Center
- Competitive Enterprise Institute
- Ethics and Public Policy Center
- National Center for Policy Analysis
- Citizens for Congressional Reform Foundation
- Manhattan Institute for Policy Research
- American Legislative Exchange Council
- Acton Institute for the Study of Religion and Liberty
- Political Economy Research Center
- Media Institute
- National Foundation for Teaching Entrepreneurship
- University of Chicago
- Defenders of Property Rights
- University of Kansas Endowment Association
- Texas Public Policy Foundation
- Center for Individual Rights

- Heartland Institute
- Texas Justice Foundation
- Institute for Policy Innovation
- Center of the American Experiment
- Atlas Economic Research Foundation
- Young America's Foundation
- Henry Hazlitt Foundation
- Atlantic Legal Foundation
- National Taxpayers Union
- Families Against Mandatory Minimums
- Philanthropy Roundtable
- Free Enterprise Institute
- John Locke Foundation
- Hudson Institute
- Alexis de Tocqueville Institution
- National Environmental Policy Institute
- Washington University
- Pacific Legal Foundation
- American Council for Capital Formation
- Institute for Political Economy
- State Policy Network
- Fraser Institute
- Mackinac Center
- Institute for Research on the Economics of Taxation
- Institute for Objectivist Studies
- Americans for Prosperity
- FreedomWorks
- Bill of Rights Institute
- Study of Political Economy and Free Enterprise
- Excellence in Economics Education

Just like the name Trump is boldly emblazoned at the top of every one of the Donald's buildings, the name Koch should be stamped on the letterhead of all too many of those organizations.

Some have a high profile; some don't. But, together, they have enabled the Koch Brothers to have a profound impact on politics and public policy.

Indeed, the Brothers have spent so much money against so many Obama initiatives—from health care to climate change—that Washington insiders refer to their multifaceted operation with awe as the "Kochtopus." Their research and money are everywhere. They have even spawned a whole new political movement.

NOT YOUR FATHER'S GOP

More than anything else, the attacks of the Obama Hate Machine show what happened when today's Republican party—which takes its marching orders from right-wing talk-show hosts and "Mama Grizzlies," and has been swallowed whole by the Tea Party—was forced to come to grips with a black man in the White House.

Make no mistake about it. The Tea Party is a creation of the Koch Brothers and their front organizations. They planted the seeds, they watered the shoots, and they nurtured them until they flowered. But in order to pull off their greatest political coup yet, the Brothers needed more than just money and misinformation. They needed a rich, loamy soil, a seedbed of discontent, for their hate to take root. They did not have to look far.

Let's face it. The Republican party of today is not the one we grew up with. It used to be the party of fiscal responsibility. Today, it's the party of out-of-control government spending. It used to be the party of social laissez-faire. Today, it's the party of Big Brother in our bedrooms, boardrooms, and chat rooms.

Yes, it still calls itself the "party of Lincoln," but it hasn't been that for a long time. Today's Republican party has its roots in the "Southern Strategy" of Richard Nixon, adopted precisely in order to pander to racism in southern states and create the politically

"Solid South." But demography is destiny, and as the southern white base of the Republican party eroded in number, the Nixonian-bred Southern Strategy ran into a brick wall—and the election of a popular black president.

At that point, the corporate-backed crazies forming the Tea Party rose up and captured control of the dessicated Republican party. And that move itself brought an important demographic into play.

Look at any breakdown of the Tea Party. Members are almost all white, social conservatives, and disgruntled Republicans— and they skew much older than the population at large. Which, of course, is ironic in itself. Because most of those opposed to "socialized health care," a key plank of the Tea Party platform, are already dependent on government health care through Medicare or Medicaid. At one Tea Party rally in Sonoma County, California, a friend of mine shouted out, "All those who want to tear up their Social Security cards, line up over here!" Nobody volunteered.

This older Tea Party generation was accustomed to a solidly white majority, and it suddenly found itself confronted with a new, multicultural, and more tolerant America—an America that was ready and willing to elect Barack Obama president. And, just as had happened in the 1920s—when America saw the revival of the KKK, a culture war over evolution fought out at the Scopes Monkey Trial, and mass opposition to the candidacy of Al Smith, the first Catholic to run for president—an older generation was afraid of, and rebelled against, the changing times.

There is no denying the strong racist element that lurks behind every Tea Party statement. They preach "fiscal austerity." Yet, as others have noted, these born-again fiscal hawks didn't make a peep when a white president, George W. Bush, turned a $236 billion surplus built up by Bill Clinton into a $1.2 trillion deficit; blew $2 trillion on a tax cut for the wealthiest 2 percent of Americans; delivered, with Medicare Part D, the biggest expansion of federal government in forty years; and led America into two foreign wars—neither of which was paid for, and both of which merely piled onto the federal debt. Only when a black man took office did they suddenly become concerned enough about federal spending to take to the streets.

But even stronger racist links were revealed by the NAACP's Institute for Research & Education on Human Rights in October 2010. In its special report, *Tea Party Nationalism,* the Institute identified several Tea Party leaders who are also active in known racist organizations. They are, among others:

- Peter Gemma, Florida: member of the ResistNet Tea Party faction, and a former marketing director for the monthly newsletter of one of the leading white-supremacist organizations, The Council of Conservative Citizens
- Billy Joe Roper, Arkansas: also a member of the ResistNet Tea Party, and a founder of the White Revolution, which still supports segregation in education
- Roán García-Quintana, South Carolina: media spokesman for the 2010 tax day Tea Party in Greenville, South Carolina, and a member of the national board of directors of the Council of Conservative Citizens

In other words, scratch below the surface of many Tea Party members and you'll find a not so closeted racist.

That's one of the "big picture" reasons why things have gotten as ugly as they have. Today's conservatives, to borrow a phrase from Bloomberg's Margaret Carlson, cannot seem to find the bottom beneath which they will not sink. And to keep their hatred against this president burning at a fever pitch, they needed more to lean on than their usual mouthpieces—people like Limbaugh and Hannity. Taking a page from their father's John Birch Society, the Koch Brothers created their own Tea Party movement.

On one level, the Tea Party is as American as apple pie. It reflects a distrust of big government and a willingness to fight against government intrusion that goes back to colonial days—and, indeed, without which spirit this nation would not even exist. Even the Gadsden flag that Tea Partiers wave at their rallies—a rattlesnake on a yellow background with the legend "Don't Tread on Me"—can be traced back to Benjamin Franklin, and was one of the first symbols of American patriotism and disagreement with the British crown.

But for all the legitimate anger that now drives the movement, it would be a big mistake to consider the Tea Party a classic, spontaneous, grassroots uprising. It is nothing of the sort. As then speaker Nancy Pelosi said, "This [Tea Party] initiative is funded by the high end—we call it Astroturf. It's not really a grassroots movement. It's Astroturf by some of the wealthiest people in America to keep the focus on tax cuts for the rich instead of for the great middle class."

From its beginning, the Tea Party was an "Astroturf" movement, created and fed from the top down by right-wing political activists and major donors with their own extreme, anti-Obama agenda—and led, of course, by two organizations and two brothers. Without them, the Tea Party would not exist.

THE FRONTS GET TO WORK

In the end, even what was widely considered the catalyst for the Tea Party movement started to appear suspicious.

On February 19, 2009, live from the floor of the Chicago Mercantile Exchange, CNBC's Rick Santelli reported that the Obama administration had just approved $300 billion to help home owners avoid foreclosure. And then he spontaneously exploded. "The government is promoting bad behavior," he bellowed. "Do we really want to subsidize the losers' mortgages?" (Note that we had already subsidized the losers on Wall Street at this point for

hundreds of millions of dollars.) Nonetheless, Santelli contin-
ued: "This is America! We're thinking of having a Chicago Tea
Party in July. All you capitalists that want to show up to Lake
Michigan, I'm gonna start organizing."

It sure made good television. Santelli was an instant folk hero.
He appeared on all the network shows. His video was a YouTube
sensation. But was it really as spontaneous as it appeared? Notice
the key phrases: "Tea Party," "We're thinking of having," and
"I'm gonna start organizing."

Within hours, a Web site called ChicagoTeaParty.com went
live. It was followed by Web sites posted by Americans for Prosperity and FreedomWorks, linking to the video and inviting
people to sign up for a "tea party" event near them: "Are you with
Rick? We are. Click here to learn more." Within a week, AFP
had organized a series of national Tea Party rallies. Were the
Web sites and rallies prepared ahead of time, just waiting for
Santelli to sound the alarm?

Yes, it's possible that all of that could have just happened—
organically—but it sure looks fishy. After researching the issue
for *Playboy,* Mark Ames and Yasha Levine concluded that Santelli's rant was about as spontaneous as the birth of the Tea
Party itself—in other words, not at all.

For a long time, both FreedomWorks and Americans for Prosperity tried to distance themselves from the Tea Party. Dick
Armey, as we saw above, insisted he was just "one" of their many
backers. And AFP denied any involvement whatsoever. In April
2009, Koch spokesperson Melissa Cohlmia told reporters, "No
funding has been provided by Koch companies, the Koch foundations, or Charles or David Koch specifically to support the tea
parties." And as late as July 2010, David Koch was telling *New
York* magazine, "I've never been to a Tea Party event. No one
representing the Tea Party has ever even approached me."

But by this time, he'd been long ago busted by ThinkProgress.
On April 9, 2009, researcher Lee Fang posted his bombshell

discovery on the ThinkProgress blog under the heading "Spontaneous Uprising? Corporate Lobbyists Helping to Orchestrate Radical Anti-Obama Tea Party Protests." Even though Tea Party rallies planned for the Washington Mall had been billed as homegrown, "bottom-up" protests growing out of citizen anger at government spending and higher taxes, Fang reported that the whole operation had been put together by FreedomWorks and Americans for Prosperity.

As Fang showed, FreedomWorks organized conference calls for state organizers and provided ideas for signs, press releases, and guidelines on how to deliver a clear message. Americans for Prosperity hosted a Web site offering "Tea Party Talking Points." It arranged for buses to transport protestors to and from Washington, while also organizing companion rallies in Arizona, New Hampshire, Missouri, Kansas, New Jersey, and other states. It also circulated a memo with instructions on how to disrupt town hall meetings. On MSNBC, Keith Olbermann described the Koch Brothers as the grand puppeteers of the Tea Party crowd, staying out of sight but "telling them what to say and which causes to take on and also giving them lots of money to do it with."

While organizing Tea Party protests on the Mall and around the country, Americans for Prosperity created still another phony front group, this one called "Patients United Now," to take to the airwaves and warn against government-controlled health care. Using Koch-supplied funds, of course, Patients United aired a TV ad called "Survivor," which repeated the old scare argument that President Obama wanted to import Canadian-style health care into the United States. (If only!) Media Matters for America, among other groups, analyzed the Patients Now spot and labeled it "strong on emotion, weak on facts." Patients United also organized three hundred rallies across the country against what they derided as "Obamacare."

Reporters soon uncovered more evidence of Koch support for the Tea Party. In her *New Yorker* article, Jane Mayer describes a

"Texas Defending the American Dream" conference sponsored in Austin over the July 4, 2009, weekend. The organizer of the event, Peggy Venable, was on the Americans for Prosperity payroll. She told the crowd, "We love what the Tea Parties are doing, because that's how we're going to take back America!" While handing out citizens awards to Tea Party activists, she even bragged, "I was part of the Tea Party before it was cool." One of the awards went to former Texas solicitor general Ted Cruz, who called Obama "the most radical president ever to occupy the Oval Office"—exactly what David Koch called him two years later.

By October 2009, at another "Defending the American Dream" gathering—this one in Crystal City, Virginia, just across the Potomac from Washington—even brother David had let the cat out of the bag, or almost. Sharing the podium with Jim DeMint and Newt Gingrich, David Koch boasted of the progress made by Americans for Prosperity: "When we founded this organization five years ago, we envisioned a mass movement, a state-based one, but national in scope, of hundreds of thousands of American citizens from all walks of life, standing up and fighting for the economic freedoms that have made our nation the most prosperous society in history." Then, carefully, without mentioning the Tea Parties by name, he added, "Thankfully, the stirrings from California to Virginia, and from Texas to Michigan, show that more and more of our fellow citizens are beginning to see the same truths we do." Later, reported Jane Mayer, he directly praised the Tea Party for demonstrating the "powerful visceral hostility in the body politic against the massive increase in government power, the massive efforts to socialize this country."

The problem for the White House was that the media gave extensive coverage to the Tea Party, its rallies and town meetings, without exposing the billionaires and their millions behind it. Grumbled then senior White House adviser David Axelrod,

"What they don't say is that, in part, this is a grassroots citizens' movement brought to you by a bunch of oil billionaires."

This was, of course, only one line of attack for the Koch Brothers machine. While they depended on the Tea Party to challenge government spending, they unleashed other forces to turn back government regulations.

The pattern is always the same. Find an issue that would harm operations of Koch Industries, form a phony "grassroots" organization to oppose it, and recruit enough brain-dead Tea Partiers to show up at the rallies. Under the slogan "Free Our Energy," one AFP group supported an increase in domestic drilling (by Koch Industries). Using the pretense of a "Save My Ballot Tour," AFP paid Joe the Plumber to travel around the country opposing the Employee Free Choice Act—because the last thing the Koch Brothers wanted was making it easier for any of their employees to join a union.

On another issue, AFP staged at least eighty "grassroots" events in opposition to proposed cap-and-trade legislation which would, in effect, make industries pay for the pollution they produce. An AFP-sponsored national "Hot Air Tour" was launched to raise doubts about global warming. AFP also railed against the presence of any U.S. government officials at international climate talks. It's estimated that, through AFP and other organizations, the Koch Brothers spent at least fifty million dollars fighting legislation on climate change.

Americans for Prosperity has also been active at the state level, supporting antienvironmental ballot measures and helping elect antilabor governors. And it played a major role, in partnership with the U.S. Chamber of Commerce, in supporting anti-Obama Republican candidates for the House and Senate in 2010.

By the time midterm elections rolled around, Americans for Prosperity was so identified with right-wing political power that President Obama referred to them by name. Denouncing the Supreme Court's *Citizens United* ruling, which allowed corporations to give anonymous, unlimited political contributions, Obama said the Court made it easy for "groups with harmless-sounding names like Americans for Prosperity."

"They don't have to say who exactly Americans for Prosperity are," the president continued. "You don't know if it's a foreign-controlled corporation. You don't know if it's a big oil company, or a big bank."

But we know now—the Brothers Koch. And we also know that if there's one thing they hate more than the president of the United States, it's any regulation that might impact their bottom line.

GLOBAL WARMING'S GOOD FOR YOU!

January 5, 2011, was a big day for John Boehner. After twenty years of climbing up and falling down the leadership ladder in the House of Representatives, he had finally made it to the top and was about to be sworn in as Speaker of the House for the 112th Congress.

It was a big day for David Koch, too. After all, he and his brother Charles had done more than any two other fat cats to help Republicans win the House—and he was there in the chamber with his top lobbyists when Speaker Boehner took the oath of office.

Not only that: Koch was awarded a private meeting with Boehner, while his top political deputy, Tim Phillips, enjoyed a one-on-one with Representative Fred Upton of Michigan, the new chair of the House Energy and Commerce Committee. Afterward, newly elected and returning Republican members of Congress trooped obediently over to the nearby Capitol Hill Club to share some wine and cheese with their billionaire benefactor and take the opportunity to kiss the ring.

David Koch deserved that royal welcome, especially from members of the Energy and Commerce Committee. The *Los*

Angeles Times reported that Koch Industries and its employees were the largest single donor to members of the panel, more generous than ExxonMobil. They shelled out $279,500 to twenty-two of the committee's thirty-one Republicans. And, just for insurance sake, they gave $32,000 to its five Democrats. Inside the Capitol, staffers started calling it the "Committee from Koch."

And the Kochs' generosity soon paid off. The budget bill passed by the Boehner-controlled House not only cut EPA's funding for the 2011 fiscal year by three billion dollars; it abolished most of the agency's authority to do its job. As decreed by House Republicans, EPA would be banned from spending any money to clean up Chesapeake Bay; from enforcing new water-quality standards in Florida; from issuing new solid-waste standards that would include coal ash from power plants as a hazardous waste; from publishing new air-quality standards for coarse particulate matter; and—biggest prize of all for Koch Industries— from regulating greenhouse-gas emissions from stationary sources.

It was a big step toward the goal Charles Koch revealed to the *Wall Street Journal*'s Stephen Moore in 2006 of eliminating 90 percent of all laws and government regulations in order to strengthen the "culture of prosperity."

The wholesale retreat from environmental protection led to this conclusion by California's Henry Waxman, ranking Democrat on the House Energy and Commerce Committee: "It apparently no longer matters in Congress what health experts and scientists think. All that seems to matter is what Koch Industries think."

Just for good measure, the House also slashed the budgets of the SEC, the IRS, and the Commodity Future Trading Commission. But it was the crackdown on the EPA that was music to the Koch Brothers' ears. They'd been fighting the EPA for years, even when their antienvironmental crusade seemed to conflict with their charitable activities. Take formaldehyde, for example. Formaldehyde is a known carcinogen—in rats and, according to a 2009 report of the National Cancer Institute, also in humans. Scientific studies led the National Institutes of Health (NIH) to recommend that it be officially listed as a carcinogen and strictly controlled by the EPA.

Enter Koch Industries, a major producer of formaldehyde ever since they purchased Georgia-Pacific in 2005. Acting through Georgia-Pacific, which manufactures 2.2 billion pounds of formaldehyde a year, Koch intervened to block the EPA from adopting new rules on the chemical until yet more studies had been conducted. During all this debate, David Koch did not recuse himself as a member of NIH's National Cancer Institute Advisory Board—even as his own company was fighting recommendations made by health professionals.

Which may not be that surprising. Because, as we've seen earlier, Koch Industries has a bad record of oil spills and air and water pollution. A 2010 University of Massachusetts at Amherst study cited it as one of the top ten air polluters in the country. And it has long been the most-outspoken corporate opponent of any climate-change legislation, because any such government program would inevitably interfere with what it believes to be its right to pollute with impunity.

One of the most damning accounts of the Kochs' role in undermining global-warming legislation came in a March 2010 study published by Greenpeace: "Koch Industries: Secretly Funding the Climate Denial Machine." In its report, Greenpeace traces almost fifty million dollars in funds allocated over the course of a decade from three different Koch-controlled foundations to climate-denial front groups working to scuttle policies aimed at stopping global warming.

The Greenpeace study shows that from 2005 to 2008, the Koch machine actually outspent ExxonMobil in funding climate-change denial: $25 million for Koch, a mere $9 million for Exxon. During this period, Koch-funded efforts included:

- Over five million dollars to the Americans for Prosperity Foundation for its "Hot Air Tour" campaign, debunking climate science and opposing climate-change legislation
- One million dollars each to the Heritage Foundation and Cato Institute for "scientific" studies questioning the reality of global warming
- $800,000 to the Manhattan Institute for hosting seminars featuring climate change–denial speakers
- $360,000 to the Pacific Research Institute for Public Policy to produce its own documentary rebutting Al Gore's *An Inconvenient Truth*
- And $365,000 to the little-known Foundation for Research on Economics and the Environment, or FREE.

Indeed, FREE, headquartered in Bozeman, Montana, operates way below the radar. Its target audience is comprised of federal judges and state supreme court justices, whom they pay to attend seminars where, according to their Web site, FREE's "scientists" apply "economics and scientific analysis to generate and explore alternative and innovative solutions to environmental problems." In other words, we'll pay you to come to Montana and learn why global warming is nothing to worry about, so you can then go home and rule accordingly.

And some judges do. Back in 1997, the EPA issued new regulations to reduce the atmospheric levels of surface ozone, a pollutant found in the emissions of oil refineries. First, the Mercatus Center filed its objection to the rule, arguing—believe it or not!—that less smog in the air would result in more cases of skin cancer. Pollution, in other words, was saving lives!

You'd think that argument would have gotten thrown out of court. But no, it made its way to the District of Columbia Circuit Court, which ruled 2-1 that the EPA had indeed overstepped its authority by cracking down on air pollution. The Constitutional

Accountability Center later revealed that the two judges in the majority had attended a Koch-funded seminar at the Koch-funded Foundation for Research on Economics and the Environment. For the Kochs, it was money well spent.

That's not the only evidence that, overall, the Koch propaganda blitz is working. In 2008, both John McCain and Barack Obama agreed that global warming was real, and man-made, and that government had to act. Most Americans agreed. Today, that situation has reversed. Obama's still pushing for climate-change legislation, but he's been blocked by Republicans in the House and Senate. Meanwhile, public opinion about climate change has shifted significantly.

An October 2009 survey by the Pew Research Center found that only 57 percent of Americans believed there was solid evidence that the Earth is getting warmer, down from 71 percent in April 2008. At the same time, fewer Americans saw global change as a serious priority. Van Jones, now with the Center for American Progress, credits anti–climate change ads paid for by the Koch Brothers with the dramatic decline in public support for action on global warming.

While they were running ads and buying off politicians, Charles and David Koch also leaned on their think tanks to muddy the scientific waters, heeding the advice of Republican pollster Frank Luntz that the key to success in this area was to convince voters that there was "no consensus about global warming within the scientific community." Thus, the Heritage Foundation argued that "scientific facts gathered in the past 10 years do not support the notion of catastrophic human-made warming." And when President Obama declared that the science on global warming is "beyond dispute," the Cato Institute took out full-page ads refuting him and dismissing any proposed global-warming legislation as expensive, ineffective, and unnecessary. And, yes, they hinted at the *s* word. It's all part of Obama's move toward socialism, Cato's president Ed Crane told *The New Yorker*'s Jane Mayer: "Global-warming theories give the government more control of the economy."

For his part, David Koch took a more upbeat note. Global warming will be good for all of us, he seriously told Andrew Goldman in a July 2010 interview with *New York* magazine. Longer growing seasons in the northern hemisphere, he argued, would more than make up for any dislocation of people from disappearing coastal cities. Concluded Koch, no doubt with a smile on his face, "The Earth will be able to support enormously more people because a far greater land area will be available to produce food."

Of course, Koch offered no information on what kind of different foods might be produced, or what other crops or livestock might be destroyed by higher temperatures. He's a billionaire. Don't bother him with details.

Nothing illustrates the Koch machine's determination to undermine the case for global warming more than the tempest it helped stir up over what came to be known as "Climategate." In November 2009, one thousand e-mails exchanged by English scientists in the Climate Research Unit of East Anglia University over thirteen years were stolen by an unknown hacker and released to the public. Climate skeptics immediately jumped on them as proving that some of the world's leading scientists themselves doubted man's contribution to global warming—and that they may even have been falsifying their data. Fox News and conservative publications had a field day, and researchers from the Koch Brothers' Cato Institute led the pack of critics on television.

But in the end, it was much ado about nothing. Five independent studies proved the e-mails had themselves been misrepresented and, in fact, proved nothing—except that even scientists can sometimes be rude in personal exchanges, as when one said he'd like to "beat the crap" out of opponent Pat Michaels, a long-time climate-change denier. Hey, join the line!

In its own investigation of the controversy, Factcheck.org analyzed one of the most quoted e-mails: "I've just completed Mike's Nature trick of adding in the real temps to each series for the last 20 years (i.e., from 1981 onwards) and from 1961 for Keith's to hide the decline." For climate-change deniers, that was the smoking gun. There it was, plain as day: a scientist admitting he had used a "trick" to "hide the decline."

But, Factcheck.org discovered, it meant nothing of the kind. The word *trick* referred to adding actual, measured instrumental data into a graph of historic temperatures—which was a "trick," or a clever thing to do. The "decline" referred to a decline in temperatures implied by measurements in the width and density of tree rings—when, in fact, temperature-instrument measurements showed just the opposite.

In fact, in the middle of Climategate, the World Meteorological Organization announced that the 2000–2009 decade would likely be the warmest on record, and that 2009 might be the fifth-warmest year ever recorded.

Still, the two or three weeks of negative publicity about the East Anglia University e-mails helped the Koch Industries cause of raising doubts about the seriousness of global warming—as did a substantial contribution to the Smithsonian.

Next time you're in Washington, be sure to stop by the Smithsonian's Museum of Natural History, one of the world's greatest museums—with an IMAX theater, a live butterfly exhibit, and classic displays of stuffed animals from around the world, cleverly and beautifully displayed.

And don't miss the new David H. Koch Hall of Human Origins, where you will learn that the temperature of the earth fluctuates up and down. Temperatures were actually hotter ten thousand years ago than they are today. Which just proves what survivors we are—or, as the exhibit reads: "Humans Evolved in Response to a Changing World." Only at the end of the exhibit are you informed that levels of carbon dioxide are higher today than they've ever been before, and are likely to increase dramatically over the next century. But there is no mention of the role man-made activities may have played in that development, nor any suggestion of how we're going to get out of it.

Surprisingly and shockingly, for such a great scientific institution, the message seems to be: "Shit happens. But we'll deal with it." Which, as Jane Mayer reported, is very similar to the conclusion found in the January 2010 newsletter of Koch Industries: "Since we can't control Mother Nature, let's figure out how to get along with her changes."

The reality, of course, is not that the Smithsonian agreed to buy into David Koch's belief that global warming is either not real or not worth worrying about. It's worse than that. The ugly reality is that David Koch was able to buy into the Smithsonian.

It just proves that in America, one man can still make a difference—especially if he has $22 billion to throw around.

FROM SACRAMENTO TO MADISON

It's not just in the nation's capital that the Koch Brothers are flexing their political muscle. They're also active in every one of the fifty states. Wherever there's a risk of increased environmental regulation, or a chance to undo existing regulations, the Koch Brothers land on state governments like a sledgehammer—and expect all of their employees to march in lockstep.

Just before the 2010 midterm elections, for example, Koch Industries sent an urgent letter to all of its fifty thousand U.S. employees, telling them how to vote and warning them of the consequences to them and their families if they did not vote the right way. This was not only a highly unusual move for any big corporation; it would have been highly illegal before the Supreme Court's *Citizens United* decision—which freed corporations to do almost anything they wanted to influence elections.

In the election packet, first reported by *The Nation*, employees were provided a list of Koch-endorsed candidates to vote for. They also received a copy of the latest company newspaper, which urged workers to vote against their own self-interest by opposing pro-worker legislation: "Similar policies that distort the labor market—such as minimum wage laws and mandated benefits—contribute to unemployment." The package also contained a bizarre historical perspective written by Charles Koch, in which he ranked the best and worst U.S. presidents in terms of their economic policies. Koch may be the only person, alive or dead, to rate as our best presidents not Abraham Lincoln, FDR, Dwight Eisenhower, or even Ronald Reagan, but Warren G. Harding and Calvin Coolidge! Most presidential historians, in fact, credit their corrupt, free-market romp as helping bring about the Great Depression.

Having done its best to keep employees in line politically—or else!—the corporation varied its election activities from state to state.

In West Virginia, Koch Industries took the lead in opposing new environmental regulations that might interfere with coal operations, including new mining safety laws proposed in the wake of the Upper Big Branch mine disaster of April 2010. Its efforts in the Mountain State have been painstakingly recorded by the *Charleston Gazette.* In typical Koch fashion, the corporation has funded several right-wing organizations with innocuous-sounding names, including the Public Policy Foundation of West Virginia. It has also subsidized several economic professors at West Virginia University. Even though government mining inspectors blamed lax enforcement at Upper Big Branch for the tragedy that cost twenty-nine miners their lives, Koch spokesmen dared to argue that more government regulations will actually cause more accidents.

New Hampshire is one of ten northeastern states participating in the Regional Greenhouse Gas Initiative, credited with cutting greenhouse-gas emissions and making improvements in energy efficiency without waiting for the federal government to act. But that may not be true much longer. Another of those Koch-created mystery organizations, the American Legislative Exchange Council, published model state legislation that would repeal the right to participate in the Regional Greenhouse Gas Initiative—a plan eagerly seized upon by the Republican-controlled state legislature, with the assistance of robocalls in support generated and paid for by—who else?—Americans for Prosperity. Governor John Lynch vowed to veto the bill, but Republicans hold a vetoproof majority in both houses of the legislature.

North Carolina saw a different side of the Koch machine, one more associated with Fred Koch, the father, than with his sons Charles and David: a direct assault on school integration. As noted above, Fred Koch was a charter member of the John Birch Society, which suspected American blacks of aiding and abetting the Communist takeover of the United States—and was, therefore, very strongly opposed to the integration of public schools. John Birchers even tried, unsuccessfully, to impeach Chief Justice Earl Warren for his role in the Supreme Court's historic *Brown v. Board of Education* decision. But some people never give up. Acting under the direction of its national board, Americans for Prosperity mobilized its local members to intervene in the school board election in Wake County, North Carolina—and succeeded in electing a new board, one dedicated to ending the county's landmark socioeconomic integration plan. In Wake County, it's back to the future with segregated schools, thanks to Americans for Prosperity and the Koch Brothers.

When you hear "Rally for Jobs," you immediately think of an event sponsored by the AFL-CIO. Right? Don't be fooled. A September 2010 series of "Rally for Jobs" events—in Ohio, Colorado, Illinois, New Mexico, New Jersey, and other states—turned out to be Koch Industries–sponsored events under a variety of shadow antienvironmental organizations. As reported by Think-Progress, the list of sponsors included FreedomWorks, Americans for Prosperity, the American Highway Uses Alliance, Americans for Tax Reform, the Institute for Policy Innovation, the National Petrochemical and Refiners Association, the National Taxpayers Association, the Texas Prosperity Project, and the Corpus Christi Chamber of Commerce—all of which were either created by or partially funded by Koch Brothers foundation funds.

In California, battles over ballot initiatives are nothing new. As a political activist and former Democratic state chair of California, I've been involved in many of them myself. But, in recent years, few have been so fierce as the battle over Proposition 23 on the November 2, 2010, ballot. Some initiatives are convoluted. Not Prop. 23. It was straightforward. It would have simply stopped in its tracks implementation of AB 32—passed by the California state legislature in 2006 and signed into law by Governor Arnold Schwarzenegger—which required that greenhouse-gas emissions in the state be cut back to 1990 levels by 2020.

The battle over Proposition 23 resembled every initiative battle in California in at least two ways. First, both sides used misleading slogans to attract voters. Supporters of the proposition called it the "California Jobs Initiative." Opponents dubbed it, more accurately, the "Dirty Energy Proposition."

Second, its place on the ballot in no way resembled the kind of volunteer, citizen-action measure that populist governor Hiram Johnson envisioned when he created the initiative process in 1911. Big oil money paid people to gather the signatures. Big oil funded the campaign and heavy TV advertising. And one of the biggest big oil contributors was Koch Industries.

Even though they have no refineries in California, the Koch Brothers were afraid of the precedent AB 32 might set for other states. So through one of their wholly owned subsidiaries, Flint Hills Resources, a Kansas-based petrochemical company, they put one million dollars on the table in another attempt to roll back the clock on efforts to curb global warming. In fact,

80 percent of the money behind Prop. 23 came from three out-of-state oil companies: Tesoro, Valero, and Koch Industries. Through Americans for Prosperity, the Kochs also lined up Tea Partiers to hold rallies in support of Prop. 23. But all their efforts failed. Voters overwhelmingly rejected the oil companies proposal, 61 to 38 percent.

West Virginia, New Hampshire, North Carolina, Ohio, California—in 2010, the Koch Brothers were everywhere, it seemed. So, too, were they in Wisconsin, where the Brothers helped install Scott Walker as governor and then turned him loose on public employees.

Koch Industries, after all, has a real interest in Wisconsin. They have three thousand employees in the state, including workers at a toilet paper factory and at gasoline-supply terminals. They own six timber plants and an extensive network of oil pipelines. And their coal company subsidiary has plants in Green Bay, Manitowoc, Ashland, and Sheboygan. They didn't want anybody to interfere with their ability to continue to pollute the Badger State.

And so they found their man in Scott Walker. Even though the Koch Industries PAC only gave Walker $43,000 directly—which was still his second-largest contribution—they gave much more help indirectly. Koch Industries gave the Republican Governors Association another $1 million, which in turn spent $3.4 million in mailers and TV ads attacking Walker's opponent.

Once in office, Walker began paying the Kochs back. He named Cathy Stepp, an arch antienvironmentalist, and chief critic of the Department of Natural Resources, to head the agency: an appointment state representative Brett Hulsey said that was "like putting Lindsay Lohan in charge of a rehab center." And Walker announced his opposition to legislation aimed at creating new clean-energy jobs for Wisconsin.

Then Walker began his front in the Koch-engineered war on state employees, similar to antiunion efforts they had already begun in Indiana, Ohio, and Pennsylvania, and following model legislation developed by another of the Kochs' antienvironmental front groups, the American Legislative Exchange Council. Planning for the union crackdown in Wisconsin began even before Walker was sworn in, when he met with officials from Americans for Prosperity who flew to Wisconsin, as AFP President Tim Phillips told the *New York Times,* in order "to encourage a union showdown."

Walker tried, unsuccessfully, to pretend that his legislation depriving public-sector workers of the right of collective bargaining for anything but their salaries was a necessary part of his efforts to balance the state budget. But that argument collapsed when it was revealed that public employees had already agreed to help eliminate the budget shortfall by contributing a larger share of their paychecks to health and retirement benefits.

Clearly, Walker's bill had nothing to do with the state budget. In fact, testifying in Washington before the House in April 2011, Walker even admitted, when pressed by Congressman Dennis Kucinich, that ending collective bargaining would, in itself, save no money. Rather, it was all about politics.

Public-employee unions were the biggest supporters of the Democratic party across the country, both in manpower and money power. If Walker and fellow Republican governors were able to weaken or destroy those unions, Democrats would suffer—and President Obama would be less likely to carry Wisconsin in 2012. That's what the whole controversy with Walker was all about.

And just in case there were any doubt about that, AFP staffer Scott Hagerstrom was dispatched to tell those attending the January 2010 conference of the Conservative Political Action Committee in Washington, "We fight these battles on taxes and regulations, but really what we would like to see is to take the unions out at the knees, so they don't have the resources to fight these battles."

Once the governor's union-busting bill was introduced, Americans for Prosperity provided funds to bring a few busloads of badly outnumbered Walker supporters to Madison. Americans for Prosperity spent $340,000 in radio and TV ads supporting the legislation. AFP also put up a "Stand with Walker" Web site. Meanwhile, Koch Industries quietly opened a lobbying office in downtown Madison.

Walker, of course, tried to deny any knowledge of the Koch Brothers, or any working relationship with them. And he got away with it for a while—until he took a private phone call from a man he thought was David Koch. On the other end of the line, however, was not David Koch, but Ian Murphy, editor of a Web site out of Buffalo, New York, called The Beast.

When he read one Democratic state senator's complaint that Walker would not take or return any phone calls, Murphy wondered whose call he might take. The answer was obvious: One from a Koch Brother! So Murphy called the governor's office, announced himself as David Koch, talked his way past a couple of aides, and snagged an appointment for a conversation with the governor himself a couple of hours later. If this was not exactly honest journalism on Murphy's part, the results were clearly embarrassing for Walker.

In his twenty-minute phone call, which Murphy dutifully recorded and published, Walker admitted working with AFP president Tim Phillips on bringing supporters to Madison, revealed plans to try to trick fourteen Democratic senators into returning to Wisconsin by promising to "talk" to them and then locking them in, and admitted he was coordinating his efforts closely with those of John Kasich of Ohio, Rick Scott of Florida, and Brian Sandoval of Nevada as part of a nationwide campaign to destroy public-employee unions. At the end of the call, "Koch" offered, "Once you crush these bastards, I'll fly you out to Cali and really show you a good time." Walker leaped at the chance. "All right, that would be outstanding!" he replied.

By this time, Walker had lived up to his reputation as a "Koch whore." This was even more evident when it was revealed that his union-busting legislation also contained a provision—totally unrelated to the budget—that would allow the state to sell or contract out management of state-owned heating, cooling, and power plants without getting bids or seeking approval of the Wisconsin Public Service Commission. Surprise, surprise: The company best poised to take advantage of that opportunity, and make millions of dollars in the process, was Koch Industries!

The Koch Brothers could no longer deny their leading role in the campaign to destroy unions in Wisconsin and other states, so they finally switched to another tactic typical of the right wing: playing the victim. In an op-ed published in the *Wall Street Journal,* Charles Koch complained, "Because of our activism, we've been vilified by various groups." And Richard Fink, executive vice president of Koch Industries, told the National Review Online, "There are serious fiscal issues at play in Wisconsin. Yet our opponents are injecting us falsely into this story."

But, they vowed, there would be no backing down. "We support Governor Walker, along with numerous other governors, who are trying to deal with the fiscal crises in their states," said Fink, echoing the pledge made by his boss in the *Wall Street Journal*: "We're determined to keep contributing and standing up for those politicians, like Wisconsin Gov. Scott Walker, who are taking these challenges seriously."

Walker finally managed to get his antiunion legislation through the legislature, with no Democratic votes. But that wasn't the end of the road for him—or the Koch Brothers. Outraged public employees and their supporters organized recall campaigns against six Republican state senators who had voted for Walker—all six of whom received substantial financial support from the Koch political machine.

During the six months leading up to the August 9, 2011, recall elections, Wisconsin was awash in outside campaign contributions. According to the Wisconsin Democracy Campaign, a total of $3.75 million was spent on all legislative or statewide races in 2010. In 2011, $35 million was spent on just six recall campaigns, over half of it provided by Koch-funded front groups like Americans for Prosperity, Citizens for a Stronger America, and The Club for Growth.

Not only that, Americans for Prosperity was charged with sending out fraudulent absentee ballot forms to 10,000 Democratic voters—instructing them to send their ballots to the wrong address by August 11, two days after the actual primary date. AFP claimed that the error was an unintentional printing mistake. In the end, Democrats won two out of six contests. And the Republican advantage in the state senate was cut from 19–14 to 17–16.

Meanwhile, the Koch Brothers political juggernaut rolled on. Koch knows, such is politics, that as long as they keep making such generous contributions, there will always be politicians who will roll over for them. But even the Koch Brothers needed the help of a few friends to fatten the political kitty.

CONSPIRING TOGETHER

I began this chapter with mention of the Koch Brothers corporate confab at Palm Springs in January 2011. It was the first of their meetings to attract any national publicity, but not the first one held.

Koch Industries began its tradition of annual seminars in Chicago in 2003, when Charles decided to pull together some like-minded corporate donors for a high level powwow. His goal, explained right-hand man Richard Fink, was "to organize people interested in market issues, explain what was at stake, and suggest ways the participants could promote free enterprise." Fifteen people showed up.

It wasn't long before Koch started holding his seminars twice a year. Again, his purpose was not so much education as fundraising. In May 2006, he told Stephen Moore of the *Wall Street Journal* that he used the seminars to recruit "captains of industry" who would "help fund free-market groups devoted to protecting the fragile infrastructure of liberty"—meaning the conservative infrastructure of front groups, political campaigns, think tanks, and media outlets he and his brother David were building.

For, speakers at their seminars, the Koch Brothers reached out not only to "captains of industry"; they also recruited prominent public and political figures, including Supreme Court Justices Antonin Scalia and Clarence Thomas, both of whom showed up at their January 2008 meeting in Palm Springs. Which turned out to be a problem for both justices. Common Cause later filed a formal request with the Justice Department to determine whether or not Thomas and Scalia had, in fact, attended Koch-sponsored events—and, if so, whether they should have recused themselves when the Supreme Court later considered the campaign-finance case *Citizens United*.

Attendance at the event represents a particular difficulty for Thomas. His office told reporters he had made only "a brief stop-by" at the Koch retreat and given a talk. His financial disclosure reports for that year, however, reveal that the Federalist Society, a conservative legal group, had reimbursed him for four days of "transportation, meals, and accommodations" that same weekend in Palm Springs—which should have been reported under federal law but was not. Four days is no "brief stop-by," especially when you consider that Thomas was featured in promotional materials for Koch events.

Also troubling was the fact that, while Thomas reported no income from his wife, Virginia, she had, in fact, been paid hundreds of thousands of dollars from conservative organizations over the years, including approximately $700,000 from the Heritage Foundation between 2003 and 2007.

Whatever happens to the legal challenge by Common Cause, both Thomas's and Scalia's actions clearly suggest a possible conflict of interest, if not an actual conflict of interest, due to their appearance at an event sponsored by the same corporate interests that would soon benefit from the *Citizens United,* decision, which allows unlimited and anonymous contributions by corporations to political candidates.

One year later, in January 2009, the Koch meeting featured a debate between Senator Jim DeMint and Senator John Cornyn on whether Republicans should support extreme right-wing, or Tea Party, candidates for the Senate, or more moderate, middle-of-the-road candidates. In that crowd, DeMint carried the day—as did Tea Partiers themselves in the midterm elections in 2010.

But if conservative Supreme Court justices or top Republican senators were the stars at earlier Koch Brothers retreats, right-wing journalists and businessmen were the major attraction at their June 2010 summit at the St. Regis, a resort in Aspen, Colorado—called expressly to plot and coordinate strategy for the midterm elections.

The list of attendees at this meeting, first reported by Think-Progress, reads like a who's who of the anti-Obama business community. Assembled at the St. Regis were 210 titans of American business, representing every industry opposed to actions taken or proposed by the Obama administration: oil and coal companies, which wanted to reverse Obama's plans for alternative energy; utilities, lined up against any regulation of greenhouse gases; banks and financial institutions, eager to overturn his Wall Street reforms; and insurance companies, pushing for repeal of health-care reform.

Also joining them were Republican campaign consultants and representatives of several Koch-funded think tanks. Other heavy hitters included David Chavern, the number-two man at the U.S. Chamber of Commerce, and Fred Malek, the principal fundraiser for Karl Rove's American Crossroads organization. The lead item on the agenda was how to take advantage of new opportunities afforded by the Supreme Court's recent *Citizens United* ruling.

Companies who brought their checkbooks to the table included the Bechtel Group, the Fluor Corporation, Amway, Gulf Stream Petroleum, Georgia-Pacific, Laredo Petroleum, BHP Petroleum, the Cintas Corporation, Home Depot, the Murfin Drilling Company, the Blackstone Group, Circuit City, Wells Fargo, the Ward Petroleum Corporation, and the Ariel Corporation. And they were obviously in a generous mood. In a follow-up memo, Charles Koch reported that participants in the Aspen conference "committed to an unprecedented level of support." Which certainly proved to be true. The Koch Brothers raised thirty million dollars at their Aspen meeting—which they matched, as pledged, with thirty million of their own. All of the funds raised were used to fuel activities of the Obama Hate Machine.

But no wonder attendees pledged so much money in Aspen. Because also present at the St. Regis was a star lineup of right-wing journalists and commentators—all flown there first-class and given luxurious quarters and a fat speaking fee—to help persuade corporate chieftains to part with their cash. A couple of them were already indirectly on the Koch payroll. Among the conservative scribes willing to suck up to the Koch Brothers:

- Charles Krauthammer: columnist for the *Washington Post* and regular commentator on Fox News
- Stephen Moore: member of the editorial board of the *Wall Street Journal,* frequent contributor to CNBC, and former fellow of the Koch-founded Cato Institute
- Michael Barone: columnist for the *Washington Examiner* and senior fellow at the American Enterprise Institute, as well as a contributor to Fox News
- Ramesh Ponnuru: senior editor for *National Review,* perhaps best known for his 2006 book about the Democratic party, *The Party of Death*

- Tim Carney: senior political columnist for the *Washington Examiner* and former editor of the "Evans-Novak Political Report" (according to ThinkProgress, Carney received fifty thousand dollars from the Koch-funded ISI Enterprise Award, another fifty thousand dollars from the Koch-funded Phillips Foundation, and once served as a paid fellow at the Koch-funded Competitive Enterprise Institute)

The biggest media star to show up and pimp for the Kochs that year was then Fox talk-show host Glenn Beck, who was more than just an invited guest. He was a true believer. Like Charles and David Koch, Beck was also a disciple of Austrian economist Friedrich von Hayek's theories about unfettered capitalism. He promoted von Hayek's book *The Road to Serfdom* so heavily on his TV and radio shows that it soared to the top of paperback sales on Amazon.com—not bad for a dry economic treatise published in 1944! Beck also shared the Koch Brothers' skepticism about global warming. As recounted by Jane Mayer in *The New Yorker*, in the middle of one segment refuting Al Gore's teachings on climate change, Beck paused to tell his audience, "I want to thank Charles Koch for this information."

The fact that right-wing media personalities were willing to travel so far and pocket money from the very interests they defend on the air every day didn't just come close to crossing the line between journalism and prostitution; it was way over the line. Had any left-leaning journalists done the same for George Soros, let's say, conservatives would have demanded their heads on a platter.

But again, no matter how powerful the people who attended and no matter how much money was raised, all Koch seminars took place way, way below the radar. They were closed to the public and members of the media (except for invited sympathetic pals). Nobody ever heard of these high-powered summits until

January 2011 at Rancho Las Palmas Resort and Spa in Rancho Mirage, California.

This was billed as the most important Koch event so far. After all, Republicans had scored big-time in November 2010, winning control of the House of Representatives and taking eleven governorships back from Democrats. They were poised to gain seats in, if not control of, the Senate in 2012. And, most important, flush with victory, they sensed an opportunity to deny Barack Obama a second term as president.

Hence the urgent message that began Charles Koch's September 24 letter of invitation: "If not us, who? If not now, when?"

For Koch, this was Armageddon. He told corporate leaders that he needed their help in Rancho Mirage "to combat what is now the greatest threat to American freedom and prosperity in our lifetimes." He reminded them that they were "under attack by the current Administration and many elected officials." He asked them to help "develop strategies to counter the most severe threats facing our free society and outline a vision of how we can foster a renewal of American free enterprise and prosperity."

But he also warned potential attendees not to come to Rancho Mirage expecting a good time. "Our ultimate goal is not 'fun in the sun.' This is a gathering of doers who are willing to engage in the hard work necessary to advance our shared principles. Success in this endeavor will require all the help we can muster." And, he might have added, all the money I can squeeze out of you.

As always, major corporate donors responded to Koch's call and showed up in droves at the Las Palmas Resort. So did newly installed House majority leader Eric Cantor and House Budget Committee chairman Paul Ryan, seeking support for his plan to end Medicare and Medicaid. Among other prominent guests were pizza king and wanna-be presidential candidate Herman Cain, Home Depot founder Ken Langone, Republican lobbyist Nancy Pfotenhauer, and Amway cofounder Richard DeVos.

What the Koch Brothers didn't count on, as recounted above, were the uninvited guests who met them at the gate. Arriving at the resort, the Brothers and their corporate buddies were met by hundreds of protestors organized by Common Cause and Code Pink, waving signs like KOCH KILLS and chanting "David and Charles Koch: Your corporate greed is making us broke." TV cameras recorded the scene. And overhead flew a blimp commissioned by Greenpeace, with photos of David and Charles and the words "Koch Brothers: Dirty Money."

For a while, at least, the sudden publicity rattled the Koch Brothers. They had earlier hired special investigators to find out who had leaked notice of the event to ThinkProgress. They hired extra security outside the hotel in Rancho Mirage and discouraged curious donors from walking outside to watch the protests.

Inside the hotel, Koch security canceled the reservation of Common Cause official Gary Ferdman and forced him to move out. They threatened to arrest Ken Vogel, a reporter for Politico, when he stopped by the registration desk and started asking questions. The Kochs also recruited a "crisis communications team"—led by former McCain campaign staffer Michael Goldfarb and seasoned Capitol Hill press secretary Ron Bonjean—to spin members of the media who came to Rancho Mirage to cover the protests. There was nothing secret or sinister going on inside, they insisted. This was just an innocent gathering of "some of America's greatest philanthropists and job creators."

No, this was a meeting of the Obama Hate Machine! And another successful one, at that. Corporations in attendance at Rancho Mirage pledged $49 million for the 2012 anti-Obama campaign.

Once in the public spotlight, however, the Koch Brothers didn't shy from publicity. They seemed to relish it. As we have seen, they popped up in Wisconsin to support embattled governor Scott Walker. Charles Koch wrote an op-ed piece in the *Wall Street Journal* defending their political agenda, under the title

"Why Koch Industries Is Speaking Out." On Wednesday, April 6, 2011, Tea Partiers held a rally in front of the U.S. Capitol to support Republican efforts to shut down the government if President Obama didn't agree to $100 billion in additional cuts in the 2011 budget. And a parade of far-right members of Congress, led by Minnesota's Michele Bachmann, showed up to throw red meat to the crowd.

The next morning, the *Washington Post* featured a color photo of one of the speakers, Bob Goodlatte of Virginia, at the podium. On the front of the podium, proudly displayed, was the name of the sponsoring organization: Americans for Prosperity.

In June 2011, the Koch Brothers gathered their millionaire buddies together again to plot, plan, and write big checks for Republican candidates. This time, they met for a much more low-key summit in Vail, Colorado. Prominent guests included Virginia governor Bob McDonnell, Florida governor Rick Scott, New Jersey governor Chris Christie, Texas governor and future presidential candidate Rick Perry, and Virginia attorney general Ken Cuccinelli, who is leading the national legal challenge to President Obama's health-care-reform program. No Supreme Court justices were on the program. Evidently, Clarence Thomas and Antonin Scalia had previous commitments.

ENJOYING THEIR SHARE OF THE SPOILS

He sure can preach when he wants to.

In his *Wall Street Journal* op-ed piece mentioned above, Charles Koch railed against corporations that accepted government handouts. "Government spending on business only aggravates the problem," he observed, while lamenting the level of national debt. "Too many businesses have successfully lobbied for special favors and treatment by seeking mandates for their products, subsidies (in the form of cash payments from the government), and regulations or tariffs to keep more efficient competitors at bay."

For companies to accept such favors from government was wrong, Koch argued. "Crony capitalism is much easier than competing in an open market. But it erodes our overall standard of living and stifles entrepreneurs by rewarding the politically favored rather than those who provide what consumers want."

There's only one problem with Charles Koch getting up on a pedestal and preaching against "crony capitalism." Because the truth is, when it comes to currying government largesse, few are more guilty of it than Charles Koch himself.

Indeed, that's the supreme irony behind the Koch Brothers' extended political empire. While they have assembled an army of think tanks and so-called grassroots organizations to fight big government, they are also first in line to take whatever big government handouts they can lay their hands on. No matter what their rhetoric says about too much government, when it comes to enjoying their share of the spoils, they are like pigs with all four feet in the trough.

As first reported by Yasha Levine and Mark Ames in *Playboy*, Georgia-Pacific, wholly owned by Koch Industries, depends on taxpayer-built roads constructed by the U.S. Forestry Service to access virgin-grown forests. Another Koch operation, Matador Cattle Company, takes advantage of a New Deal program to graze cattle on federal lands for free.

During the George W. Bush administration, Koch Industries was awarded a lucrative contract to supply the Strategic Petroleum Reserve with eight million barrels of crude oil. Even though the Koch oil company is a relatively small one, it also landed significant contracts to buy crude oil from Iraqi oil fields.

Koch Industries is also expected to benefit from various levels of government assistance in building the Keystone XL Pipeline, which will connect Koch-owned tar sands–mining operations in Canada to Koch-owned refineries in Texas. Much of the right-of-way for the pipeline was obtained by state exercise of eminent domain. The Kansas legislature has granted the pipeline a ten-year property-tax exemption, a special corporate favor that will cost Kansas taxpayers fifty million dollars in revenue.

According to ThinkProgress, Koch Industries has also received $85 million in contracts from federal agencies, mainly the Department of Defense. It also, of course, like other energy companies, benefits from billions of dollars in tax subsidies for oil and ethanol production.

Even after creating the Tea Party and directing its attacks against President Obama's health-care-reform legislation, once the bill was passed, Koch Industries, eager for another free lunch, applied for health-reform subsidies provided under the law. No, they have no shame.

However, the fact that the Koch Brothers do not hesitate to suck at the public teat, while condemning others for it, should really come as no surprise. When you look at it closely, it's apparent that even their so-called philanthropy is entirely self-serving.

GOD HELPS THOSE WHO HELP THEMSELVES?

No doubt, Charles and David Koch hope someday to join the pantheon of great and revered American philanthropists. But no matter how much money they give away, they're never going to make it. There's one simple reason they won't. Yes, the Kochs—David in particular—have given millions to the arts and cancer research, but, unlike Andrew Carnegie, who used his fortune to build 2,509 public libraries, 1,689 of them in the United States, unlike John D. Rockefeller, who built the University of Chicago, Rockefeller University, and established the Rockefeller Foundation to fund medical research, education, and scientific research, and unlike David Packard, who left behind the great Monterey Bay Aquarium and the Children's Hospital at Stanford University, it seems like pretty much every dollar that Charles and David Koch have given, through their foundations, to organizations involved with public policy has been spent in pure self-interest, trying to improve their bottom line.

Impressed by his example of philanthropy, a young John D. Rockefeller once wrote to Andrew Carnegie, "The time will come when men of wealth will more generally be willing to use it for the good of others." Charles and David Koch, men of enormous wealth, have chosen instead to use their vast resources solely for their own good.

In this chapter, I have mentioned a few of the many organizations created and funded by the Koch machine. They range from think tanks to research organizations to political organizations to organizations whose purpose is to craft model legislation. They number in the dozens. But they all have one thing in common: They are all part of the same agenda. Every one of them, whatever its special angle, was created to attack workers' rights, support total, unfettered capitalism, and promote deregulation, especially when it comes to any attempts by the government to curb global warming.

The Cato Institute, for example, the first and still most important Koch-built institution, leads the field in planting seeds of doubt about global warming and opposing any congressional or state efforts to reduce greenhouse-gas emissions. That's money in the bank for the big-polluting Koch oil refineries and power plants.

The Mercatus Center, at George Mason University, is funded as a tax-exempt research operation. But its main mission seems to be attempting to weaken the EPA's authority to regulate air and water pollution—thereby preventing the EPA from cracking down on Georgia-Pacific's paper mills.

Americans for Prosperity and FreedomWorks are, supposedly, two grassroots organizations, creators and chief funding sources of the Tea Party. But notice the only issues they get involved in: opposing Obama health care, opposing Obama climate legislation, opposing Obama campaign-spending reforms, opposing

Obama budget proposals. If it doesn't affect Koch Industries' bottom line, you won't find the Tea Party, Americans for Prosperity, or FreedomWorks involved.

And the Koch Brothers do all of this, remember, through tax-exempt foundations. In fact, they target their public-policy philanthropy so narrowly and so much to their own advantage that some have questioned the legality of their enterprise, given IRS rules and regulations. By law, tax-exempt foundations must support exclusively nonpartisan activities that serve the "public welfare," not the political agenda of their founders.

As Mayer reports in *The New Yorker,* a 2004 report of the National Committee for Responsive Philanthropy blasted activities of the combined Koch foundations as being entirely self-serving: "These foundations give money to nonprofit organizations that do research and advocacy on issues that impact the profit margin of Koch Industries." And, they could have added, American taxpayers should not give them a tax break for fueling their own partisan political machine.

Mayer also quotes one environmental lawyer who has tangled with the Mercatus Center over EPA issues. He calls it "a means of laundering economic aims." And he explains how it works: "You take corporate money and give it to a neutral-sounding think tank." Then the think tank turns around and uses that tax-exempt money to hire people "with pedigrees and academic degrees who put out credible-seeming studies. But they all coincide perfectly with the economic interests of their funders." And that describes the Koch Brothers in a nutshell.

AMERICA'S SPECIAL-INTEREST POLITICAL JUGGERNAUT

Complaining about the political abuse directed his way, the legendary Chicago mayor Richard J. Daley once complained, "They have vilified me. They have crucified me. Yes, they have even criticized me."

Charles and David Koch might say the same thing. Crucified? Maybe not. But they have been vilified. They have been criticized. They have been accused of breaking the law. Nevertheless, you can't deny that they have not only survived all the attacks but have emerged as the single most powerful force in American politics today—and Barack Obama's most potent enemy.

Rob Stein, a brilliant political strategist who researched the Lewis Powell model and founded the Democracy Alliance to counteract it from the Left, describes the Kochs as "the epicenter of the anti-Obama movement"—and of the broader antiprogressivism movement.

Bob Edgar, a former Democratic congressman from Pennsylvania, now president of Common Cause, sees a similar threat. "This is a dangerous moment in American history," he told the *New York Times,* citing the Kochs' capacity to hide their corporate welfare behind a facade of phony grassroots political organizations. "It is not that these folks don't have a right to participate in politics," he explained. "But they are moving democracy into the control of more wealthy corporate hands."

Like every other big corporation, Koch Industries makes its political contributions to candidates directly through its political action committee, or Koch PAC. And those contributions are significant. Using data compiled by the Center for Responsive Politics, the Oil Change International Web site created an offshoot site called Dirty Energy Money. It listed total contributions to members of Congress by Koch PAC from 1999 through 2010 as $4,665,104. Those checks went, in various amounts, to 250 congressional candidates, ranging from $237,366 to Republican congressman Todd Tiahrt and $94,650 to Republican senator Pat Roberts, both of Kansas, to $5,000 to Democratic congressman Brian Baird of Washington State. All in all, 84 percent of Koch PAC contributions went to Republicans.

But, in the case of the Koch Brothers, that is only the tip of the iceberg. As we have seen, in addition to campaign contributions made by Koch Industries and its employees through Koch PAC, Charles and David Koch dominate the political process in two other, even more powerful ways: through the many tax-exempt, yet overtly political, groups they fund through their foundations, and through the millions of dollars they contribute to political organizations like Karl Rove's American Crossroads or the U.S. Chamber of Commerce.

At a certain level, corporations have always been part of the political process and have supported political candidates, mostly Republicans. The big difference today is *Citizens United v. Federal Elections Commission*, decided 5–4 by the Roberts Supreme Court on January 21, 2010. Now it's a whole new, wild, and unruly ball game—where anything goes and nobody knows.

Citizens United was not just a random ruling. It was carefully engineered by Chief Justice John Roberts himself as a vehicle for totally dismantling existing limits on corporate campaign contributions. In fact, the case first came before the Court as a routine review of a district court ruling against the political organization Citizens United for violating the McCain-Feingold Act by airing its corporate-sponsored campaign ad "Hillary: The Movie" during the 2008 Democratic primaries. (The full name of the organization, Citizens United Not Timid, was chosen by Republican dirty trickster Roger Stone, mainly for its acronym.) But after an initial hearing on that matter alone, Roberts, long an opponent of restrictions on campaign contributions, saw his opportunity, and ordered all parties to return six months later for a broader debate on campaign-finance laws in general.

The result: the *Citizens United* decision. It wiped out the McCain-Feingold Act, adopted by Congress in 2002, and radically changed campaign contributions in two ways. First, it declared that corporations and unions should be treated the same as individuals under the law—and should therefore be permitted to spend as much as they like to support or defeat candidates for federal office. Second, it affirmed the right of so-called 501(c)(4) organizations to raise money in support or opposition to candidates—without disclosing the names of their donors.

Those two provisions combined opened the floodgates to a tidal wave of secret corporate campaign contributions—far outweighing the ability of ordinary Americans, or even labor unions, to compete.

The bare majority decision prompted a blistering dissent by Justice John Paul Stevens, who made the rare move of insisting on reading his remarks out loud from the bench. He concluded, "At bottom, the Court's opinion is thus a rejection of the common sense of the American people, who have recognized a need to prevent corporations from undermining self government since the founding, and who have fought against the distinctive corrupting potential of corporate electioneering since the days of Theodore Roosevelt. It is a strange time to repudiate that common sense. While American democracy is imperfect, few outside the majority of this Court would have thought its flaws included a dearth of corporate money in politics."

Just six days later, in his 2010 State of the Union address, President Obama made the even rarer move of publicly condemning a Supreme Court decision while members of the Court sat right in front of him. "Last week, the Supreme Court reversed a century of law to open the floodgates for special interests— including foreign corporations—to spend without limit in our elections," he told the nation. "Well, I don't think American elections should be bankrolled by America's most powerful interests, or worse, by foreign entities."

No matter how hard Justice Samuel Alito shook his head in disagreement, the president turned out to be right on the money. The 2010 midterm elections were, in fact, "bankrolled by America's most powerful interests," most likely with some of the funds coming from foreign corporations—and the names of many donors will never be revealed.

Shortly after the midterm elections, the extent of corporate influence in those 2010 elections was spelled out in a report issued by People for the American Way: *Citizens Blindsided: Secret Corporate Money in the 2010 Elections and America's New Shadow Democracy.* It's the first look at post–*Citizens United* electoral politics, and the political picture it paints is frightening to anyone who cares about representative democracy.

Among the report's main findings:

- Outside groups, or so-called super PACs, spent a total of $450 million in the 2010 elections, of which $126 million was, thanks to *Citizens United,* undisclosed.
- In the ninety days remaining before the midterm elections, the twenty largest conservative outside groups ran 144,182 television ads. Seventy-seven percent of the funding for those ads came from organizations that do not disclose their donors.
- Anonymously funded pro-Republican groups outspent their pro-Democratic counterparts by a 6–1 margin. According to the Center for Responsive Politics, eight of the top ten groups that did not disclose their sources of funding directed the bulk of their money to GOP candidates.
- Most super PAC ads were not only for pro-Republican candidates; they were also dishonest. Politifact concluded that "ads from super pacs and other political groups targeting the 2010 midterm election[s] were overwhelmingly spreading exaggerations and falsehoods."

The People for the American Way report profiles sixteen of the biggest super PACs, including the three that, because of the personalities involved, received the most public attention.

- American Crossroads and Crossroads GPS. When he left the White House, Karl Rove didn't leave politics. He just switched to a greener pasture—much greener, in fact. With former RNC

Chair Ed Gillespie, he founded the two Crossroads organizations in direct response to new opportunities created by the *Citizens United* decision. Between the two, they raised and spent $32 million in 2010, most of it through American Crossroads, which, as a 501(c)(4), is not required to disclose its donors.

- Americans for Prosperity. As we have seen, this is the political arm of the Koch Brothers. AFP spent $6 million on campaign ads against Democrats running for Congress in competitive districts. Previously, it had spent $750,000 on an ad claiming that President Obama's "government-run health care" would prove harmful to cancer patients, especially women with breast cancer. In addition, AFP spent $45 million in 2010 on related political campaign activity nationwide.
- U.S. Chamber of Commerce. With a lot of help from their friends, Charles and David Koch, the Chamber spent $32 million on campaign ads in 2010—93 percent of them on behalf of Republican candidates. What's unknown is how much of those funds came from foreign-owned corporations.

Lee Fang of ThinkProgress was the first to note that the U.S. Chamber of Commerce actually raised political funds from two foreign sources: foreign-owned corporations and chapters of the Chamber located in dozens of countries overseas. From available records, we know that the Chamber raised a minimum $885,000 from foreign sources in 2010—and all of those funds were deposited in the same 501(c)(3) trade association account used by the Chamber to pay for political ads. The Chamber refused, however, to provide documentation proving that none of their foreign-source funds were mingled with contributions received from American corporations—which, even after *Citizens United,* would still be illegal.

With the help of the Supreme Court, then, the Koch Brothers'

Hate Machine was off to a strong start in 2010—and it promises to be even more powerful next time at bat. Through all their front groups, Charles and David Koch spent an estimated $45 million attacking Democratic candidates in 2010. After their winter meeting in Rancho Mirage, they pledged to spend $88 million in 2012.

As Ronald Reagan said, "You ain't seen nothin' yet!"

NO MORE "CRONY CAPITALISM"

Which gets us back once again to the warning issued by Charles Koch in his remarkable op-ed in the March 1, 2011, *Wall Street Journal*, quoted above.

Koch himself acknowledges that American corporations today have been able to use their considerable financial clout to win too many concessions from government. It's not good for taxpayers, and it's not good for business, either, says the *Journal*, summing up Koch's article, because "crony capitalism and bloated government prevent entrepreneurs from producing the products and services that make people's lives better."

Following Koch's own logic, it's clear that the massive influence of big corporations on our political process must be curbed immediately. And we need to take a stand against wealthy plutocrats who would subvert the American political system to make themselves even richer. On that point, at least, it seems, we and the Brothers Koch can agree. As Charles Koch himself might say, "If not us, who? If not now, when?"

What's especially sad is the fact that this undemocratic corporate takeover of our political system, led in large part by the Koch Brothers, received so little attention in the media—which was more interested in the latest opinion polls or the wild charges being traded by candidates than in the secret forces flooding the airwaves with an unprecedented number of campaign commercials.

It's sad but not surprising. Because, in many ways, the mainstream media was little more than a partner in crime when it came to the Obama attack squads.

The truth is that even with their huge, secret financial advantage, the various elements of the Obama Hate Machine could never have been so successful without the willing assistance of its chief enabler: the media.

6

THE ROLE OF THE MEDIA

> What do I regret? Well, I regret that in our attempt to estab-
> lish some standards, we didn't make them stick. We couldn't
> find a way to pass them on to another generation.
>
> —WALTER CRONKITE

When the story of the Koch's secret meetings broke in October 2010, you didn't read about it first in the *New York Times* or the *Washington Post*. You didn't hear about it on ABC or NBC or CBS, nor on CNN or MSNBC. And you definitely didn't hear about it on Fox News. In fact, the story was broken by Lee Fang, a smart young blogger for the Center for American Progress, who had been working the Koch beat for months.

Fang's hard work in getting this scoop demonstrates how the Internet and the world of blogging have changed the way news breaks these days. But it also begs the question: How did all of the traditional media outlets miss such an important story? Shouldn't it be news when almost every prominent right-wing corporate donor in the country is meeting in secret—joined by top Republican leaders of Congress, leading conservative jour-nalists and talk hosts, and even justices of the Supreme Court—to undermine the president of the United States?

But even after Fang broke this important story, it didn't make much in the way of news until January 2011. Then the campaign-finance organization Common Cause worked hard to raise awareness of the 2011 Koch meeting and generate the protests discussed in the previous chapter. With protesters on-site at the Koch compound, all of a sudden it was a story. Cameras and newspaper writers flocked to Palm Springs to capture the now-sensational scene. Because, in today's media, a story isn't a story until it's "Made for Television."

To understand the media's considerable role in helping the Obama Hate Machine undermine our president, you first have to understand the lay of the land in the world of media today, and how far the profession has fallen since its glory days. And to explain that, we need to go back a few years.

THE HALCYON DAYS

Believe it or not, there was once a time when journalists were seen as statesmen, and even heroes. After all, every schoolboy in America knows that Superman's day job was a reporter for the *Daily Planet*.

As beloved as Clark Kent was to Metropolis, so was CBS's Walter Cronkite to America. Every night, families gathered around the television to listen to Cronkite tell them the news of the day. Cronkite was widely considered the most trusted man in the nation. And when he delivered his nightly sign-off, "And that's the way it is," America believed him—so much so that when Cronkite famously questioned the Vietnam War effort after the Tet Offensive in 1968, President Lyndon Johnson was rumored to have said, "If I've lost Cronkite, I've lost Middle America." He announced within a month he would not be running for reelection.

Although one can't be certain whether or not it was Cronkite's defection that ultimately brought down Lyndon Johnson, we know for a fact that two newspapermen did just that to his successor, Richard Nixon. The gumshoe detective work of *Washington Post* writers Bob Woodward and Carl Bernstein in uncovering the Watergate scandal was immortalized in our popular culture: first in their book *All the President's Men,* and then in the movie version, where handsome movie stars Robert Redford and Dustin Hoffman played the *Post*'s dynamic duo.

Back then, journalists were considered dogged seekers of truth, men and women who would leave no stone unturned in their quest to find the story. They were the Fourth Estate, the nation's watchdog. They were the ones who stood up for the little guy, who spoke truth to power, let the chips fall where they may. There were journalists like David Halberstam, who exposed the mind-set that led America into Vietnam in his 1972 book, *The Best and the Brightest,* and Edward R. Murrow, who famously questioned the tactics of powerful Wisconsin senator and Red-baiter Joseph McCarthy on his television show *See It Now*—and ended McCarthy's political career.

It is telling that when actor-director George Clooney (the son of a journalist and news anchor) made a movie that enshrined newsmen as heroes again in 2005's *Good Night, and Good Luck,* it told the story of Murrow in black and white. Because, for many of us, those days, indeed, seem a long time ago.

THE DAILY PAPER NO MORE

So what happened? How did journalism fall off its golden pedestal? How did we get from Walter Cronkite to Glenn Beck?

There are many reasons. It would take another entire book to tell the whole story. But perhaps most important, the business of journalism has fundamentally changed over the past forty years—due mainly to new technologies and increased competition.

Thanks to new technologies, media outlets have proliferated. Where once there were only three networks, now there are dozens, even hundreds, of cable-television channels where Americans can get their news. Never again will one anchor carry the audience and have the gravitas of Walter Cronkite, or Chet Huntley

and David Brinkley, due to the sheer fact that the American television audience has by now segmented and segmented again.

The same goes for newspapers. It used to be that families had
access only to the paper delivered to their front door every
morning. That was their window on the world. But now, thanks
to the Internet, men and women in, say, Topeka, Kansas, can go
online and read any paper they desire—the *New York Times* or
the *Washington Post, The Guardian* or the *Jerusalem Post.*

In fact, these Topekans can, with very few exceptions, read
any of these newspapers for free. Or they can just get their news
from a Web site portal or blog, perhaps one that fits their ideo-
logical predispositions, like the Drudge Report or Firedoglake.

In short, there are now more media outlets than ever, fighting
over an evermore distracted and dwindling base of paying customers. This has changed the media ecosystem in many ways.

With so much competition and such a declining revenue
stream, many newspapers have been forced into bankruptcy. At
the very least, they've been forced to lay off large numbers of
their staffs, which has severely diminished the quality of their
reporting. Local newspapers have been hit especially hard, particularly with Web sites like craigslist, eBay, and Monster.com
replacing the classified ads that drove much of local papers' revenue.

Paradoxically, all of this hypercompetition has also led to
consolidation. As newspapers and magazines have gotten into
financial trouble, many of them have been gobbled up by bigger
fish and turned into simple moneymaking schemes rather than
legitimate newspapers. Their local staffs have been cut to the
bone, and they are now just reprint farms for other papers
owned by the same company.

Competition has had other ill effects, as well. With so many
media outlets to choose from, newspapers and cable TV look for
headlines and stories that will grab people's attention. Nuanced
discussion of substantive issues tends to go out the window, and

dramatic conflict and spectacle are the order of the day, particularly if it looks good—or very, very bad—on television. This hyper-competition has also fueled a race to the bottom in terms of what issues the media covers, with tabloid sensibilities leading the way. Everyone knows that sex and violence sells, so that's what media outlets deliver, lest their competitors beat them out of the juiciest stories. Local television news in particular has devolved into a rattling off of every violent crime, fire, or car crash in the area. And at every level, sensationalism now trumps substance across the board.

This focus on the shocking and scandalous impacts political coverage in at least a couple of ways: what's covered and who's covered. It seems hard to believe now, for example, that in Franklin Roosevelt's day, many Americans had no idea the president was physically handicapped. That's because the president's press secretary, Stephen Early, asked journalists not to report this fact . . . and so they didn't. Similarly, John F. Kennedy's many health issues—and private peccadilloes—were kept out of the press as well, on the assumption that they were personal business and did not really constitute news.

For better or worse, this is emphatically not the way things are today, where our political leaders are in the public eye 24/7, and any indiscretion—or even any passing, careless remark—is immediately fired around the world as news on Twitter or Facebook.

It also means that people who would once have been ignored as kooks now get taken seriously as candidates, simply because they say outrageous things or make "good television." One need only remember the inordinate attention Donald Trump received in the spring of 2011, when he was making noises about running for president. No way was he a serious candidate. Everybody knew his candidacy was a joke. Yet because he was Donald Trump and willing to challenge President Obama's birth certificate, he was given time on every network to spout his nonsense—time denied more qualified potential candidates like Mitch Daniels, Jon Huntsman, or Haley Barbour.

WORKING 'ROUND THE CLOCK

Even as media outlets have proliferated, the journalism profession has also been hit hard by another technological development—twenty-four-hour news.

Gone are the days when people expected a daily update on the events of the day, either in the morning or at the news hour. Now, thanks to television, radio, and especially the Internet, the news cycle has accelerated at a breakneck pace. A story breaks on Twitter at 10:00 A.M. and is old hat by the time Brian Williams or Diane Sawyer actually begins the evening newscast. Something happens in Libya or Belgium or Bahrain, and it is instantly transmitted back to homes and workplaces all across America.

In other words, nowadays people expect to get the news immediately, as soon as it happens. And so we have several twenty-four-hour cable news channels, which are ready to run with any story the moment it breaks. Normally, this would be considered a great development for journalism—until you realize that all of these networks now have twenty-four hours of airtime to fill, every hour of every day, whether there's new news or not.

With so much time to fill, cable television has adopted politics as its full-time obsession. Only politics can help it fill twenty-four hours a day, seven days a week. Facts don't matter. If there is no political "news" on a given day, there is no end of political speculation, nor any end of "political strategists" willing to speculate—even though many of them have never walked into a campaign headquarters, let alone worked on a campaign or run for public office.

As Fox News was the first to figure out, it's not enough to report on politics. To be successful, cable news must also take sides. Fox went first. Launched by Rupert Murdoch and Roger Ailes in 1996, it loudly and immediately staked its claim as America's conservative twenty-four-hour Republican party cable channel—ending up today as vehemently anti–Barack Obama as it was passionately pro–George W. Bush back then. People only laughed at its slogan, "Fair and Balanced," because everybody who ever watched it knows Fox is anything but. Indeed, it blows its Hate Obama trumpet from the opening of *Fox & Friends* in the morning to the closing credits of *On the Record*, with Greta van Susteren, late at night.

It took MSNBC seven years to get smart and start to lean left, providing a liberal alternative to Fox News with strong prime-time shows hosted by Chris Matthews, Ed Schultz, Keith Olbermann (for a few years), Rachel Maddow, and Lawrence O'Donnell. Still, unlike Fox News, MSNBC does not totally lean in one political direction. It starts the day with *Morning Joe,* an entertaining conservative/liberal mix, and then provides classic news coverage until Chris Matthews and *Hardball* at 5:00 P.M.

Meanwhile, stuck in the middle and struggling to survive, there's CNN. Back in the days when I was cohost of *Crossfire* and the network also featured *Capital Gang, Inside Politics,* and *The Spin Room,* CNN was far and away number one in political coverage. But CNN lost its edge when it dropped its signature political shows and tried to muddle its way through the middle, without taking sides. In fact, CNN messily fired Lou Dobbs, their one host who did dare to express his opinions, no matter how obnoxious. CNN learned the hard way that in cable television today Americans don't want wishy-washy; they want hard-edged opinion—just what CNN is afraid to deliver.

THE GREEN CHEESE FALLACY

Market segmentation, competition, new technologies, the twenty-four-hour news cycle—all of these developments have irrevocably transformed the way journalism works since "Uncle Walter" addressed the nation every night.

Because of these trends, some of the most successful news outlets today, like Fox and MSNBC, have returned to even older models of journalism—the blatantly partisan papers of Jefferson's and Adams' era, or the fact-free, sensationalistic "yellow journalism" that helped to spur the Spanish-American War—"If you furnish the pictures, I'll furnish the war"—and make William Randolph Hearst a very wealthy man at the turn of the twentieth century.

These may or may not be welcome developments for journalism. But for all the terrible things you can say about Fox News, at least Roger Ailes's baby has the virtue of being honestly dishonest. Nobody at Fox still argues that its "Fair and Balanced" slogan actually reflects what shows up on their air anymore. They no longer pretend to be an impartial news organization.

As I said above, everyone knows Fox News hates President Obama and everything he stands for, and that they go out of their way to attack him whenever possible. They do this to the point of self-parody.

When Barack Obama and his wife, Michelle, bumped fists on the campaign trail in June 2008, a moment that suggested a playful tenderness and camaraderie in their marriage, a Fox News morning host called it a possible "terrorist fist jab."

In November 2010, the president wrote a picture book for children entitled *Of Thee I Sing: A Letter to My Daughters,* which chronicled the life story of thirteen famous Americans from the past. Since one of these thirteen was the Sioux Indian chief Sitting Bull, the Fox News headline screamed "Obama Praises Indian Chief Who Defeated U.S. General."

These are just two examples. There are dozens, even hundreds, more. But here's the problem. Yes, Fox News and right-wing blogs always lead the way in trumpeting, and often making up, charges against Obama. But they'd never get so much traction for their perpetual anti-Obama crusade were it not for the complicity of the rest of the media.

Unwittingly, and almost despite themselves, all of the other networks become part of the Obama Hate Machine by being only too willing to report on or repeat the bogus attacks first seen on Fox, thereby giving them more airtime and more credibility.

This is due to one of the most unfortunate transformations in journalism over the past four decades—one that Democratic strategist and CNN contributor Paul Begala aptly called "the Neil Armstrong principle" during the 2008 election, or, as I like to think of it, the "Green Cheese Fallacy."

"If John McCain and Sarah Palin were to say the moon was made of green cheese," Begala wrote in September 2008, "we can be certain that Barack Obama and Joe Biden would pounce on it, and point out it's actually made of rock. And you just know the headline in the paper the next day would read: 'CANDIDATES CLASH ON LUNAR LANDSCAPE.'

"Why doesn't somebody call Neil Armstrong? He's been there. Or go to the Smithsonian and open the glass case that contains a piece of the moon. The moon is a rock. That's a fact, Jack. . . . Facts ought not be debatable. The media have an obligation to point out when a politician is lying about a matter of fact, but the right-wing attack machine has so cowed some of them you can almost hear them moo."

So true. And why does this happen? Because the media outlets that are still trying to stay "impartial" often do not seem to understand that they are using the term differently from the way newsmen of old did. In Walter Cronkite's day, being impartial meant holding up what politicians said to the truth. If somebody was lying, they would and should get called on it.

But now, unfortunately, members of the "impartial" news media think they are doing their job if they just report on what everyone is saying, whether or not what is being said has any actual basis in fact. In this manner, Republican lies are repeated over and over again by the so-called impartial media, going three or four times around the world before the truth can even get its boots on. And the stating of those known factual errors is defended in the name of the First Amendment—as if the right of free speech includes the right of politicians to tell lies and the right of the media to broadcast them.

A shocking illustration of this disregard for the truth occurred in April 2011, during the debate over funding for the last six months of FY 2011. As part of any agreement, Republicans demanded elimination of any federal funding for Planned Parenthood. And, on the floor of the Senate, Senator Jon Kyl explained why: "You don't have to go to Planned Parenthood to get your cholesterol or your blood pressure checked. If you want an abortion, you go to Planned Parenthood. And that's well over 90% of what Planned Parenthood does."

Wow! Ninety percent of Planned Parenthood's clinic work is abortion? Well, not exactly. It's actually 3 percent. But, when confronted by CNN with the facts, Kyl's office issued an official explanation: The senator's "remark was not intended to be a factual statement, but rather to illustrate that Planned Parenthood, an organization that receives millions in taxpayer dollars, does subsidize abortion."

In other words, Kyl knowingly and deliberately told a lie. And all the networks knowingly and deliberately broadcast it. Only CNN bothered to check and report the facts.

We saw another blatant example of this during the 2008 campaign. At one point, CNN's Anderson Cooper asked frequent contributor Candy Crowley which campaign was telling more lies at that moment, McCain's or Obama's. To any objective observer, the answer was very clearly the McCain-Palin ticket. Nonetheless, Crowley's answer was instructive and telling: "I'm not going to be the one to tell you whether it's equal or not."

She's not? Why not? "I honestly think that voters need to be out there and say, Ok, here's what McCain says, everybody says it's a lie, here are the facts of the matter." Crowley, a damned good reporter and anchor, was shirking her duty. As Greg Sargent of Talking Points Memo correctly pointed out, "If CNN reporters don't think this is their role, whose job is it, then?"

Sadly, the Green Cheese Fallacy is pervasive throughout the contemporary news media. In fact, it is arguably one of the main reasons why we ended up in a protracted war of choice in Iraq. When Bush administration officials told bald-faced lies to journalists about the existence of WMD in Iraq, many, including those at the mighty *New York Times*, never tried to figure out if these claims had any basis in fact. They just wrote down what they heard, and expected Americans to figure out for themselves if any of these claims were true or not.

Looking back on the lead-up to the Iraq War, NBC's David Gregory actually had the temerity to argue that he thought the press had done a good job. How could he make such a case? When bird-dogged by Salon.com's indispensable columnist, Glenn Greenwald, Gregory said in May 2008, "I think there are a lot of critics who think that [in the run-up to the Iraq War] . . . if we did not stand up and say this is bogus, and you're a liar, and why are you doing this, that we didn't do our job. I respectfully disagree. It's not our role."

It is not your role? That would sound ludicrous to a journalist of Cronkite's day. It sounds ludicrous to me, as well! That's precisely their job. But that's how the vast majority of the members of today's so-called impartial news media view their jobs. Whether they are overworked, underpaid, or just plain lazy, far too many members of the media simply act as stenographers today. They repeat what they are told, whether or not it has any basis in reality. I see it happening every day in the White House briefing room.

THE MYTH OF THE LIBERAL MEDIA

One of the reasons journalists repeat these lies so often is because there is nothing that today's self-professed impartial journalists are more afraid of than being branded as part of the "liberal media."

This is an unfortunate trend I covered in my 2001 book, *Spin This!* As I wrote then, whenever somebody asks me about the "liberal media," I say, "You want to meet the liberal media? Here I am!" Now, thanks to MSNBC, thanks to progressive talk radio, and thanks to progressive Internet sites like Firedoglake, Talking Points Memo, Mother Jones, and the Huffington Post, the ranks of self-professed liberals in journalism have grown a little bigger. But liberals are still a minority in the press, in part because Republicans have been gaming the system for decades now.

As William Kristol told *The New Yorker,* "The liberal media were never that powerful, and the whole thing was often used as an excuse by conservatives for conservative failures." Former RNC chairman Rich Bond compared complaints about the liberal media to working the referees at a basketball game. "If you watch any great coach," said Bond, "what they try to do is work the refs. Maybe the refs will cut you a little slack next time."

After decades of abuse, many theoretically impartial media outlets have been battered into submission. They will do anything the right wing wants, just so they don't come across as "liberals."

How else to explain CNN's hiring a right-wing extremist like Erick Erickson, founder of the conservative blog Red State.com, to appear on its network as a political commentator? See, we're not liberals! We have Erick Erickson! Mind you, this is a man who once referred to a Supreme Court justice, David Souter, as "a goat-fucking child molester"—and he's the same man who threatened to take out his wife's shotgun and confront any census worker who appeared at his front door. Imagine a liberal saying anything like that and still holding down a job on a network.

For that matter, how else to explain the long, sad, extended political fifteen minutes of vice presidential candidate Sarah Palin? But we will get to her in a moment.

THE PRESS AND THE PRIMARY

All of these bad habits of the contemporary media—a preference for conflict, substance-free sensationalism, a disregard for figuring out facts, a fear of seeming in any way "liberal"—predated the political rise of Barack Obama. But, as a candidate and as president, he has had to deal constantly with the ugly consequences of this decline in journalism. Because the press has either abdicated or failed in its responsibilities as the Fourth Estate, the Obama Hate Machine has become more powerful than ever. In fact, without the willing role of the American media, the Obama Hate Machine would not exist.

Looking back on the 2008 election, it often seems like the press was a net benefit for candidate Obama. After all, he was the new political superstar, electrifying crowds across the country. *Saturday Night Live* ran a skit in which members of the press gave Obama comfy pillows to rest on rather than asking him tough questions. And we all remember that MSNBC's Chris Matthews told us about the thrill that ran up his leg whenever Obama spoke. Yes, Obama did receive a lot of glowing press coverage. Yet, it's also true that Obama experienced a bumpier road with the press than is originally remembered.

The problems began with the interminably long primary battle between Obama and the woman who would become his secretary of state, Hillary Clinton. As everyone remembers, Obama won a surprise upset in Iowa, but Hillary came roaring back to win New Hampshire. From then on, we had an epic Democratic contest on our hands, and there is nothing the press loves more than a dogfight. The way it was reported at the time, we had a hard-fought, razor-close barn burner of a primary all the way from January to June—and the press ate up every minute of it. Clinton! Obama! Come watch the sparks fly on CNN!

Unfortunately for Hillary Clinton, the raw arithmetic confronting her candidacy told a very different story from the one that was being reported. According to Democratic party rules, unlike the winner-take-all rules in most Republican primaries, the number of delegates won in each state were apportioned by the percentages of the final vote tally each candidate won. Say Hillary Clinton won a state with ten delegates by a 60–40 margin. Instead of winning all ten delegates from that state, she would win six of them, and Obama would win four.

What this meant in practice was that once Obama racked up a delegate lead, which he did early on, Clinton was, for all intent and purposes, drawing dead. Fight as hard as she might—and she did!—there was simply no realistic mathematical way for her to get the delegates she needed to win the nomination.

Unfortunately for Clinton, it seems her campaign manager, Mark Penn, didn't even understand the rules of the contest when formulating his strategy. As *Time*'s Karen Tumulty reported in May 2008, Penn thought as late as 2007 that Hillary could make up the early difference by winning all of California's 370 delegates. "How can it possibly be," asked Clinton insider Harold Ickes—who had earlier written the Democratic party's primary rules—"that the much vaunted chief strategist doesn't understand proportional allocation?"

In any case, Clinton's campaign was in deep trouble after Super Tuesday in early February, when she failed to land a knockout blow. By mid-February, Obama had a lead of over one hundred delegates, and some members of the Clinton campaign conceded to the *New York Times*'s Adam Nagourney that they would most likely never be able to catch up. When Texas and Ohio voted on March 4 and Clinton did not win by the overwhelming margins she needed to be viable again, the Democratic primary was, for all intent and purposes, over. As they say, "nothin' left but the cryin.'"

And, yet, with very few exceptions, like MSNBC's then delegate guru Chuck Todd, much of the press continued for several months thereafter to act as if the Democratic primary was still up in the air. After all, it filled the twenty-four-hour-news cycle nicely. And besides, the Clinton campaign said publicly many times over that their campaign was still winnable, even if, mathematically, it wasn't. As Candy Crowley and David Gregory have reminded us, who are journalists to decide whether or not such self-serving statements are factually correct?

Now, I thought Hillary was a good candidate and believe she would have made an outstanding president. I voted for her in the primary. And if she wanted to go the distance, that was her prerogative. But that doesn't mean the press should have taken her campaign's statements at face value and simply repeated them without qualification for viewers and readers.

To be fair, Clinton was by no means spared the vicissitudes of the press corps, either. Wherever there was an opportunity to highlight a conflict for sensationalist purposes, the press jumped on it—as when, during the lead-up to the South Carolina primary, every word out of Bill Clinton's mouth was somehow parsed and reported as "playing the race card."

In fact, both candidates had to deal with the broken press throughout the Democratic primary. For its part, the Obama campaign had to consistently push back against the "impartial" media pushing forth right-wing talking points. For example, CNN, ABC, and, of course, Fox News all reported on the "controversy" surrounding Obama's decision not to wear a flag pin. (MSNBC's Chuck Todd correctly called this "the media getting a classic case of the Drudges.")

CNN's Josh Levs, meanwhile, spoke darkly of the "rumors" surrounding Obama's "patriotism." (Gee, where do you think those rumors started?) In a February 2008 debate, the late Tim Russert kept questioning Obama about an endorsement recently given by Louis Farrakhan—without mentioning that Obama had already denounced Farrakhan's "unacceptable and reprehensible" comments, this in the very article Russert was reading from.

Others in the impartial media began to ridicule the adulation Obama was receiving from his crowds. "Isn't there a natural limit to our enthusiasm for this kind of sweeping phenomenon?" whined John Dickerson of Slate. "There was something just a wee bit creepy about the mass messianism," wrote ostensibly liberal pundit Joe Klein, while ABC's Jake Tapper talked of Obama supporters' "Helter-Skelter, cult-ish qualities."

It is hard to pick a moment when press coverage of the Democratic primary hit its nadir, but it might well have been during a debate between Barack Obama and Hillary Clinton hosted by ABC News in April of 2008 and anchored by Charlie Gibson and George Stephanopoulos. To the shock and disgust of many Democrats watching, the two highly-respected anchors spent almost the entire first hour of the debate forcing Obama to respond to discredited right-wing talking points.

The questioning began with Charlie Gibson's asking Obama if he really believed, as he had said ten days earlier in San Francisco, that working-class Americans were bitter and clung to their guns and religion. Stephanopoulos later rationalized that as the starting point for the debate by noting, "When these comments from Senator Obama broke on Friday, Senator McCain's campaign immediately said that it was going to be a killer issue in November." But that didn't mean that ABC had to take its marching orders from the McCain campaign.

The questioning then moved on to Jeremiah Wright. Stephanopoulos asked in a follow-up, "Do you think Reverend Wright loves America as much as you do?" And later: "Do you believe he is as patriotic as you are?"

Then, finally, both anchors moved to "serious" issues: flag la-

pel pins! Charlie Gibson first played videotape of a question submitted ahead of time and selected by ABC executives, over all
other issues, as worthy of the first voter question to Obama:
"Senator Obama: I have a question, and I want to know if you
believe in the American flag." After acknowledging that Obama,
in fact, was wearing an American flag pin on his lapel, Charlie
Gibson still pressed further: "How do you convince Democrats
that this would not be a vulnerability?"

Obama avowed that he "revered" the American flag and went
on at length to establish his American bona fides. But that wasn't
enough. George Stephanopoulos felt compelled to pounce next
to "a follow-up on this issue, the general theme of patriotism in
your relationships." His question, of course, was about the right-
wing's favorite, and so beat-to-death straw man, William Ayers.
"Can you explain that relationship for the voters, and explain to
Democrats why it won't be a problem?"

At this point, a rightfully exasperated Obama sighed and
said, "The notion that somehow as a consequence of me knowing somebody who engaged in detestable acts 40 years ago, when
I was 8 years old, somehow reflects on me and my values doesn't
make much sense, George." Indeed, it didn't make any sense at
all, until Stephanopoulos later admitted the Ayers question had
been suggested by none other than Sean Hannity.

While the questioning, for the most part, turned to real, honest-
to-goodness issues after that, Charlie Gibson continued to use
right-wing talking points to frame questions put to both Democratic candidates. On taxes, Gibson defended the Republican
mantra of cutting taxes for the wealthiest of Americans: "Those
are a heck of a lot of people between $97,000 and $200[,000] and
$250,000. If you raise the payroll taxes, that's going to raise
taxes on them." And when the discussion turned to gun control,
Gibson tried hard to get Obama and Clinton to admit, as right-
wingers claimed, that, given the chance, they'd gladly take everyone's firearms away. Both declined the opportunity.

Even by the low standards we've grown accustomed to from the media, ABC's debate was judged a disaster. Josh Marshall of Talking Points Memo deemed it "genuinely awful." As Todd Beeton of the progressive site MyDD put it, "I feel like taking a shower after that debate. It was tabloid hour on ABC, and certainly Obama did get the bulk of the more disgusting questions." And Greg Mitchell, editor of *Editor & Publisher,* called the evening "perhaps the most embarrassing performance by the media in a major presidential debate in years. . . . [Gibson, Stephanopoulos,] and their network, should hang their collective heads in shame."

Even right-wing pundit Jonah Goldberg of *National Review* had to concede that ABC was doing their dirty work. "I'm no left-wing blogger," he wrote, "but I can only imagine how furious they must be with the debate so far. Nothing on any issues. Just a lot of box-checking on how the candidates will respond to various Republican talking points come the fall. Now I think a lot of those Republican talking points are valid and legitimate. But if I were a 'fighting Dem' who thinks all of these topics are despicable distractions from the 'real issues,' I would find this debate to be nothing but Republican water-carrying."

When Jonah Goldberg comes across as the voice of reason, you know you're in trouble. But in this case, he was absolutely correct.

Then again, it was hardly the first time the media had agreed to carry water for Republicans—especially when the Republican happened to be media darling John McCain.

RIDING THE TIRE SWING

While Obama and Clinton were slugging it out in Ohio and Texas in late February, many political reporters took the opportunity to spend a day at a barbecue held by Republican candidate John McCain, who at that point was very close to sewing up the GOP nomination. Here is the first paragraph of the hard-hitting dispatch filed about that incident by *Time* magazine's Holly Bailey:

> There are worse ways to spend a sunny Sunday afternoon than swinging lazily back and forth on a tire swing strung up under a massive sycamore tree in a quiet Arizona canyon, the sound of a gushing stream nearby. Almost grazing the ground and hung on rope that looked to have been tied and retied again over the years, the swing belonged to John McCain, who stood several dozen yards away, carefully monitoring giant slabs of pork ribs on a smoking grill.

How appropriate! A collection of journalists is given a chance to spend a day with one of the three most likely candidates to be the next president of the United States—and the only person doing any grilling is John McCain.

"Reporters were given surprisingly free rein on the McCain property," Bailey continued. "Members of the press were allowed to roam around, availing themselves of the opportunity to take rides on the tire swing and exploring his house, which features a mat outside the door that says, 'Geezer (formerly known as Stud Muffin) Lives Here.'"

Stud Muffin! Yessir! That's the kind of hard-hitting stuff we expect from *Time* magazine. "Riding on the tire swing" quickly became shorthand in blogger circles for this kind of incestuous relationship between journalist and candidate.

And that exemplifies the cozy relationship the senator from Arizona has always enjoyed with the national news media. It started long before his presidential run in 2000, continued for the next eight years (to the total dismay of the Bush White House), and endures today, even after his embarrassing run for president. In fact, the older and crankier John McCain gets, the more airtime he gets.

Here's one more example of the media's love affair with

McCain. Jon Friedman of MarketWatch, who accompanied Mc-
Cain on a senatorial junket in 2005, couldn't disguise his puppy
love:

> At the conference McCain worked hard to show the editors and
> publishers that he is a regular guy. He spent hours shooting
> craps in full view of dozens of fairly stunned (and impressed)
> conference attendees on Sunday night. They cheered him on—
> and he in turn gave vocal encouragement to the other bettors at
> the table. . . . I wished I'd had the presence of mind to hammer
> him on Karl Rove, the Iraq elections or the White House's per-
> formance during the early stages of the Hurricane Katrina di-
> saster. But to tell the truth, McCain was having too much fun
> and so was everyone else to bother with the heavy stuff.

Aw, shucks, don't bug the guy when he's playing craps! He
only wants to be leader of the Free World someday. And who
cares about the "heavy stuff" anyway?

But give McCain credit for this: More than most politicians, he
recognized early on the importance of scratching the media watchdog's tummy and coddling it into submission. I experienced that
firsthand in the 2000 New Hampshire primary, when I joined
other reporters on his campaign bus, "The Straight Talk Express,"
where McCain would hold forth in between town hall meetings
on any topic and on the record. That's why he could proudly tell
Newsweek's Evan Thomas that the media was "his base."

So when Obama finally emerged the undisputed victor in the
Democratic primary, he still had an uphill climb ahead of him
with the media. Looking back just a few years later, it seems almost inevitable that Obama, the rising star, would beat McCain,
the aging war hero. But that wasn't necessarily the case at the
time. In fact, Obama's victory was secured by only two unrelated events in the fall: the frightening Wall Street meltdown in
September—to which McCain cluelessly replied that "the funda-

mentals of our economy are strong"—and his earlier disastrous selection of Governor Sarah Palin of Alaska as a running mate.

In fact, the Center for Media and Public Affairs at George Mason University found that over the first six weeks of the general-election campaign, the networks were much harder on Obama than on John McCain. According to its analysis of television campaign coverage, "Since the primaries ended, on-air evaluations of Barack Obama have been 72% negative (vs. 28% positive). That's worse than John McCain's coverage, which has been 57% negative (vs. 43% positive) during the same time period."

So much for that pro-Obama media bias.

According to a study by the Tyndall Report over that same period, Obama received about twice as much media time as John McCain—but that doesn't mean it was all favorable. As media observer Andrew Tyndall wrote then, "Obama gets more positive coverage, more negative coverage, and more trivial coverage. Who else has stories filed about them on how he shakes hands with his wife? Or whether Jesse Jackson wants to castrate him? Or how he is lampooned on the cover of *The New Yorker*?"

And, of course, that doesn't take into account the extraordinary influence of Fox News, which increasingly over the course of the campaign painted Barack Obama as the most dangerous man ever to run for president. Suddenly facing the prospect of their worst fears come true, Fox unleashed an ugly direct assault on Obama, one that continues unabated to this day.

If you believed what was broadcast on the "Fair and Balanced" network, Obama was a pal and supporter of terrorists. He was a student of radical organizer Saul Alinsky. He was a Muslim in Christian clothing. With his pastor Jeremiah Wright, he advocated the violent overthrow of the U.S. government. His wife, Michelle, had vowed that she and her husband, if successful, would use the powers of the presidency to "bring down Whitey." And Obama himself wasn't even born in the United States, and was therefore ineligible to be president.

None of this barrage of ugly charges was true, of course. But that did not matter to Fox—it is not in the truth business. Unfortunately, efforts by media outlets to get the story right did not improve much even after Obama became president.

LOOKING FOR OUTRAGE

Barack Obama's inauguration in January 2009 was a transcendent moment for America, indeed for the whole world, and the press captured it as such. For the first time in our history, an African-American man was entering the nation's highest office. The press worked hard to capture that clear, chilly January morning in all its glory. It was, and remains, a great American story.

But nature and the press abhor a vacuum, and once Obama was in office, the press needed a new angle. As a party, the Republicans seemed in disarray—so much, in fact, that in May 2009, soon after Arlen Specter defected to the Democrats, *Time* magazine published an article entitled "Republicans in Distress." "These days," wrote *Time*'s Michael Grunwald, "Republicans have the desperate aura of an endangered species."

But the political irrelevance of the GOP was more than just a problem for the Right. It also posed a problem for the national news media, who for so long now had dumbed their mission down merely to repeating what one party said and then what the other said. The result was that in the early days of the Obama administration the so-called impartial media was forced to help fan the flames of opposition to the new president and his agenda—if only to fill their available airtime and stir up a little controversy that might convince viewers to hang around and not disappear for the next four years.

At first, very early in Obama's presidency, the mainstream press decided to follow Fox's lead—race to the bottom?—and see if they could tag the president as a socialist. After all, as we saw earlier, right-wing pundits had been warning for months about

Obama's socialist tendencies. Sure enough, not to be outdone by Fox, *Newsweek* ran a cover story in early February 2009, declaring "We are all Socialists Now." And, in an exclusive interview with President Obama, a reporter for the *New York Times*, arguably the world's greatest newspaper, actually asked him directly if he was, in fact, a socialist. "Are you now, or have you ever been . . . ?"

Stunned by the question, an angry Obama called the *Times* back to set the record straight. "It was hard for me to believe that you were entirely serious about that socialist question," he told them, correctly pointing out that "it wasn't under me that we started buying a bunch of shares of banks. And it wasn't on my watch that we passed a massive new entitlement, Medicare Part D, the prescription drug plan, without a source of funding."

The socialism label was an obvious canard during the 2008 campaign. It was even more so in February 2009. So the press had to start looking elsewhere for headline-generating controversy. Fortunately for them, Americans for Prosperity and other branches of the Koch Hate Machine were just getting ready to unleash their "Astroturf" Tea Party. And former vice presidential candidate Sarah Palin was still eager to get back in the limelight any way she could. An ever-desperate media leaped at both opportunities.

TALE OF THE TEA

The Tea Party started drawing media attention on tax day 2009, when all three network news shows featured stories on the smattering of protests across the country—protests that were heavily promoted by hosts on Fox News. Glenn Beck even headlined the biggest event, held at the Alamo.

But the "movement" really came into its own during the long, hot August of 2009, when Congress took its annual recess— meaning, for cable TV, a long, hot summer of almost no political news. Desperate to fill the void, assignment editors started sending reporters to cover town hall meetings scheduled by members of Congress back home in their districts. These are normally the most boring events imaginable. Two things made a difference that summer. One, they focused mainly on health-care reform, because that was the main issue before Congress at that time. And two, the presence of TV cameras, which helped to create as many protests as they covered.

It reminded me of an experience I had early in my broadcast career, when I was a political commentator on KABC-TV in Los Angeles. Whatever story I was reporting on required a "stand-up" in front of Los Angeles City Hall. When I arrived with my crew, we noticed about two hundred elderly Asian-Americans just sitting quietly on the steps, as if they were waiting for a tour to begin or something. So we piled out of the van, the crew set up the camera, and I grabbed the mike and began my spiel, when suddenly all two hundred people stood up, picked up protest signs they'd been sitting on, and started marching and chanting behind me.

It was an instant protest! Actually, it was a protest in waiting—waiting only for the presence of a TV camera, any TV camera, to make it happen. And so it was with the so-called spontaneous protests of the summer of 2009.

According to the lazy and gullible mainstream media, these protestors were true-blue grassroots activists, direct descendants of the Boston Tea Party participants, and they were flocking to these gatherings enthusiastically and on their own, genuinely angry with big government spending and demanding that Congress "keep government out of their health care."

Enthusiastically? Maybe. On their own? No way.

Now, granted, it was August. And, as I said, Congress was in recess. The president was on Martha's Vineyard with his family. There was no news, yet still twenty-four hours of airtime needed to be filled every day. But that's no excuse. Somebody should have told the truth: that these protests were not "grassroots" protests at all. As we saw in the previous chapter, they were organized by FreedomWorks and Americans for Prosperity, both funded by the Koch Brothers, with additional support from health-care providers and insurance companies banding together to kill President Obama's proposed health-care-reform plan.

The truth was so obvious, but I didn't see one reporter or anchor ask the obvious questions: Why did some of the same protestors show up at town halls in different states? How did they know where they were taking place, in other districts and other states? Who paid for the busses to take them there? And, by the way, since the vast majority of protestors were seniors, how many of those demanding that government get out of their health care were willing to burn their own Medicare cards? After all, Medicare is government health care, and has been since 1965.

Yet, sadly, nobody exposed the truth about the town halls— not the big three networks, certainly not Fox, not CNN, not even MSNBC. They all treated the summer protests as a genuine expression of democracy in action, rather than a diabolically planned and brilliantly executed Republican opposition strategy.

Writing on the Tea Party protests for *Newsweek* that August, historian Rick Perlstein put the blame squarely where it belonged: on the national news media. "Conservatives have become adept at playing the media for suckers," he noted, "getting inside the heads of editors and reporters, haunting them with the thought that maybe they are out-of-touch cosmopolitans." And so these Tea Party protests, while clearly an "orchestration of incivility" organized by right-wing elites, were just as much a creation of the media.

In previous decades, Perlstein argued, "the media didn't adjudicate the ever-present underbrush of American paranoia as a set of 'conservative claims' to weigh, horse-race-style, against liberal claims. Back then, a more confident media unequivocally labeled the civic outrage represented by such discourse as 'extremist'—out of bounds. The tree of crazy is an ever-present aspect of America's flora. Only now, it's being watered by misguided he-said-she-said reporting and taking over the forest."

And take over the forest it did, for a little while at least. Throughout the health-care debate, the press covered every single Tea Party gathering, no matter how large or small, as if it were a meeting of the Founding Fathers.

Sure enough, when between sixty and seventy thousand Tea Partiers descended on the Washington Mall in September 2009 for the "9/12 Rally," it was a huge story, breathlessly covered by the networks, newspapers, and cable news. Yet when 200,000 Americans marched for gay rights on the Mall just one month later, they got almost no coverage. It was the same story for the 200,000 Americans who turned out for reasonable (read: non-Republican) immigration reform in 2010. And look at the media silence that greeted the huge labor protests in Madison, Wisconsin, in the winter of 2011. Curiously enough, only when Americans for Prosperity bussed about one hundred people to stage a counter "Tea Party" protest did the national media deem the protests against Governor Scott Walker's attempt to destroy public-sector unions worthy of airtime.

The determination to cover any Tea Party event like it was major news reached parody levels in March 2011, when organizers announced a massive rally on the National Mall of Tea Partiers from around the country—you know, "Americans just like you!"—to protest a possible budget deal between the Democratic Senate and the Republican House. Fox News even decided to cover the entire event live.

What an embarrassment, then, when only a few dozen people showed up! Various media outlets were reduced to reporting on the "dozens of Tea Party supporters gathered outside the Capitol." *Dozens?* You can get more people at a bar mitzvah. But, to their credit, several news reports did note that there were two reporters present for each protestor. Fox News, meanwhile, stuck with live cameras and blamed the rainy Washington weather for the poor turnout—ignoring the fact that 100,000 protestors turned out in Madison, despite the snow and near-zero temperatures.

It was bad enough when cable channels were misreporting the size or authenticity of Tea Party events. But sometimes it was even worse than that. As reported by Talking Points Memo's Zachary Roth, there were cases where media outlets were not just covering Tea Party events; they were creating them out of whole cloth. In August of 2009, Roth reported, Tea Party Patriots national coordinator, Jenny Beth Martin, posted the following memo to a Tea Party Google group: "We have a media request for an event this week that will have lots of energy and lots of anger. This is for CNBC." In other words: Please, please produce something to fill our dead air!

CNBC may have been the only cable channel to solicit angry protests for their TV cameras to cover (although we can't really be sure.) But all of the media was complicit in helping to foment and legitimatize the Tea Party. In their eagerness to cover this groundswell of anger and acknowledge a powerful new force in American politics, most outlets failed to mention the "Astroturfing" behind the Tea Party events. And even fewer took time to challenge the pure nonsense spewed daily by Tea Party activists.

Throughout the protests of summer 2010, you would see one hundred protestors on the news complaining about how President Obama had raised taxes for average Americans—before anyone would point out that, under Obama's stimulus package, 95 percent of Americans actually got a tax cut! That may sound like campaign rhetoric, but, in fact, it's true.

In his January 27, 2010, State of the Union address, President Obama said, "We cut taxes. We cut taxes for 95 percent of working families. We cut taxes for small businesses. We cut taxes for first-time homebuyers. We cut taxes for parents trying to care for their children. We cut taxes for 8 million Americans paying for college." Obama did so not by sending everyone a check, but by

264 THE OBAMA HATE MACHINE

reducing the amount withheld for Social Security—which meant everyone's payroll tax went down a little bit in the spring of 2009. Politifact immediately jumped on Obama's claim, put it through its fact-check wringer, and reported, "We rate Obama's statement true."

Nevertheless, because the media didn't do its job of reporting the truth—and, frankly, because the Obama administration didn't do a good job of making its case—Obama's tax cut remained one of the biggest secrets of his first term. In February 2010, only 12 percent of Americans knew Obama had actually cut their taxes. Eighty-eight percent were still complaining about a tax hike!

In the same vein, on any given day you could find a dozen right-wing talking heads on TV calling Obama an antibusiness socialist. Yet rarely did any reporter take the time to point out that, in fact, that was a big fat lie. The fact is—forget the politics, the fact is, as documented by the *New York Times*—that U.S. corporate profits hit an all time high at the end of 2010. And financial firms, those rescued by Obama under the TARP bailout of Wall Street, experienced some of the biggest gains. Overall, corporations reported an annualized $1.68 trillion in profit in the fourth quarter of 2010, surpassing the previous record of $1.65 trillion in the third quarter of 2006.

But, of course, investors in the stock market lost their shirts under President Obama. Right? Wrong! In fact, just the opposite is true. Leading up to Obama's State of the Union address in January 2011, the *San Francisco Chronicle* compared market performance during the first two years of the last ten presidents. Granted, the market's only one indicator of the health of the economy, but it's still an important and highly followed indicator. The results, therefore, may surprise you.

- John F. Kennedy—up 6.4 percent
- Lyndon Johnson—up 33 percent

- Richard Nixon—down 8.7 percent
- Gerald Ford—up 26.5 percent
- Jimmy Carter—down 12.7 percent
- Ronald Reagan—up 12.6 percent
- George H. W. Bush—up 17.6 percent
- Bill Clinton—up 19.4 percent
- George W. Bush—down 20.3 percent

And Barack Obama? During his first two years, the market soared 48.7 percent! That's partly a result of how low Bush's policies had taken the economy, of course, but it's also proof that Obama's policies were working and the economy was coming back strong. Bet you never heard that on the Fox Business Channel. And you never heard it from Larry Kudlow on CNBC, either.

In the light of such dramatic results, and such a triumph for capitalism, how could the Koch Brothers continue to paint Obama as the enemy of American business? And how could so many in the media continue to parrot their lies without taking the trouble to discover and report the truth? Because the corporate-funded Obama Hate Machine was in full gear.

Finally, as we've seen and has been reputed elsewhere, Republicans are still, in print and on television, accusing President Obama of engineering a "government takeover of health care," when his plan has no new government component whatsoever. Then, in a brazen display of hypocrisy, they also accused him of trying to undermine Medicare, when House Republicans actually adopted a plan that would destroy Medicare altogether. And the "impartial" media let the charges fly without saying a word about the truth.

In short, 99.44 percent of the Tea Party's talking points were total nonsense—and yet the media refused to call them on it. As Rick Perlstein said in *Newsweek*, "Good thing our leaders weren't so cowardly in 1964, or we would never have passed a civil rights bill—because of complaints over the provisions in it that would enslave whites."

Not only did reporters fail to do their job of exposing Tea Party lies but too often they were more than willing to pile on. After an Obama press conference in March 2009, for example, the Associated Press's Ron Fournier published his analysis, entitled "Teleprompter Telegraphs Obama's Caution"—in which he repeated the by-now-standard Tea Party myth that Obama was the first president to use a teleprompter, when in fact the ubiquitous speech-making device has been used by every president since they were invented. Fournier even called it Obama's "familiar crutch."

As it happens, when it came to spouting nonsense and telling lies, the Republicans had a new rising star. And she was about to come up with a real humdinger. . . . You betcha!

PALIN AND THE DEATH PANELS

Perhaps the only subject the media loved to cover more than the Tea Party itself was its self-anointed queen.

In fact, it was in that Tea Party August of 2009 when former governor Sarah Palin added to the folklore about the health-care-reform debate with her now-famous Facebook entry, worth repeating here: "The America I know and love is not one in which my parents or my baby with Down Syndrome will have to stand in front of Obama's 'death panel' so his bureaucrats can decide, based on a subjective judgment of their 'level of productivity in society,' whether they are worthy of health care. Such a system is downright evil."

That's a total straw man. As I pointed out earlier, nothing even remotely close to "death panels" was contained in the legislation. Nothing. Nada. Zip. She made it up. Or, more likely, somebody made it up for her. It was a total fabrication.

In fact, Palin's "death panel" comment was later singled out by

Politifact.com—the nonpartisan, Pulitzer Prize–winning Truth-O-Meter run by the *St. Petersburg Times,* which I consult often and trust completely—as "the biggest political lie of the year."

If the media had been doing its job, such a bold, outright lie would never have gotten off the ground. Yet Palin's charge, ignited by Fox News, took off like wildfire—recycled nonstop, yet never shot down, by the "mainstream media." Opportunistic right-wingers repeated and amplified on the charge. On ABC's *This Week,* Newt Gingrich told George Stephanopolous, "You're asking us to trust turning power over to the government, when there are clearly people in America who believe in establishing euthanasia." Comparisons were made to Nazi Germany. Suddenly, the White House and Democrats were forced on the defensive as millions of seniors began to fear they might be the next ones hauled before a death panel. And many still believe it.

In a *New York Times* op-ed about his "Near Death-Panel Experience" in November 2009, Democratic representative Earl Blumenauer—who authored the original end-of-life counseling provisions in the bill—argued correctly that "the news media was a particular culprit" in the death-panel drama. "This was not just Fox News," he pointed out. "Seemingly all the national news organizations monitored any meetings they could find between lawmakers and constituents, looking for flare-ups, for YouTube moments. The meetings that involved thoughtful exchanges or even support for the proposals would never find their way on air; coverage was given only to the most outrageous behavior, furthering distorting the true picture."

Blumenauer concluded, "The 'death panel' episode shows how the news media, after aiding and abetting falsehood, were unable to perform their traditional role of reporting the facts. By lavishing uncritical attention on the most exaggerated claims and extreme behavior, they unleashed something that the truth could not dispel."

Of course, most of the media did not even try to absorb this lesson. They just kept on writing stories about whatever ridiculous new thing Sarah Palin had to say, whether or not her insights had any basis in fact. Every inane pronouncement from the Oracle of Wasilla was elevated to the level of newsworthy content—from when she demanded that President Obama "refudiate" the NAACP's criticism of the Tea Party to when she accused journalists of manufacturing a "blood libel" against her, after the tragic shooting of Congresswoman Gabrielle Giffords.

Eventually, in January 2011, *Washington Post* columnist Dana Milbank took that important first step and at least admitted the media had a problem. "I have written about her in 42 columns since Sen. John McCain picked her as his vice-presidential running mate in 2008," he wrote. "I've mentioned her in dozens more blog posts, Web chats, and TV and radio appearances. I feel powerless to control my obsession, even though it cheapens and demeans me. But today is the first day of the rest of my life. And so, I hereby pledge that, beginning on Feb. 1, 2011, I will not mention Sarah Palin—in print, online or on television— for one month. Furthermore, I call on others in the news media to join me in this pledge of a Palin-free February. With enough support, I believe we may even be able to extend the moratorium beyond one month, but we are up against a powerful compulsion, and we must take this struggle day by day." And so Dana Milbank bravely gave up Sarah Palin for a whole month. And he and other political reporters started obsessing over Congresswoman Michele Bachmann instead. This is progress?

THE DUMBING DOWN OF AMERICAN POLITICS

I know, it sounds like an oxymoron to talk about the "dumbing down of American politics." How could it get any dumber?

But, seriously, it didn't always used to be this dumb. I remember being mesmerized by the intelligent speeches of Adlai Stevenson when I was a kid. As a young adult, like millions of others, I was inspired by the wit and wisdom of John F. Kennedy. I got involved in politics out of admiration for Eugene McCarthy. As an adult, I have valued the leadership of Bill and Hillary Clinton, Teddy Kennedy, Joe Biden, Jerry Brown, Nancy Pelosi, Barack Obama, and so many more.

Michele Bachmann doesn't deserve to be in the same room with any of them. And that's not a sexist remark, either! Although I've been accused of that.

Appearing as a guest on CNN's *Reliable Sources* on March 27, 2011, I was asked by host Howard Kurtz why the media was paying so much attention to Michele Bachmann's flirting with running for president when Tim Pawlenty, who had actually announced an exploratory committee for president, was getting no attention at all.

"Because the media really wants her to become a candidate," I responded, "because she's such a laughing stock. I think it's the dumbing down of American politics." At which point, I was immediately accused of making a "sexist" remark by fellow panelists Jennifer Rubin of the *Washington Post* and Jane Hall of American University.

Nonsense! As I shot back to Rubin and Hall, "I don't think it's sexism to say she's not a serious candidate." And she's not. And she's proved it over and over again—almost every time she opens her mouth, in fact.

I credit the Web site BuzzFeed for collecting the craziest things Michele Bachmann has ever said. Here from a long list are a few classic gems:

- "I wish the American media would take a great look at the views of the people in Congress and find out: are they pro-America or anti-America?"

- "I want people in Minnesota armed and dangerous on this issue of the energy tax because we need to fight back."
- "But we also know that the very Founders that wrote those documents worked tirelessly until slavery was no more in the United States."
- "Pelosi is committed to her global warming fanaticism to the point where she has said, she has even said, that she is trying to save the planet. We all know that someone did that 2,000 years ago."
- "This cannot pass. What we have to do today is make a covenant, to slit our wrists, be blood brothers on this thing. This will not pass. We will do whatever it takes to make sure this doesn't pass."
- "And what a bizarre time we're in, when a judge will say to little children that you cannot say the pledge of allegiance, but you must learn that homosexuality is normal and you should try it."
- "If we took away the minimum wage—if conceivably it was gone—we could potentially virtually wipe out unemployment completely because we would be able to offer jobs at whatever level."

Okay, Okay. We could go on and on. But you get the point. She's batshit crazy. Now here's what's really scary: She home-schooled her kids! OMG! Those poor children probably think the American Revolution ended slavery.

Only Michele Bachmann could make Sarah Palin look like a Rhodes scholar. She makes Christine O'Donnell look like a rocket scientist.

I'm sorry, but I'll say it again: She's a laughingstock. She represents the dumbing down of American politics. She should not be taken seriously. And to prove that's not a sexist remark: I don't think Paul Ryan should be taken seriously, either.

A SERIOUS MAN

It wasn't just Michele Bachmann who became the media's new right-wing sweetheart in early 2011.

Unfortunately for America, just as the press was beginning to swear off their heroinlike Sarah Palin addiction, many of them found their new conservative methadone in Wisconsin congressman Paul Ryan.

Mainly by virtue of endlessly repeating trite homilies from the World According to Ayn Rand—Limited government! Don't tax the rich!—every time he was in front of a TV camera, Paul Ryan had already developed a growing reputation in media circles as an intelligent conservative. Which, of course, is not hard when your competition is Sarah Palin, Michele Bachmann, and Glenn Beck. Among conservatives, *intelligent* is a relative term. Or, as they say: In the land of the blind, the one-eyed man is king.

So when, in April 2011, Congressman Ryan published his 2012 budget blueprint, brimming over with imaginary numbers and right-wing talking points, Beltway pundits fell over themselves to praise the man and his new budget like he was Moses carrying the Ten Commandments.

You know Ryan. He's the guy with the "jet black hair and a touch of Eagle Scout to him," gushed *Time* magazine. He's the congressman from Wisconsin with "the piercing blue eyes, love for heavy metal on his iPod and a reputation among Democrats, including President Obama, as a Republican who has put forward budget ideas that are thoughtful and serious," babbled the *New York Times*. And he put forth a budget plan, crowed the normally restrained columnist David Brooks, that is "the most comprehensive and most courageous budget reform proposal any of us have seen in our lifetimes."

And they were hardly alone. *Time*'s Joe Klein called Ryan's plan "without question, an act of political courage." *Newsweek*'s

Fareed Zakaria declared it "courageous." Even self-proclaimed liberal Jacob Weisberg of Slate felt compelled to praise Ryan's plan as "brave, radical, and smart." Weisberg wrote, "[M]ore than anyone else in politics, Rep. Ryan has made a serious attempt to grapple with the long-term fiscal issue the country faces." And Chris Licht, then executive producer of MSNBC's *Morning Joe,* may have summed it all up best when, after Ryan appeared on the program, he whispered in Joe Scarborough's ear, "I'm in love."

Oh, give me a break. Get a hotel room! Or do your job!

As MSNBC's Rachel Maddow pointed out, after denouncing what she called the "smoochy smoochy love bubble" reporters had created around Ryan, "If the Beltway media could stop making out with Paul Ryan long enough to look at what's actually in his budget proposal, they might notice that some of the important numbers in it appear to be made up."

Indeed, the closer you examined Ryan's plan, the sooner you realized there was nothing bold, comprehensive, courageous, or even original about it. It was nothing but a collection of all the recycled, right-wing, rejected Republican policies of the past rolled into one document—most of which are less applicable today than when they were first proposed by Ronald Reagan over thirty years ago.

For a long time, Republicans threatened to get rid of Medicare—even though it's the single most effective program in government today. Ryan finally went over the cliff. He proposed shutting down Medicare as we know it and forcing seniors instead, armed with a voucher that would cover only 32 percent of their health-care needs, to go shopping for the best health-care deal they could wrangle out of private insurance companies.

Ryan proposed shutting shut down Medicaid, too, by turning the whole program over to states—and we all know how flush states are with cash these days. He also called for repeal of Obama's health-care-reform plan, even though the Congressional Budget Office concluded that repeal would actually add $230 billion to the deficit over the next decade. Two-thirds of Ryan's projected cuts, in fact, came from programs serving the middle class and the poor—while he proposed no cuts at all in the massive Pentagon budget.

As for new sources of revenue, there weren't any. In true Tea Party fashion, Ryan pretended we could get rid of the deficit by budget cuts alone. In fact, his plan would have further slashed revenues by offering the wealthiest Americans yet another tax cut, and lowering the tax rate for big corporations, even though most of them don't pay their fair share today, if they pay any taxes at all.

The biggest secret about the Ryan plan was that when it came to balancing the deficit, it was a total con job. Especially because it contained no new sources of revenue, it would have taken forever to kick in. The Republican Study Committee in the House—hardly a bunch of wild-eyed liberals—estimated that Ryan's scheme would actually not balance the federal budget until 2050—or maybe even 2080!—and would require raising the debt ceiling multiple times.

Even that didn't stop the media from loving Ryan's plan and treating it with as much reverence as they'd treat a new American Constitution. The morning after the Republican-controlled House approved the Ryan budget package, the *New York Times* headline read HOUSE APPROVES REPUBLICAN PLAN TO CUT TRIL- LIONS. By any correct standard of journalism, or truth, it should have read HOUSE APPROVES REPUBLICAN PLAN TO DESTROY MEDI- CARE.

Before writing that morning's headline, maybe the *Times* editor should have referred to the *Times* and CBS poll of January 2011. The vast majority said they wanted to save Medicare. And in order to fix it, they preferred raising taxes over cutting benefits, 64–24. In other words, they prefered President Obama's approach over Paul Ryan's approach almost three to one. Maybe the accurate headline would be: BY VOTING TO DESTROY MEDICARE, REPUBLICANS COMMIT POLITICAL SUICIDE.

As it turned out, it wasn't long before many Republicans came to that very conclusion—after feeling the wrath of senior citizens who showed up at congressional town meetings during the spring break of 2011. Ryan himself, in fact, had to be escorted out of a town meeting in his own district by local police officers after angry seniors disrupted his PowerPoint presentation. Many other members had similar experiences to the extent to which they were forced to cancel scheduled town hall gatherings or accept only questions submitted in writing ahead of time.

When Congress reconvened two weeks later, it was almost comical watching Republicans try to distance themselves from Ryan. Eric Cantor admitted that since it was obvious the Ryan plan was going nowhere, Republicans were going to have to look somewhere else for budget cuts. Speaker Boehner dismissed the whole anti-Medicare package as "Paul's idea," one of many on the table. And Ryan himself insisted it was merely a "starting point" for discussion.

But by that time, it was too late for Republicans to run from Ryan's proposal. Because, on April 15, before leaving on spring break, they'd already voted for it, 235–193—with all Democrats and four Republicans voting against it. Abolishing Medicare was already the official Republican party deficit-reduction plan. Their names were recorded as yes votes, and they couldn't deny it.

Other Republicans saw the danger. Within a month, presidential candidate Newt Gingrich, who had actually made noises about getting rid of Medicare when he was Speaker of the House in the 1990s, told NBC's David Gregory on *Meet the Press* that the Ryan plan was "too big a jump" for the American people— thereby becoming the first leading Republican outside of Congress to throw Paul Ryan under the bus.

At that moment, the entire political dynamic for 2012 changed. Republicans were suddenly playing defense, not offense. Democrats were able to paint every House and Senate race as a choice between those who would save Medicare and those who had already voted to destroy it. And political commentators openly began to discuss the possibility that, rather than losing control of both the House and the Senate in 2012, Democrats might actually win back leadership of the House and increase their margin in the Senate.

The point here is that the vast majority of Americans recognized the Ryan plan as dangerous and rejected it right away, while most political reporters were still describing it as "bold." It wasn't bold. It was unrealistic. It was cruel. It was reckless. It was politically suicidal. The public understood that. The media missed it.

But there was something even more fundamentally wrong about the media's slobbering over Ryan's deficit-reduction plan: the fact that, by doing so, members of the press bought into the Tea Party argument that this was the single most important issue facing the American people. Unfortunately, a few months later, President Obama fell into the same trap and spent weeks trying to reach a compromise debt reduction deal with Republicans Congress—again, all based on the premise that cutting the debt is America's number-one challenge. In fact, it's not. On every opinion survey, jobs ranks as the public's number-one concern. Balancing the budget ranks as two, three, four, or even five on the list.

Not only that: While the idea of balancing the budget gets broad public support, there is vast disagreement over how to do so—and little support for many of the budget-balancing ideas put forth in Congress. According to a *Washington Post* poll conducted in December 2010, only 36 percent supported reducing Social Security benefits, only 44 percent supported cutting defense spending or agricultural subsidies, and only 21 percent supported raising gas taxes. In other words, Americans are sending a clear message to their representatives: Balance the budget, yes. Just don't cut any programs we care about or depend on. Which completely undercuts the impression we get from too many Washington reporters—who are divorced from reality to begin with!—that the American people are obsessed with cutting the deficit and debt reduction and are willing to support any cuts to entitlements necessary to get the job done.

That's not the case, says economist Jamie Galbraith, son of the great John Kenneth Galbraith. In fact, in an interview with the *Washington Post's* Ezra Klein, he argued that the danger of the deficit is actually "zero. It's not overstated. It's completely misstated." Writing in *The Nation,* Galbraith elaborated: "[T]he frame of the [deficit] debate is between those who think the witches have taken over the entire community and the whole lot of them should be burned and those who think there are only a few witches and burning just a few of them would be enough to appease the demons. There are a few of us operating safely removed from the bonfires who maintain there is no such thing as witchcraft.'"

In other words, according to Galbraith, deficits don't matter! Instead of worrying about them all the time, Galbraith argues, "we should be focusing on real problems and not fake ones. We have serious problems. Unemployment is at 10 percent. If we got busy and worked out things for the unemployed to do, we'd be much better off. And we can certainly afford it. We have an impending energy crisis and a climate crisis. We could spend a generation fixing those problems in a way that would rebuild our country, too."

That's a powerful progressive argument, but one you never hear from the punditocracy. They're too busy prescribing cuts to Social Security and "shared sacrifice," because they think that is what "serious" people in Washington are supposed to do. At least that's what their hero, Paul Ryan, tells them.

Not everybody saw the media's infatuation with Paul Ryan as all bad. As economist Dean Baker, codirector of the Center for Economic and Policy Research, pointed out, it may serve to highlight very dramatically shortcomings in political reporting today. "Almost everything in the plan has been tried and failed,"

Baker wrote, "yet many pundits will applaud the plan as brave, innovative, and creative. In making these pronouncements these pundits will immediately reveal themselves as worthless hacks who either lack the ability or desire to do their own thinking . . . For this reason we owe Mr. Ryan a debt of gratitude."

With his usual insight, columnist Paul Krugman noted that reporters loved Ryan because he ratified their necessary world-view that not all right-wingers were crazy, like Sarah Palin or Michele Bachmann. There were actually some bright ones out there. Or at least one: Paul Ryan. Krugman noted and reprinted a comment someone had posted on the blog of UC Berkeley economist Brad DeLong. "The Beltway NEEDS Ryan," correctly observed DeLong's anonymous follower. "They need to have 'intelligent,' 'thoughtful' conservatives to lavish praise on to show they aren't part of the 'liberal media.' And they need him to create the 'balance' which is at the heart of their world. Not all Republicans are batshit crazy, thumping their bibles and shouting angry nonsense about the conspiracy of global warming—why, look at Paul Ryan! The Republican proposals and solutions are just as valid and well thought out as the Democratic ones. He said/she said forever!"

If Paul Ryan didn't exist, in other words, reporters would have to invent him. His "serious" demeanor and Hollywood good looks provide just the cover they need in order to ignore the facts, pretend to be objective, simply repeat what right-wingers say, and suggest that proposals of the Tea Party should really be taken seriously.

It's a lack of journalistic integrity that drives me crazy. And I see it every day, in the very belly of the beast.

THE PRESS CORPS

Since the early days of the Obama administration, I've had the honor of being a member of the White House press corps.

It wasn't something I'd always sought. Under Bill Clinton or George W. Bush, I never attended a single briefing. But, encouraged by C-Span's Steve Scully, former president of the White House Correspondents Association, to take a closer look at the Obama administration, I applied for a White House pass, got one, and now attend the briefings on almost a daily basis. I'm the only radio talk-show host to do so. I truly consider it an honor to be there. And I admire the work of those full-time correspondents, print and media, who cover the White House 24/7, travel with the president, put in the long hours, often in cramped quarters, and keep the American people up-to-date on the latest political and policy news from 1600 Pennsylvania Avenue.

At the same time, it's not always pretty.

First, let's agree on this. No matter who is president, no matter which party is in power, it's not the media's job simply to report or repeat whatever the White House says. It is the media's job to challenge, to probe, to test, to ask the tough questions. I firmly believe, for example, that if reporters had done a better job of challenging President Bush's assertions about weapons of mass destruction during the run-up to the war in Iraq, it would have been much harder, perhaps impossible, for him to con the American people and Congress into supporting the invasion of Iraq.

Similarly, when President Obama first promised to close the prison at Guantánamo Bay in January 2009 and try terrorist suspects in federal criminal courts—and then, in April 2011, did a complete 180, keeping Gitmo open and resurrecting military tribunals—it was important for reporters to press the administration on what went wrong.

When President Obama made a forceful argument that a "public plan option" was an essential part of any health-care plan, in order to allow consumers the benefit of choice and competition—and then abandoned the public option—every reporter worth his or her salt should have demanded to know why he caved.

And when Obama said we couldn't afford extending George Bush's tax cuts for the rich—and then turned around and extended them anyway—reporters should have been expected to ask, "What the hell?" And should have been fired if they didn't.

And don't worry, reporters do ask those tough questions at the White House. But what I see too often are questions that do little more than repeat Republican talking points, no matter how invalid.

Questions like: "Speaker Boehner says that the president's proposed budget cuts are only 'smoke and mirrors.' Is he correct?"

Or: "The president says he's willing to compromise. Yet he criticized the plan Republicans have put on the table. Isn't he being hypocritical by refusing to accept their plan?"

Or: "If raising the debt ceiling is so important, why doesn't the president just give Republicans whatever budget cuts they demand as the price for doing so?"

Yes, believe it or not, I have heard all three of those questions posed by the world's most prestigious gathering of reporters.

The case that really drove me crazy was media coverage of the BP oil spill in the Gulf. Republicans in Congress, egged on by right-wing talk-show hosts, were trying hard to turn this into Obama's Katrina—making him look bad for a slow response and, in retrospect, making George W. Bush look good. It was a real stretch at best, but they nonetheless got a lot of help from the White House press corps.

Day after day, Press Secretary Robert Gibbs was pounded with the question, "What took you so long to respond?" In fact, the federal government—in the form of the Coast Guard—was on the scene immediately, trying to save lives and get the fire under control. Within days, under leadership of Coast Guard admiral Thad Allen, a flotilla of ships had been assembled to begin containing and cleaning up the spill. And several other federal agencies and departments—EPA, NOAA, Interior, Homeland Security, FEMA— each had hundreds of personnel in the Gulf region.

Given that BP Horizon was the deepest underwater oil well ever drilled, and that this was the largest oil spill in U.S. history—twenty times larger than the *Exxon Valdez* spill—we were lucky there was not more long-term damage done to the important Gulf economy. In part, that was due to favorable wind and wave conditions. But it was mainly due to the overwhelming, rapid, and lasting response of federal agencies, which worked closely with state and local governments. This was not another Katrina. This was the way Katrina should have been handled. So it was doubly disappointing that when Republicans tried to play political games with BP, some reporters were only too willing to carry their water and blame it all on Obama. In fact, the permit for BP Horizon as well as the lax rules putting the company in charge of all cleanup, and trusting them to have all the necessary cleanup equipment, were issued by the Bush Department of the Interior.

So what do you do when the first-ever deepwater well in American waters blows up in your face? You certainly don't rush into handing out other permits. The responsible thing to do is to declare a time-out, so you can review the existing technology and procedures in place and make a determination that it's indeed safe to move forward. Which is exactly what President Obama did. He declared a six-month moratorium on deepwater drilling.

And wouldn't you know it? Those same political enemies who first accused him of not doing enough in the Gulf now accused him of doing too much. And their talking points were duly repeated and amplified at the next White House briefing.

Again, reporters should never swallow, hook, line and sinker, anything any president says. But they should never swallow, hook, line and sinker everything his political enemies say, either—and thus give their purely political remarks instant credibility.

But that's what I've seen happen all too often during these first years of the Obama presidency. If reporters can't do better than parroting what the political opposition says, they might as well surrender their seats in the briefing room and let Republican press secretaries take their places. Who needs a middleman?

WE NEED A BETTER PRESS

There are many more examples of where members of the media have fallen down on the job by merely repeating, rather than countering, the lies of the far right. Bloviating about "death panels" or "socialism" may make for provocative radio or television, but it does a disservice to the public. But, time and again, the press would rather repeat patently idiotic statements than actually report the facts.

The point is, all members of the media bear some responsibility for the lies and unprecedented barrage of hatred that has been directed against Barack Obama. Yes, blame the Kochs for funding it and Fox News for promoting it. But the rest of the media has helped them spread it. The Obama Hate Machine has rolled through on their watch.

CONCLUSION: TOWARD A POLITICS
OF CIVILITY

As we began with a massive rally held in Washington—the inauguration of President Barack Obama—let us close with one there, too.

On October 30, 2010, hundreds of thousands gathered on the Washington Mall to answer *Daily Show* host Jon Stewart's call to "Restore Sanity" to American politics. Stewart sidekick and fellow *Comedy Central* host Stephen Colbert shared the stage, under the slightly more ominous banner "Restore Sanity . . . and/or Fear."

It was a festive event. The crowd was a lot less earnest or emotional than those at most political rallies I've attended. They were just out for a good time, and they were in a great celebratory mood. It was more like the crowd at a rock concert, except there were people of all ages and colors, milling around, watching the stage or the monitors, enjoying one another's company.

Walking among them, I realized that they fit perfectly the advance description of the gathering Stewart had posted on his Web site: "Ours is a rally for the people who've been too busy to go to rallies, who actually have lives and families and jobs (or are looking for jobs)—not so much the Silent Majority as the Busy Majority. If we had to sum up the political view of our participants in a single sentence . . . we couldn't. That's sort of the point."

They gathered on the Mall for no cause other than Stewart's call for a "return to reason in America." They asked for nothing more than common sense, courtesy, and civility. If there was one overriding message, it was simply "Let's take it down a notch."

For me, the best part were the handmade signs people carried. In a way, Stewart's rally was the counterpoint to the big Tea Party rally Glenn Beck had staged at the Lincoln Memorial in August. For that event, Beck had expressly begged people not to bring signs—because he didn't want the embarrassment of having to explain or defend all the ugly, racist anti-Obama posters Tea Partiers would have inevitably brought to the Mall.

Stewart and Colbert did just the opposite. Go for it. Show your creativity. Make us laugh. Bring your signs, they encouraged their followers. And people outdid themselves. Many signs that I saw related to current events. In response to Delaware senate candidate Christine O'Donnell's making headlines by condemning masturbation as a sin, one man's sign declared I MASTURBATE AND I VOTE (ALTHOUGH NOT USUALLY AT THE SAME TIME). Another man's sign simply identified him as a member of a new political organization: ATHEISTS FOR MASTURBATION.

With my iPhone, I took photos of signs on gays in the military: JUST ASK, JUST TELL.

On politics: DON'T TEABAG ME.

On anger: I'M MAD AS HELL AND I'M GOING TO TAKE A DEEP BREATH AND COUNT TO 10.

On taxes: TAXES ARE OK.

On the media: THINK OUTSIDE THE FOX.

And even on cuisine: THANK GOD FOR MEXICAN FOOD.

But one sign in particular caught my attention and perhaps best captured the spirit of the day. Off to the side of the crowd, a young woman stood by herself, carrying a homemade placard that read IF YOU'RE NOT WITH US.... YOU MAY HAVE AN EQUALLY VALID WORLDVIEW WORTH CONSIDERING.

Of course, I laughed out loud. But, in a sense, as much as Jon Stewart and Stephen Colbert, she spoke for everyone there. Because the very fact that so many people showed up was in itself a plea for civility and a break from the politics of today—which has become so ugly, especially, but not exclusively, toward the forty-fourth president of the United States.

Don't get me wrong. I'm not against spirited and lively political debate. In fact, I've made a good living at it: on CNN's *Crossfire*, on MSNBC's *Buchanan and Press*, as a guest on countless other TV shows, and on my own nationally syndicated radio show. I love debating the issues. The tougher, more passionate, more hard-hitting, the better. By helping to create a better-informed electorate, it's healthy for our democracy.

After all, most of us have strong political opinions. So there's nothing wrong with expressing them—flat out, as robust as you dare. No shrinking violet need apply.

It's okay to disagree. It's okay to have a different point of view. It's more than okay to disagree with the way President Obama wants to fix health care or immigration or the economy. In fact, I love seeing protestors on Pennsylvania Avenue, standing in front of the White House every day. That's what democracy's all about. Put your own ideas forward and make your best case.

But it's not okay or necessary to try to destroy him, or to condemn him as a Communist, a fascist, a socialist, a Marxist, a Nazi, a Muslim, or an America-hating terrorist in the process. That reminds me of another sign seen at the Stewart/Colbert rally, carried by a World War II vet: I FOUGHT NAZIS . . . AND THEY DIDN'T LOOK LIKE OBAMA.

The ultimate irony, as historians will no doubt show, is that Barack Obama in no way resembles the radical left-wing caricature his enemies draw of him. Not even close. In fact, nobody's been more disappointed in him than those on the Left—because he moved too slowly on some issues, or not at all, or because he completely folded on others.

Look at his record. Obama's no radical. I wish he were. By most definitions, he's not even a liberal. He's a classic, genuine, albeit frustrating, middle-of-the-roader. As president, for example, he refused to indict George W. Bush and Dick Cheney for war crimes. Except for banning torture, he continued most of their policies related to terrorism and national security. And not only did he fail to take the lead on three favorite liberal causes—supporting same-sex marriage, a single-payer system, and restoration of the Fairness Doctrine—he took them all off the table.

Obama's no knee-jerk Democrat. I wish he were. In 2010, he refused to endorse Frank Caprio, the Democratic candidate for governor of Rhode Island, because, in the Senate, Obama had become friends with Republican Lincoln Chafee, who ended up defeating Caprio.

Obama's no Democratic party ideologue. I wish he were. He honestly wants and tries hard to govern in a postpartisan or transpartisan manner. This led him to spend (or waste, in my opinion) far too much time trying to line up Republican support for his health-care proposal—when he should have known from the beginning that there was no way either John Boehner or Mitch McConnell would allow any Republican to vote for it. And don't forget his total cave-in on the Bush tax cuts for the wealthy: agreeing at the last minute to extend them, after campaigning against them in 2008 and arguing for two years in the White House that we could not afford them. Nor his surrender on the debt reduction deal reached with Congress in July 2011. After correctly insisting on a "balanced" approach that contained both deep program cuts and new tax revenues, Obama agreed to massive cuts with zero revenue. He tried hard to convince skeptical Democrats it was a fair deal, while John Boehner gloated to House Republicans that he got "98 percent" of what he demanded.

Sometimes, it seems, Obama believes in bipartisanship to the point of being naïve.

At the same time, Obama is certainly no shaky patriot. Indeed, he's just the opposite. Given his own life story, he knows more than most people the incredible opportunities that exist only here in America. And that personal experience has imbued in him a deep and abiding love for his country, one that nobody should ever challenge.

As he so often does, Obama himself said it best. When he walked out onstage in Chicago's Grant Park on election night 2008, having just become the first black man elected president of the United States, he began by telling the world, "If there is anyone out there who still doubts that America is a place where all things are possible; who still wonders if the dream of our founders is alive in our time; who still questions the power of our democracy, tonight is your answer."

Little did Obama know at the time that the greatest challenge of his presidency would not be solving the serious problems facing the nation: problems like the economy, the deficit, education, environment, education, immigration.

No, the greatest challenge of his presidency would be dealing, instead, with the unprecedented barrage of hatred leveled against him. It remains his challenge, and ours, today—as I was reminded while making final revisions to this book.

In April 2011, members of the Republican party's central committee in Orange County, California, received an e-mail from fellow member Marilyn Davenport with this message: "Now you know why—No birth certificate!" In the e-mail was a family photo of Obama and his parents, with all three depicted as chimpanzees.

At first, Davenport refused to apologize, insisting she just meant it as a joke: "I am not a racist. I have friends who are black." Later, she did apologize, but she refused to resign from the committee and continued to deny she was a racist, yet she said she still wasn't convinced that Obama was an American citizen.

Clearly and sadly, when it comes to political differences with President Barack Obama, we still have a long way to go to get away from the politics of personal destruction and back to debating public policy.

BIBLIOGRAPHY

In addition to the many anti-Obama books identified in chapter 4, the following works were helpful in crafting this volume.

Alter, Jonathan. *The Promise: President Obama, Year One.* New York: Simon & Schuster, 2010.

Anonymous. [Mark Salter]. *O.: A Presidential Novel.* New York: Simon & Schuster, 2011.

Badger, Anthony J. *FDR: The First Hundred Days.* New York: Hill & Wang, 2008.

Brookhiser, Richard. *America's First Dynasty: The Adamses, 1735–1918.* New York: Free Press, 2002.

Chernow, Ron. *Washington: A Life.* New York: Penguin, 2010.

Conason, Joe, and Gene Lyons. *The Hunting of the President: The Ten-Year Campaign to Destroy Bill and Hillary Clinton.* New York: St. Martin's Press, 2000.

Ellis, Joseph J. *First Family: Abigail and John Adams.* New York: Alfred A. Knopf, 2010.

———. *Passionate Sage: The Character and Legacy of John Adams.* New York: W. W. Norton, 1993.

Long, Kim. *The Almanac of Political Corruption, Scandals and Dirty Politics.* New York: Delacorte, 2007.

McCullough, David. *John Adams.* New York: Simon & Schuster, 2001.

Milbank, Dana. *Tears of a Clown: Glenn Beck and the Tea Bagging of America.* New York: Doubleday, 2010.

Obama, Barack. *Dreams from My Father: A Story of Race and Inheritance.* New York: Crown, July 1995.

Phillips-Fein, Kim. *Invisible Hands: The Making of the Conservative Movement from the New Deal to Reagan.* New York: W. W. Norton, 2009.

Remnick, David. *The Bridge: The Life and Rise of Barack Obama.* New York: Vintage, 2010.

Smith, Page. *John Adams.* 2 vols. New York: Doubleday, 1962.

Tagg, Larry. *The Unpopular Mr. Lincoln: The Story of America's Most Reviled President.* New York: Savas Beatie, 2009.

White, Ronald C., Jr. *Lincoln's Greatest Speech: The Second Inaugural.* New York: Simon & Schuster, 2002.

Wilson, John K. *The Most Dangerous Man in America: Rush Limbaugh's Assault on Reason.* New York: St. Martin's Press, 2011.

Wolf, Richard. *Revival: The Struggle for Survival Inside the Obama White House.* New York: Crown, 2010.

Wright, John. *The Obama Haters: Behind the Right-Wing Campaign of Lies, Innuendo & Racism.* Washington: Potomac Books, 2011.

INDEX